World
AN ILLUSTRATED GUIDE
History

Publisher and Creative Director: Nick Wells
Project Editor: Cat Emslie
Art Director: Mike Spender
Layout Design: Dave Jones
Digital Design and Production: Chris Herbert
Proofreader: Dawn Laker
Indexer: Jayne Moss

This is a **STAR FIRE** book
First published in 2001, then 2003
This edition published in 2007

07 09 11 10 08

1 3 5 7 9 10 8 6 4 2

STAR FIRE
Crabtree Hall, Crabtree Lane, Fulham
London, SW6 6TY, United Kingdom
www.star-fire.co.uk

Star Fire is part of
The Foundry Creative Media Company Limited

Copyright © 2007 The Foundry Creative Media Company Ltd

ISBN 948 1 84451 926 2

All rights reserved. No part of this publication may be reproduced, stored
in a retrieval system, or transmitted in any form or by any means, electronic,
mechanical, photocopying, recording or otherwise, without the prior
permission of the publisher.

A copy of the CIP data for this book is available from the British Library

Printed in Dubai

World History
AN ILLUSTRATED GUIDE

Guy de la Bédoyère, Alan Brown, Gerard Cheshire, Ingrid Cranfield,
Judith Hodge, Michael Kerrigan, Jon Sutherland

General Editor: Patrick O'Brien

STAR FIRE

CONTENTS

Introduction 6

Politics 8

Religion 32

Royalty 50

Science and Industry 86

Society and Culture 102

War 138

Glossary 182

Bibliography 185

Authors 187

Credits 188

Index 189

INTRODUCTION

As the global integration of nations and communities accelerates, the demand for concise information about the history of our interdependent world from schools and universities, and for an educated public at large, becomes clear and urgent.

Several developments promote a need for histories of the world. Firstly the sheer number of publications and the volume of data about the past stimulates demand for compressed, attractively presented but reliable sources of information about a universal past. Secondly, the branching out of history's traditional concerns (namely with states, warfare and diplomacy) in order to take into account a plurality of contemporary interests, such as ecology, evolutionary biology, ethnology, botany, the health and wealth of populations, human rights, gender, family systems, private life, fashion, popular music, to name but a few, points the study of history towards comparisons across cultures and national histories. Thirdly, in an age of travel and electronic communication, the young quickly acquire portfolios of knowledge and develop curiosities about other places, peoples and cultures. These new generations are less easily persuaded to feed on diets of national, let alone regional and parochial histories, than previous ones. Thus, schools and universities need to provide spatially unfettered, ready access to the kind of historical understanding that will satisfy the capacious interests of this generation. To nourish the cosmopolitan sensibility required for the next millennium, history needs to be widened and repositioned to bring it into fruitful exchange with geography, geology, evolutionary biology and the social sciences. Barriers between archaeology, ancient, classical, medieval, early modern, contemporary and other 'packages' of traditional, but now anachronistic histories must be dismantled.

As new technologies enable our world to 'shrink', for problem after problem and subject after subject, national frameworks for political action and academic enquiry are recognized as unsatisfactory. People require historical perspectives on the ubiquitous technological, political and economic forces that are now clearly transcending and transforming traditional frameworks for human behaviour and reshaping personal identities around the world.

Thus this excellent work of reference to world history is not only propitious, but it has been well designed, structured and written by a team of experts in order to help teachers of history in high schools and universities communicate a truly global historical perspective to their pupils and to students in general. Histories of the world cannot be taught or read without a clear comprehension of the chronologies and spatial parameters within which political, economic, social and cultural activities of different empires, states and peoples have evolved over very long timespans. This book is an ideal text for the easy acquisition of basic facts upon which an understanding of world history can be built and studied. It encapsulates hard knowledge and reunifies history with

geography, providing a perspective which goes back to classical civilizations in order to help its readers appreciate the significance of people, places and locations for seminal events in world history.

Works of reference must be accurate, accessible and display the unfurling chronology of world history in words, illustrations, maps and captions that are memorable. The team of historians, illustrators, cartographers and editors who collaborated in the production of this book set out to produce a popular work of reference that could be adopted for undergraduate and high school courses in world history.

World History is a concise, fully-illustrated, up-to-date, single volume reference book for readers aged 16 and above. It features: over 700 clearly written entries, compiled and authenticated by professional historians and more than 300 colour illustrations, covering millennia of history, from Ancient Egypt to the present day.

The entries provide readers with authoritative, yet accessible, information on every period in history. Due weight has been given to all regions of the world – Europe, the Americas, China, India, Russia, the Middle East, Southeast Asia and Asia. Entries have been organized alphabetically to enable fast fact-finding, while cross-references give directions to associated entries and illustrations. References to people, dates and events from Ancient Egypt to the present day cover every inhabited continent on the planet and have been organized into six major themes: Politics, Religion, Royalty, Science & Industry, Society & Culture and War.

Although books on world history must accord prominence to such traditional, historical topics as the rise and decline of empires, states and civilizations, a serious effort has been made to include the communal concerns of mankind, including religion, economic welfare, trade, technology, health, the status of women, human rights, etc.

World History offers chronologies, perspectives and geographical parameters which aim to subdue the excesses of nationalism, ethnicity, chauvinism and condescension. The length and breadth of this world history, covering, as it does, all continents with a chronology which goes back hundreds of years, works to separate the provincial from the universal, the episodic from the recurrent. It will elaborate upon the decline as well as the rise of societies, nations, cultures and civilizations. This volume contributes towards rapidly growing aspirations for an education in universal history and will also contribute towards the nurturing of a cosmopolitan sensibility for the twenty-first century.

Patrick K. O'Brien FBA
Centennial Professor of Economic History, London School of Economics; Convenor of the Programme in Global History at the Institute of Historical Research, University of London

KEY DATES

1789	❖	First French Revolution
1907	❖	Triple Entente signed between Britain, Russia and France
1916	❖	Easter Rising in Ireland
1917	❖	Russian Bolshevik Revolution
1917	❖	Balfour Declaration
1919	❖	League of Nations established
1933	❖	Nazi Party established in Germany
1938	❖	Munich Agreement signed
1939	❖	Nazi-Soviet Pact signed
1945	❖	Arab League formed
1945	❖	World's first atomic bomb dropped on Hiroshima, Japan
1945	❖	Iron Curtain 'raised'
1945	❖	United Nations formed
1945	❖	Yalta Conference
1947	❖	Indian independence declared; formation of Pakistan
1948–49	❖	Berlin Airlift
1949	❖	NATO formed
1949	❖	People's Republic of China founded
1949	❖	German Democratic Republic established
1955	❖	Warsaw Pact signed

POLITICS

1956	❖	Suez Crisis
1957	❖	Treaty of Rome and formation of the EEC
1961	❖	Berlin Wall raised
1962	❖	Cuban Missile Crisis
1963	❖	Assassination of John F. Kennedy
1969–79	❖	SALT negotiations between the USA and the Soviet Union
1972	❖	Bloody Sunday, Northern Ireland
1972–74	❖	Watergate Scandal, USA
1989	❖	End of the Berlin Wall
1991	❖	Maastricht Treaty signed; EEC now known as the EU

Marxism (1844)

Doctrines of Karl Marx and Friedrich Engels. Arguably, Karl Marx created his own vision of Communism in 1844, following a period as editor of a Cologne newspaper. Marxism has come to mean the political doctrines of the Soviet Union (1917–91) and other Communist or Socialist countries. Although complex and revised by many other writers, Marxism encompasses views on class, economics, art, capitalism, materialism and dialectics. Marx believed that the class struggle would lead to a classless society where those who use their energies to create would benefit directly from what they have achieved. Capitalism was the last stage before this would happen.

❖ see BOLSHEVIKS p18

Taiping Rebellion (1850–64)

Chinese popular revolt. A radical new Chinese movement, the Taiping T'ien-kuoç declared itself a new dynasty in 1851. The group's fanatical religious leader and his followers observed strict moral rules and shared all property. By 1853 they had amassed an army of one million, which attacked and captured the major city of Nanjing. In 1864 the city was reclaimed by pro-government troops, and the movement collapsed. But the Ch'ing dynasty was irretrievably damaged by the rebellion, a forerunner of Chinese Communism.

Woodrow Wilson (1856–1924)

28th US president (1913–21). As US leader during World War I, Wilson reluctantly declared war against Germany in 1917. He delivered a famous speech, 'The Fourteen Points' (guidelines for a peace settlement), attended the 1919 Paris Peace Conference, and founded the League of Nations, the predecessor of the United Nations.

❖ see LEAGUE OF NATIONS p21, WORLD WAR I p164

Theodore Roosevelt (1858–1919)

26th US president (1901–09). He was the Republican president who passed legislation curbing the powers of big corporations in the USA, and introduced food and drug regulations. Roosevelt was very active in international affairs. He helped create the Panama Canal in 1902 and played a central role in ending the Russo-Japanese War.

❖ see RUSSO-JAPANESE WAR p162

Ku Klux Klan (1866 and 1915 onwards)

Terrorist organization. Taking its name from the Greek word for 'circle', it was established by Confederate soldiers but became an underground resistance movement aiming to restore white supremacy and terrorize non-whites in the southern states of America. Originally led by the Confederate General, Nathan Bedford-Forrest, their first Grand Wizard, they dressed in robes and sheets to prevent Federal troops from identifying them. White supremacy had been achieved by the 1870s and the Klan diminished. In 1915 a new Klan arose to counter what they saw as a change in the ethnic character of America as a result of immigration. Membership peaked in the 1920s with four million members being opposed to Jews, Roman Catholics and all foreigners. It resurged in the 1960s and was responsible for shootings and bombings in the south. Lyndon Johnson renounced the organization on nationwide television. The Klan is still active, having strong alliances with right-wing extremists and neo-Nazis.

Neville Chamberlain (1869–1940)

British politician. He became prime minister in 1937, following two stints as Conservative chancellor. Chamberlain was responsible for the policy of 'appeasement' towards Hitler: this resulted in the 1938 Munich Pact that abandoned Czechoslovakia to Germany. On his return to London he announced that he had achieved 'peace in our time', then resigned when World War II broke out the following year.

❖ see WORLD WAR I p164

Mahatma Gandhi (1869–1948)

Indian political and spiritual leader. Called 'the Mahatma' ('great-souled'), Gandhi fought for Indian independence from

Great Britain through a policy of non-violence or passive resistance. In 1915 he returned to India from South Africa, where he had been a human rights lawyer defending the country's Indian community, and became leader of the Indian National Congress party. He denounced Western dress and customs, aiming to lead a simple spiritual life. He preached religious tolerance and advocated the end of India's caste system. Gandhi organized civil disobedience and hunger strikes, and was imprisoned a number of times by the British authorities, including a spell during World War II when he refused to co-operate. He was a major influence in the negotiations for independence in 1947, but was deeply distressed by the religious partition of the country into Pakistan and India. Violence broke out between Hindus and Muslims and Gandhi was assassinated by a Hindu nationalist.

Home Rule (1870)

Movement by Irish nationalists to secure self-government. The modern movement began in 1870 and its vocal leader Charles Stewart Parnell unified the Irish Parliamentary party and publicized the cause. Prime Minister Gladstone was converted and introduced the first Home Rule Bill (1886), but it failed to pass; the second bill (1893) was defeated by the House of Lords. This defeat led to the rise of revolutionary factions, seeking alternatives to constitutional means to achieve self-government. It was a long wait until the third bill (1912), and when it was passed, Protestant Ulster threatened civil war. The Lords excluded Ulster, but the bill was interrupted by World War I. After years of conflict, the fourth bill (1920) gave a form of home rule to the six counties of Northern Ireland, though they remained part of Britain. The Anglo-Irish treaty in 1921 recognized the 26 southern counties as the Irish Free State.

Vladimir Ilyich Lenin (1870–1924)

Russian revolutionary and political theoretician. Lenin created the Soviet Union and headed its first government (1917–24). After the failure of the 1905 revolution, he spent time in exile where he wrote many revolutionary pamphlets, including *State and Revolution*, his most important contribution to Marxist political theory. Lenin adapted Marxism to Russian conditions to create Leninism. In 1917 the Bolsheviks came to power and Lenin was finally able to put his theories into practice, although civil war broke out between 1918–21. After the war, Lenin introduced the New Economic Policy, which returned the Soviet Union to a market economy, at the same time insisting on single party rule.

❖ see BOLSHEVIKS p18, MARXISM p10

BELOW: *Vladimir Lenin changed the face of Imperial Russia by ensuring all businesses became property of the State.*

POLITICS

Jan Christian Smuts (1870–1950)

South African soldier and prime minister (1919–24 and 1939–48). Smuts was an outstanding military commander and treaty negotiator. He served in both the Boer War and World War I and was a member of the Imperial War Cabinet in 1917. Smuts was a signatory to the peace treaties following both world wars, and was influential in the development of the United Nations.

❖ see BOER WAR p161

Rasputin (1872–1916)

Mysterious Russian figure associated with the court of Tsar Nicholas II. Rasputin was reputed to be a saint, a mystic and a healer. He achieved fame after apparently healing the Tsar's son who was a haemophiliac. Rasputin became great friends with the Tsarina and was said to exert influence over the Tsar's political decisions. He was assassinated in 1916, but he survived poisoning and being shot, and finally died only when he was thrown into the Neva River.

❖ see NICHOLAS II OF RUSSIA p84

Winston Churchill (1874–1965)

British statesman. Churchill was first elected to parliament in 1900. During World War I he was in charge of the Admiralty (1911–15), but resigned after the failed Dardanelles campaign. His political career was similarly chequered: he served in both Liberal and Conservative cabinets, including a stint as Chancellor of the Exchequer (1924–29). Churchill replaced Chamberlain as prime minister in 1940 and is best remembered for his outstanding leadership during World War II. Labour won the post-war election in 1945, but Churchill was again prime minister from 1951–55. He wrote many biographies and memoirs and won the Nobel Prize for Literature in 1953.

❖ see DARDANELLES CAMPAIGN p166, WORLD WAR I p164, WORLD WAR II p172

BELOW: *Winston Churchill, one of Britain's most influential statesmen.*

RIGHT: *Grigori Efimovich Rasputin.*

ABOVE: *Leon Trotsky.*

Treaty of San Stefano (1878)

Peace treaty signed following the last of the Russo-Turkish wars. The agreement between Prussia and the Ottoman Empire saw significant changes to national boundaries within Eastern Europe. Bulgaria was enlarged and became an independent state; Serbia and Montenegro were given greater territories. The Ottoman Empire was made to pay a large compensation.

❖ see RUSSO-TURKISH WAR p158

Leon Trotsky (1879–1940)

Adopted name of Lev Davidovich Bronstein, Russian revolutionary and Communist theorist. Trotsky was one of the leaders in Russia's October Revolution (1917) and in the civil war that followed (1918–20). After Lenin's death (1924), Trotsky lost the battle for power to Joseph Stalin and was exiled to Mexico. He continued to oppose Stalin and criticized the Soviet regime in his writing until his assassination with an ice pick, probably carried out at Stalin's instigation.

❖ see VLADIMIR ILYICH LENIN p11

LEFT: *Soviet leader, Joseph Stalin.*

Joseph Stalin (1879–1953)

Leader of the USSR (1929–53). In 1929, Stalin introduced the first Five-Year Plan which enforced the government control of agriculture. Farmers resisted by destroying stock and crops: a huge famine resulted and millions of peasants were detained in Siberian labour camps. During the 1930s' 'Great Purge', secret police arrested citizens suspected of challenging the government, and millions were killed. In World War II, Stalin aligned the USSR with the Allies, and was one of the three world leaders at the 1945 Yalta Conference. In the post-war period, Stalin succeeded in isolating the USSR from the West during a period known as the Cold War.

❖ see COLD WAR p100, WORLD WAR II p172

Franklin D. Roosevelt (1882–1945)

32nd US president (1933–45). Roosevelt was the longest-serving US leader. He was elected four times for a 12-year period during the Depression and World War II. In 1933 Roosevelt launched the New Deal, which provided relief for the unemployed and those faced with losing their farms and homes. He later placed heavier taxes on the wealthy and introduced social security. Roosevelt was reluctant to involve the USA in World War II, but after the bombing of Pearl Harbor in 1941, he sent American troops to Europe. Along with Churchill and Stalin, Roosevelt became one of the 'Big Three' Allied leaders during the war.

❖ see GREAT DEPRESSION p134, NEW DEAL p135, WORLD WAR II p172

RIGHT: *Benito Mussolini, leader of the Fascist Party in Italy, became Aldolf Hitler's principal ally during World War II.*

Benito Mussolini (1883–1945)

Italian dictator (1922–43). Mussolini was the leader (Il Duce) of Italian Fascism, which he founded in 1919. His Blackshirt militia, supported by landowners and industrialists, terrorized socialist and peasant groups. He formed a coalition government in 1922, and by 1926 had created a totalitarian, single-party state. Mussolini invaded Ethiopia (1935–36), but the Italian army suffered many defeats in World War II, which they entered in 1940 in support of Germany. Mussolini was forced to resign from the Fascist Council in 1943. With German help he set up a republican government in northern Italy, but was captured in 1945 and executed by the partisans.

❖ see WORLD WAR II p172

WORLD HISTORY

Jawaharlal Nehru (1889–1964)

Prime minister of India (1947–64). Nehru led the socialist wing of the Congress party and was second only in influence to Gandhi, though his approach to politics was more secular. He was imprisoned many times during the fight for Indian independence and became the new republic's first prime minister. Nehru isolated Western powers with his foreign policy of non-alignment and finally drove the Portuguese out of Goa. His daughter was Indira Gandhi, who also became prime minister.

❖ see INDIAN INDEPENDENCE p26, INDIRA GANDHI p20.

BELOW: *General Dwight Eisenhower commanded the Allied forces in Italy during World War II and was later elected 34th US president.*

Dwight Eisenhower (1890–1969)

American general and US president (1953–61). Commander of US forces during World War II, 'Ike' Eisenhower was appointed supreme commander of the Allied forces and planned the cross-channel invasion of France on D-Day. He organized NATO's defence forces after the war, then won the 1952 presidential election. Despite ending the Korean War, he continued Harry S. Truman's Cold War policy and the Eisenhower doctrine committed the USA to containing Communism in the Middle East. He won a second term with ease in 1956. Civil rights were coming to the fore and Eisenhower sent federal troops to Little Rock, Arkansas, to enforce a court-ordered school desegregation.

❖ see COLD WAR p100, D-DAY p175, WORLD WAR II p172

Charles de Gaulle (1890–1970)

French general and statesman. De Gaulle was an army officer in World War I and, while in exile, head of the French Resistance during World War II. A chequered political career followed, including stints as president and provisional head of state. De Gaulle became president (with a new constitution that strengthened the role) in 1958. He was determined to resolve the crisis created by the civil war in Algeria (a French colony) and in 1962, he negotiated Algeria's independence. De Gaulle's high spending on nuclear defence, among other things, sparked demonstrations by workers and students in 1968 that nearly brought down his government. He resigned the following year.

❖ see WORLD WAR II p172

RIGHT: *Charles de Gaulle on the cover of* **TIME** *magazine. De Gaulle became leader of the French troops during the German occupation of France. He was head of the provisional French government from 1944–46.*

Francisco Franco (1892–1975)

Spanish dictator (1939–75). As army general, Franco led the Nationalist rebels to victory in the Spanish Civil War (1936–39). With help from a fascist Italy and Nazi Germany, Franco invaded Spain from Morocco and established a corporate state. He kept Spain officially out of World War II, although he sent aid to the German side, and in 1947 he declared Spain a kingdom and himself regent. In 1969 he named Prince Juan Carlos as his successor.

❖ see SPANISH CIVIL WAR p169, WORLD WAR II p172

Marshal Tito (1892–1980)

Yugoslav military commander and premier (1953–1980). Marshal Tito fought in World War I and the Russian Civil War. During World War II as leader of the partisans, he fought valiantly against the Nazis, and in 1941 he headed Yugoslavia's first Communist government. In 1948, following his expulsion by Stalin from the Communist eastern bloc, Tito developed a freer style of Communist rule. His policy of non-alignment built up groups of neutral countries between the Communist East and capitalist West.

RIGHT:
Marshal Tito.

Dual Entente (1893)

Franco-Russian Alliance signed by France and Russia in 1893. In 1907 the alliance was joined by Britain, becoming the Triple Entente. Then in 1911 the Triple Entente became a military alliance as the threat of war loomed large. It formed the basis for the Allied Powers who entered World War I against the Central Powers – Germany and Austria-Hungary. The Russian Revolution of 1917 saw the end of the Triple Entente.

❖ see TRIPLE ENTENTE p19, WORLD WAR I p164

Mao Zedong (1893–1976)

Founder of the People's Republic of China; Chinese leader (1949–76). Mao Zedong has been described as the 'architect of the New China'. A member of the Chinese Communist Party in 1921, he became a dedicated Communist and expert soldier. After heading the famous Long March in 1934–35 (a 15,520 km/9,700 mile trek) Mao became the Communist Party leader.

In 1949, Mao became the Communist Party Chairman and declared the People's Republic of China. Under Mao's radical reforms, all land was distributed to the peasants, farms run communally and industry controlled by the State.

Two of Mao's national campaigns, 'The Great Leap Forward' (1958) and the 'Cultural Revolution' (1966–76), failed in advancing China. They led to the collapse of the economy and the execution of millions – and widespread unrest resulted.

ABOVE: *Nikita Khrushchev.*

Nikita Khrushchev (1894–1971)

Premier of the USSR (1958–64). Khrushchev rose rapidly in the Communist Party, directing the second five-year plan and the Red Army's southern front during World War II. He became the Soviet agricultural expert when he was charged with restoring agricultural production after the war. After Stalin's death Khrushchev was appointed head of the Communist Party, but he denounced Stalin and demoted many of his supporters. He was made Soviet premier on the resignation of Bulganin in 1958, until he himself was deposed in 1964 following accusations of political error over the Cuban Missile Crisis. He was dropped from the party in 1966.

❖ see CUBAN MISSILE CRISIS p29

Fulgencio Batista (1901–73)

Cuban dictator. Batista twice ruled Cuba, the first time (1933–44) as an effective reformer, the second (1952–59) as a brutal dictator. During his eight-year absence from government, there was an upsurge in corruption and a breakdown of public services. Batista's return to power was welcomed, until he embezzled huge sums from Cuba's booming economy and suppressed the press and Congress. Fidel Castro's long guerilla campaign finally toppled him in 1958.

Ayatollah Ruh Allah Khomeini (1902–89)

'Ayatollah' means 'signs of God' and contemporary ayatollahs are the caretakers for the Imam who will return at the end of time. In Shiite hierarchy there were 12 imams, the last of whom disappeared. The application of the title 'Ayatollah' appears to depend upon the personality and charisma of the scholar as well as recognition by the community. Ayatollah Khomeini was the main opponent of the Shah of Iran before the Shah's overthrow; exiled in 1964 until finally returning in 1979. After the revolution in 1978–79, Khomeini was recognized as Vilayat Faqih – the supreme representative in Iran of the Hidden (12th) Imam. His opposition to the West and his promotion of his form of Islam has had a powerful bearing on the portrayal of Islam in the West.

ABOVE: *The Ayatollah Khomeini opposed the Shah of Iran who was later overthrown and exiled to the USA.*

Bolsheviks (1903–52)

Political and military group that seized power in Russia in 1917. The Bolsheviks, meaning 'one of the majority', originated in 1903 under the leadership of Vladimir Ilyich Lenin. From the beginning, the party was highly centralized, disciplined and professional. The group insisted that party membership of the Russian Social Democratic Workers Party should be restricted to professional revolutionaries. By 1912, the group was still small despite its high-profile leader. In 1917, after the February Revolution that signalled Lenin's return to Russia, the Bolsheviks had gained control of the key worker councils in Petrograd and Moscow. This assured Russia's exit from World War I. After the October Revolution, the Bolsheviks suppressed other political rivals and took power. They became the Russian Communist Party of Bolsheviks in 1918 and the All Union Communist Party of Bolsheviks in 1925. The term disappeared when they were renamed the Communist Party of the Soviet Union in October 1952.

❖ see VLADIMIR ILYICH LENIN p11, NICHOLAS II OF RUSSIA p84, RUSSIAN REVOLUTION p168, WORLD WAR I p164

Entente Cordiale (1904)

Unofficial alliance between France and Great Britain. Britain became a component of the Triple Entente, along with France and Russia, in 1907, seven years before the outbreak of World War I. In 1904, Britain and France made an agreement called the Entente Cordiale (French for 'Friendly Agreement') to show goodwill between nations. The Entente Cordiale recognized British interests in Egypt and French interests in Morocco, with a mutual understanding that each would be left to their own devices.

❖ see DUAL ENTENTE p16, TRIPLE ENTENTE p19, WORLD WAR I p164

LEFT: *King Edward VII, seen here greeting President Poincare of France at Portsmouth, used his personal influence to help cement the Entente Cordiale.*

Triple Entente (1907)

The Triple Entente – Triple 'Agreement' – was signed between Britain, France and Russia in 1907. It would last until 1917, with the start of the Russian Bolshevik Revolution. It was a military alliance, especially after 1911 when the threat of the Central Powers, Germany and Austria-Hungary, became more apparent in the build-up to World War I. Before Britain joined, France and Russia were the members of the Dual Entente, signed back in 1893.

❖ see BOLSHEVIKS p18, RUSSIAN REVOLUTION p168

Kuomintang (1911)

Chinese name for the Nationalist People's Party. The party was founded by Sun Yat-sen, a revolutionary leader who overthrew the Manchu dynasty in 1911 and set up a republican government. In the 1920s, sharp divisions arose between the right-wing and the Communist elements in the party. The leader of the right-wing faction, Chiang Kai-shek, threw out the Communists in 1927 and began a campaign to unify the whole country under the Kuomintang. The nationalist regime was finally defeated by Mao Zedong in 1949 and Kuomintang supporters (an estimated two million people) withdrew to the island of Taiwan, which was fortified with US economic aid. Chiang Kai-shek continued to rule until his death in 1975.

Willy Brandt (1913–92)

German political leader. A Social Democrat, Brandt was elected mayor of West Berlin (1957–66) where he came to international attention over his handling of the Berlin Wall crisis. The main objective of his political career (he was West German foreign minister, 1966–69, and chancellor, 1969–74) was his Ostpolitik (eastern policy) – a desire to improve relations with East Germany and the Soviet Union. Brandt was forced to resign after the discovery of an East German spy in his government.

❖ see BERLIN WALL p28, COLD WAR p100

RIGHT: *Willy Brandt, a Social Democrat and former German chancellor, is best remembered for his efforts to improve East-West relations between Germany and the Soviet Union at the height of the Cold War.*

Richard Nixon (1913–94)

37th US president (1969–74). Under threat of impeachment over the Watergate scandal, Nixon became the first American president to resign from office. He was vice-president to Eisenhower (1953–61) but lost the presidential election to John F. Kennedy in 1960. He won in 1968 and again in 1972. The Nixon Doctrine called for the US withdrawal from Vietnam and he forged new links with China. Nixon's time in office was cut short by the Watergate scandal, which uncovered many dirty tricks by the Republicans: burglary and wiretapping the Democrats' headquarters (at the Watergate offices); a 'slush fund' for discrediting his political opponents during Nixon's re-election campaign; and the subsequent cover-up operation authorized by the president. The existence of the Watergate tapes (Nixon's taped phone conversations) and his reluctance to release them untampered to the investigating committee led to a likely impeachment. Nixon resigned but was later pardoned by his successor, Gerald Ford.

❖ see WATERGATE p30

POLITICS

Easter Rising (1916)

Republican uprising against the British Government in Ireland. The revolt, also known as the Easter Rebellion, began on 24 April, Easter Monday. The plan was for a nationwide uprising by a number of organizations but, due to a series of mishaps, it only took place in Dublin. The leaders Patrick Pearse and Tom Clarke – with about 1,800 men – seized the Dublin General Post Office and other strategic points in the city centre. There was fighting for a week while British troops put down the insurrection and the leaders were all executed. Although the uprising itself had been unpopular, the executions fuelled the Irish cause and the government collapsed.

John F. Kennedy (1917–63)

35th US president (1961–63). At 43, Kennedy was the youngest ever president. Many of his domestic reforms, such as civil rights and extra spending on education and welfare, stalled in Congress. His time was spent dealing with foreign affairs, including the Bay of Pigs invasion, the Cuban Missile Crisis (1962) – the peaceful outcome of which was a personal triumph for Kennedy - and increasing the number of US military advisers to South Vietnam to 16,000 (1963). Kennedy was assassinated while campaigning for a second term.

❖ see BAY OF PIGS p177, CUBAN MISSILE CRISIS p29

Indira Gandhi (1917–84)

Indian politician. Daughter of India's first prime minister Jawaharlal Nehru, she herself served two terms as prime minister (1966–77 and 1980–84). Her government became increasingly authoritarian. When faced with questions over the validity of her re-election in 1975, she declared a state of emergency, suspending civil rights and imprisoning her opponents. She was defeated in 1977, mainly due to her unpopular programme of social and economic reforms. Gandhi was re-elected in 1980, but assassinated four years later by her Sikh bodyguards following her use of troops to attack the Golden Temple in Amritsar, the Sikhs' holiest shrine. Her son Rajiv succeeded her as prime minister.

ABOVE: *John F. Kennedy.*
ABOVE RIGHT: *The tenth meeting of the League of Nations at Geneva.*

Nicolae Ceausescu (1918–89)

Communist leader of Romania. Ceausescu was a Communist youth movement member, imprisoned in 1936 and 1940. He escaped from prison in 1944 and served as secretary of the Union of Communist Youth (1944–45), minister of agriculture (1948–50) and deputy minister of the armed forces (1950–54). He succeeded Gheorghiu-Dej as leader (March 1965), head of state (1967) and president of Romania (1974). He was shot by a firing squad, along with his wife, having been convicted of mass murder and other crimes in Timisoara (1989).

❖ see MARXISM p10

Abdel Nasser (1918–70)

President of Egypt (1956–70). Nasser was the driving force behind the 1952 coup to oust King Faruk. He then negotiated a treaty with the British to end their 72-year occupation of Egypt. His policy of non-alignment brought conflict with the British and the USA, who withdrew finance for the Aswan Dam. In order to raise money for the project, Nasser nationalized the Suez Canal, which led to an armed response from France, Britain and Israel. The three countries were forced to withdraw by the USA, but a UN force remained. Tensions erupted again in 1967 when Israel attacked Egypt in the Six-Day War, occupying the entire Sinai Peninsula.

❖ see SIX-DAY WAR p179, SUEZ CRISIS p28

League of Nations (1919)

Organization established for international co-operation. In an attempt to prevent another world conflict, a covenant was drawn up by Allied Powers at the Paris Peace Conference (1919) covering collective security, dispute arbitration, open diplomacy and armament reduction. New members were assimilated during the 1920s; the League's headquarters were based in Geneva with the aim of preserving the covenant established in the peace treaties following World War I. A series of failures to maintain this status quo during the 1930s forced the League to cease its activities during World War II, being replaced in 1946 by the United Nations.

❖ see UNITED NATIONS p25, WORLD WAR I p164

Eva Perón (1919–52)

Wife of Argentine president Juan Perón. During her husband's first term as president, 'Evita' (as she was known) became a powerful political figure in her own right and a champion of the poor. She never held an official government post, but virtually ran the health and labour ministries. She awarded large wage increases to the unions and set up thousands of hospitals, schools and orphanages. Evita helped women get the vote and set up the Peronista Feminist Party in 1949. She was nominated for vice president in 1951, but was opposed by the army. She died of cancer soon after.

Ernesto 'Che' Guevara (1928–67)

Cuban revolutionary. Argentine-born doctor and political activist, Ernesto 'Che' Guevara joined Cuban brothers Fidel and Raul Castro in their guerilla campaign to overthrow Fulgencio Batista. He was Castro's chief lieutenant in the revolution (1956–59) and served as minister of industry (1961–65) in the new government. He left Cuba to train revolutionaries in Africa and Latin America, but was caught and executed by the Bolivian army in 1967.

❖ see FULGENCIO BATISTA p17

Boris Yeltsin (1931–2007)

President of Russia (1991–2000) An outspoken critic of the traditional Soviet structure, Yeltsin was elected president of Russia in 1991. He was a key figure in the break-up of the Soviet Union and moved Russia towards a market economy. In 1993 he introduced both a new parliament and constitution. Despite ill-health and growing unpopularity due to the long war in Chechnya, Yeltsin was re-elected in 1996. He resigned in 2000, naming Vladimir Putin as his successor.

Nazi Party (1933–45)

German political party. The abbreviated name of the National Socialist Party, the Nazis governed Germany under the brutal dictatorship of Adolf Hitler from 1933 to 1945. The Party ideology included state control over the individual, enforced by violent repression and racism, a policy that resulted in the deaths of, among others, six million Jews in concentration camps. The party was banned in Germany after World War II, though neo-Nazism gained some popularity following reunification, and groups have also sprung up in other countries.

❖ see CONCENTRATION CAMPS p171, ADOLF HITLER p159, WORLD WAR II p172

LEFT: *Che Guevara, Cuban revolutionary and writer, joined forces with the Castro brothers in the 1960s and formed a guerilla movement to depose Batista.*

Munich Agreement (1938)

Pact signed by Germany, Italy, France and Britain in which Czechoslovakia was forced to surrender its Sudetenland region to Hitler. Britain and France, still recovering from World War I, were desperate to avoid confrontation with Germany and agreed on this policy of appeasement in return for Hitler's promise not to claim any other territory. The Munich pact was nullified when German troops marched into Czechoslovakia in March 1939 and claimed the rest of the country.

❖ see WORLD WAR II p172

Nazi-Soviet Pact (1939)

Treaty of non-aggression between Germany and the Soviet Union. The secret pact was signed a few days before the outbreak of World War II and divided Eastern Europe into separate German and Soviet spheres of influence. This enabled Hitler to invade Poland from the east and partition the country. The pact dissolved when Germany invaded the Soviet Union in 1941. Until 1989, the USSR denied the pact's existence as it was evidence of its annexation of the Baltic States.

❖ see NAZI PARTY p22, WORLD WAR II p172

Arab League (1945)

Organization of Arab countries, formed in 1945 to co-ordinate political and economic interests. Its 21 members include nearly all of the Arab states and the Palestine Liberation Organization, and its headquarters are in Cairo. In 1948, league members attacked the newly formed Jewish state of Israel. Egypt was suspended (1979–89) following its peace agreement with Israel, and the headquarters were moved to Tunis. The Iraqi invasion of Kuwait in 1990 and subsequent involvement of Western countries (invited by Saudi Arabia) caused a deep rift between members.

❖ see GULF WAR p181

RIGHT: *A uniform bearing a swastika, the symbol of the Nazi Party.*

Iron Curtain (1945)

Political and military barrier put up by the Soviet Union after World War II to seal itself off from Western Europe. Although the term had been in use before, it was popularized by Winston Churchill's speech in 1946: 'From Stettin in the Baltic to Trieste in the Adriatic an iron curtain has descended across the continent.' The Berlin Wall, built in 1961, reinforced the concept, which largely ceased to exist following the 1989 fall of Communism in both the USSR and its satellite states. The 'bamboo curtain' has also been used to describe the barrier between Communist China and other countries.

❖ see BERLIN WALL p28, COLD WAR p100

Potsdam Conference (1945)

Meeting convened at the end of World War II to organize the administration of post-war Germany. Leaders of the main Allied Powers – US president Harry S. Truman, Winston Churchill (and later Clement Attlee) from Britain and the USSR's premier Joseph Stalin – divided Germany into 'zones of occupation' to be controlled by military forces from each of the delegate countries, plus France. The conference's aims failed in practice due to difficulties among the occupying powers and the unclear wording of the final declaration.

❖ see WINSTON CHURCHILL p12, JOSEPH STALIN p14, WORLD WAR II p172

BELOW: *A street poster depicts Communist leaders during the iron-curtain era when Europe was split into the USSR-backed East and the US-backed West.*

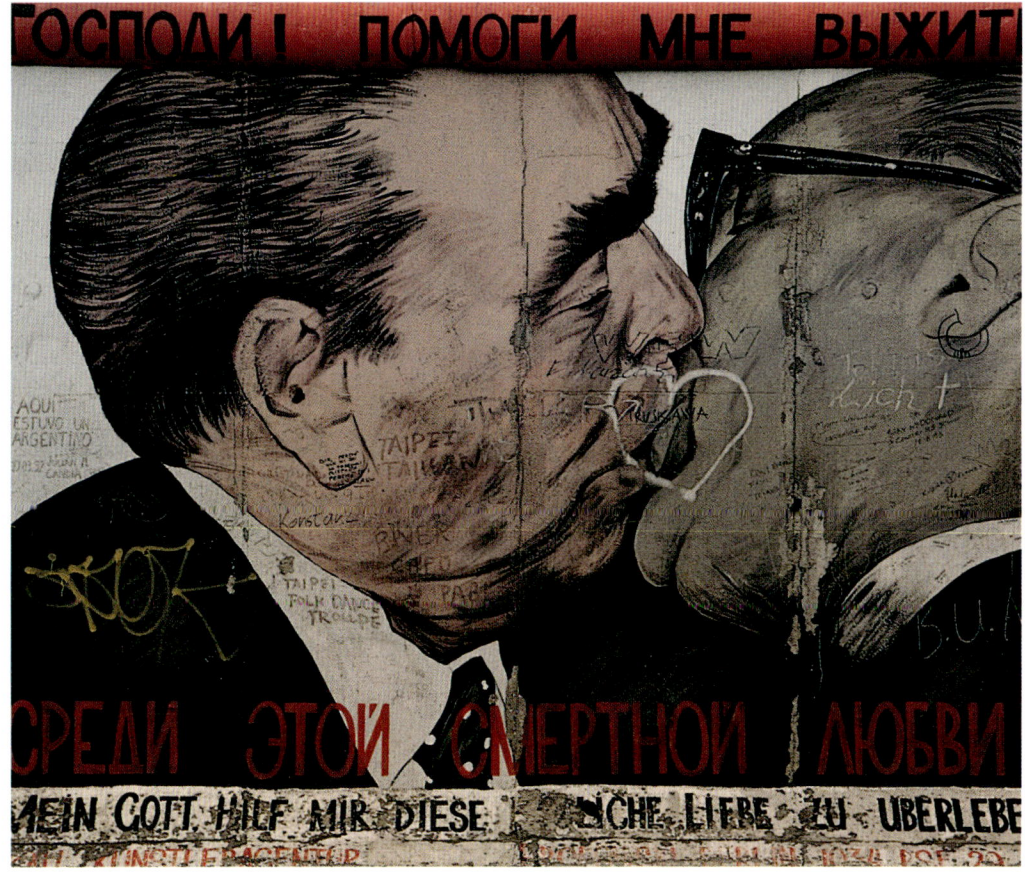

United Nations (1945)

International association of nations. After World War II, the United Nations was created to prevent another international conflict. The organization has representatives from nearly every country in the world and aims to work as an independent body preserving peace. The UN Charter, devised in 1945, was signed by 50 nations – today there are more than 185 member countries. The UN also provides aid and support to developing nations.

The central body of the United Nations is divided into six sections: the General Assembly (international forum); the Security Council (peacekeeping wing); the Secretariat (administrative branch); the Economic and Social Council (contains aid agencies); the International Court of Justice; and the Trusteeship Council. The Economic and Social Council oversees a huge number of agencies such as UNICEF, WHO, the World Bank and UNESCO. These groups provide loans, personnel, food and medical supplies, and much more, to areas in need.

The Security Council has a major function within the United Nations, helping settle major conflicts and making decisions regarding UN peacekeeping troops. There are 15 member countries, five of which are permanent: France, China, Russia, Britain and the USA. If one of the permanent delegates opposes a decision, they use the power of 'veto': this has blocked many UN recommendations.

❖ see WORLD WAR II p172

Yalta Conference (1945)

Meeting between British prime minister Winston Churchill, US president Franklin D. Roosevelt and Soviet premier Joseph Stalin. Critical decisions made during this conference remained secret until the end of World War II. The Yalta delegates demanded Germany's unconditional surrender and made plans to divide Germany into four occupied zones under Berlin's control. These and other agreements were widely disputed and led to criticism of Roosevelt in the United States.

❖ see WINSTON CHURCHILL p12, FRANKLIN D. ROOSEVELT p14, WORLD WAR II p172

BELOW: *A propaganda poster issued shortly after the end of World War II, at the formation of the United Nations. It promotes the idea of international co-operation and mutual support.*

POLITICS

ABOVE: *US President Bill Clinton enjoyed two terms in office.*

Bill Clinton (b. 1946)

Former US president (1993–2001). First elected Arkansas governor in 1976, he defeated George Bush in 1993. Clinton's battles with a Republican-dominated Congress meant he was unable to pass healthcare reforms, although he did increase the minimum wage. Foreign policy successes included restoring relations with Vietnam and a role as peacemaker in Bosnia and Northern Ireland. But his presidency was dogged by scandal, including the Whitewater Case and his affair with Monica Lewinsky. Clinton was the first sitting president to testify before a grand jury and he narrowly avoided impeachment after committing perjury. His wife, Hillary Rodham Clinton, is Senator of New York.

Indian Independence (1947)

Creation of modern-day India and Pakistan. Political riots and uprisings became intense in India after World War I, Gandhi calling the Indian people to counter British repression with passive resistance. During the 1920s and 1930s civil disobedience led to the imprisonment of Gandhi and nearly 30,000 Indian nationalists. Despite autonomous legislative bodies being established (1935), when World War II broke out the Viceroy of India declared war on Germany without consulting elected Indian councils. During the war, anti-British agitation continued. By 1945, Gandhi and other leaders had been released. India and Pakistan were established as independent countries in 1947.

❖ see BRITISH EMPIRE p124, WORLD WAR I p164, WORLD WAR II p172

Organizations of American States (1948)

Organization formed to foster co-operation, both economic and military, among north, central and south American states. The OAS grew out of the Pan-American Union, a defence pact the USA felt was in need of reinforcement at the onset of the Cold War in 1948. Its founding principle was to consider an attack on one American state as an attack on all. The organization aimed to prevent the spread of Communism, and Cuba was suspended in 1961 when a Marxist government came to power. Canada finally joined in 1990. Since the collapse of the Soviet Union, the OAS has focused on encouraging democracy and monitoring elections in its member states.

❖ see COLD WAR p100

North Atlantic Treaty Organization (NATO) (1949)

Organization set up to implement the North Atlantic Treaty (1949). The treaty established Western Europe's military answer to the Warsaw Pact alliance, led by the Soviet Union. The wartime armies of Britain, France and the USA had been drastically reduced at the end of World

War II. In contrast, the Soviets had a huge army in Eastern Europe to reinforce Communist control of the region. NATO's answer was to deploy US nuclear weapons: its numbers were always fewer than the Warsaw Pact's huge ground forces, but NATO had superior weaponry. The Cold War stand-off came to an end in 1989 when the USSR fell apart. In the 1990s, NATO's role changed to that of peacekeeper with operations in places like Bosnia. Russia opposed applications to join NATO from Eastern European countries, such as Poland, Hungary and the Czech Republic, but all three joined in 1999. By 2001, NATO membership stood at 19.

❖ see WARSAW PACT p27, WORLD WAR II p172

German Democratic Republic (1949)

Official name of East Germany. Established in 1949 from the former Soviet occupation zone, East Germany was a satellite state of the USSR. The Berlin Wall was built in 1961 to halt the flow of refugees to West Germany, and as leader (1971–89), Eric Honecker presided over one of the most politically repressive police states in the Soviet bloc. In 1989, Honecker was ousted, the hated secret police disbanded and the borders were reopened. Reunification with West Germany occurred the following year.

❖ see BERLIN WALL p28, COLD WAR p100

Warsaw Pact (1955)

Military alliance between the Soviet Union and Eastern European Communist countries. The pact was signed by the USSR and Albania, Bulgaria, the former Czechoslovakia, the former East Germany, Hungary, Poland and Romania in response to the rearmament of West Germany and its admission to NATO (the North Atlantic Treaty Organization). The real function of the agreement was to strengthen the Soviet hold over its satellites. Although the Warsaw Pact was renewed in 1985, the political transformation of Eastern Europe in 1989 profoundly weakened the organization and it was dissolved on 1 July 1991.

❖ see WORLD WAR II p172

BELOW: *Sikh and Hindu students take to the streets of Lahore, shouting anti-Pakistan slogans and brandishing weapons during their fight for Indian independence in 1947.*

POLITICS

Suez Crisis (1956)

International conflict centred on the Suez Canal in Egypt. The canal, an important passageway for oil tankers, was the centre of an international dispute from July–December 1956. Britain and France, joint controllers of the canal, developed a dispute with Egyptian President Nasser following the US and British withdrawal from a major Egyptian construction project, the Aswan High Dam. Nasser retaliated by nationalizing the canal and taking control of the Suez Canal Company. In October 1956, Israeli troops invaded Egypt and occupied the canal zone, to be joined by French and British military. The United Nations denounced the action, and evacuated the European troops in December.

❖ see ABDEL NASSER p21

Berlin Wall (1961–89)

Wall that divided East and West Berlin. Between 1949–61 about 2.5 million East Germans defected to West Germany. To stop this exodus, the East German authorities built a 47 km (29 mile) wall on 12 August 1961. About 5,000 East Germans managed to cross it, but about the same number were caught. Over 100 people were killed attempting the escape. The Wall remained a symbol of division until it was dismantled following the collapse of the East German Communist regime in 1989.

❖ see COLD WAR p100, IRON CURTAIN p24

ABOVE: *The Suez Canal is an artificially-built waterway which connects the Mediterranean Sea with the Gulf of Suez.*

RIGHT: *A former symbol of suppression, hatred and division: the ramparts of the Berlin Wall in East Berlin.*

Cuban Missile Crisis (1962)

Cold War confrontation between the US and Soviet Union. After the unsuccessful Bay of Pigs invasion to oust him by US-backed Cuban exiles, Fidel Castro began acquiring weapons from the Soviet Union. In 1962, Soviet missiles with nuclear warheads trained on American cities were secretly stationed in Cuba. US spy planes detected these and President Kennedy demanded their removal. After six tense days – during which the world came close to nuclear war – the Soviets agreed to dismantle the missile sites. In return, the USA removed its own nuclear missiles from Turkey.

❖ see BAY OF PIGS INVASION p177, JOHN F. KENNEDY p20

Strategic Arms Limitations Talks (SALT) (1969–79)

Two long series of arms negotiations between the USA and the Soviet Union. In 1972, the SALT I agreements were signed in Moscow by President Nixon and General Secretary Brezhnev. Two major pacts resulted: the Treaty on Anti-Ballistic Missile Systems and the Interim Agreement on Limitation of Strategic Offensive Weapons. In 1979, SALT II was signed; this agreement set controls on missiles with multiple warheads.

❖ see RICHARD NIXON p19

POLITICS

Bloody Sunday (1972)

Day on which demonstrators were killed by British Army in Northern Ireland. On Sunday 30 January 1972, British soldiers shot at a crowd of 300,000 Catholic demonstrators in Londonderry and killed 13 people. The authorities claimed the dead were 'gunmen' although weapons were never found on them. Subsequent inquiries have been inconclusive. The Irish Ambassador in London was recalled to Dublin and the British Embassy in Dublin was burned down. The year following Bloody Sunday showed a sharp increase in sectarian violence, with the Irish Republican Army (IRA) finding many new recruits among nationalists who now turned to direct action to expel British troops.

BELOW: *A funeral procession for those who fell during Bloody Sunday in 1972, when 13 Irish demonstrators were gunned down by British soldiers in Northern Ireland.*

Watergate (1972–74)

US political scandal that led to President Nixon's resignation. The story began with the arrest of five men for burglary and wiretapping at the Democrat Party's national headquarters in the Watergate offices in Washington. Nixon's secret attempts to cover up his administration's involvement in the affair, including 'hush money' to the Watergate burglars, were uncovered by news reporters Carl Bernstein and Bob Woodward, who were fed information by a source known only as 'Deep Throat'. Nixon obstructed the FBI's attempts to get hold of his taped conversations, finally releasing some that implicated him in the Watergate affair. He resigned on 8 August 1974 before he was impeached.

❖ see RICHARD NIXON p19

Khmer Rouge (1975–79)

Communist rulers of Cambodia. Cambodia was granted independence by France in 1953. Pol Pot, an urban radical and Communist, became Secretary General of the party in 1963. With a war raging in Vietnam, the Cambodian monarch, Sihanouk, attempted to keep the country out of the war. A right-wing military coup, led by the US-backed General Lon Nol, overthrew Sihanouk in 1970 and the Khmer Rouge fought a civil war that finally defeated Lon Nol after the capture of the capital, Phnom Penh. During the next four years, at least 1.7 million Cambodians were killed. Among them intellectuals were massacred and minorities wiped out. Buddhism was suppressed and the Khmer Rouge began to attack its neighbouring countries, including Vietnam, Thailand and Laos. After a rebellion in 1978, the Vietnamese invaded, and eventually Pol Pot was arrested in 1997 and sentenced to life imprisonment for his crimes. The rebels took power after January 1979.

Tiananmen Square Massacre (1989)

Chinese people's demonstration that ended in killings by the army. In April 1989, students began a huge pro-democracy demonstration that continued for two months. They were calling for political reform and the resignation of the Communist leadership. The students were joined by workers, intellectuals and civil servants, and their numbers swelled to over one million in Tiananmen Square, which is the largest public square in the world. Premier Deng Xiaoping responded by instating martial law on 20 May and then sending in the army on the night of 3 and 4 June to quell the unrest. As many as 2,000 unarmed protesters were killed and many student leaders arrested.

Maastricht Treaty (1991)

Historic document signed by members of the European Community (EC) in the Dutch city of Maastricht. The city was put on the map when it hosted an important summit between the 12 members of the EC, convened to accelerate their economic and political integration. The resulting treaty, officially called the Treaty on European Union, granted European citizenship to citizens of each member country. This allowed greater freedom for people to move between countries in order to live, work or study.

BELOW: *Propagandist literature in favour of the Maastricht Referendum.*

POLITICS

KEY DATES

1900 BC	❖	Birth of Abraham
722 BC	❖	Jewish diaspora begins
566 BC	❖	Death of the Buddha (historical)
c. AD 31	❖	Death of Jesus Christ
AD 70	❖	Siege and destruction of Jerusalem
AD 325	❖	Council of Nicaea
AD 632	❖	Death of the prophet Muhammad
6th century	❖	Benedictine order established
9th century	❖	Holy Roman Empire established
1096	❖	Crusades begin
1226	❖	Death of St Francis of Assisi
1232	❖	Beginning of the Roman Catholic Inquisition
1378	❖	The Great Schism
1515	❖	Martin Luther nails his '95 Theses' to the door at Wittenberg
1534	❖	Henry VIII severs ties with Rome
1539	❖	Death of Guru Nanak, founder of the Sikh religion
1546	❖	Death of Martin Luther

RELIGION

1564	❖	Death of Jean Calvin
1545–63	❖	Council of Trent
1691	❖	Death of George Fox, founder of the Quakers
1844	❖	Death of Joseph Smith, founder of the Mormon Movement
1844	❖	Foundation of the Baha'i movement
1920	❖	Birth of Pope John Paul II
1935	❖	Birth of the Dalai Lama
1975	❖	Death of Haile Selassie
1997	❖	Death of Mother Theresa

Bible

The Christian Bible is a library of books (from a Greek word meaning 'books') of many different styles. It had taken its present form by the second century AD. The Christian Bible contains the Old and New Testaments; for Christians, the New Testament is more important. It contains four Gospels (accounts of Jesus's life and teachings) and a number of letters from the early years of the Church. The Gospels are very different from one another but they all focus on Jesus as the Messiah who brings freedom from sin and the possibility of eternal life to those who follow him. It is the only written source for knowledge of Jesus. Christians interpret the Bible differently, but all accept that the Gospels represent Jesus as revealing God's love for the world. It is the central resource and inspiration of the Christian faith. The Christian Old Testament corresponds to the Jewish (Hebrew) Bible.

❖ see JESUS CHRIST p35

Abraham (c. 1900 BC)

Abraham was born in Mesopotamia around 1900 BC. The Old Testament tells how God appeared to him and offered him and his people the Promised Land in Canaan. The Bible also tells of how Abraham was instructed by God to sacrifice his son Isaac, which the prophet was about to do when angels intervened and saved him.

Jerusalem

Capital of the State of Israel. Captured by King David (c. 1000 BC), its origins go back to 1800 BC and it was the site of Solomon's Temple (c. 950 BC). Jerusalem was destroyed by the Babylonians in 587 BC and partially restored by Nehemiah in 445–433 BC. Herod the Great carried out a re-building programme. In AD 70 the Temple and city were destroyed by the Romans under Titus. Only the Western Wall of the old city remains today. After the Bar Kochba

ABOVE: *The cover of the tenth-century Echternact Bible.*

ABOVE: *A devout Jewish man worships by the Wailing Wall in Jerusalem.*

revolt (AD 132–135) it was renamed 'Aolia Capitolina' by Hadrian and all Jews were expelled.

For Christians, Jerusalem is the city of Jesus's death and resurrection. The Jewish–Christian Church existed there until the exile under Hadrian. The Christian centre of the city is the Church of the Holy Sepulchre (purported to be built over the burial place of Jesus). Jerusalem is a potent Christian symbol as a place of pilgrimage.

Jerusalem is not mentioned in the Qur'an, but is the third most important city for Muslims. Muhammad's Night Journey took place there and originally it was the direction of Muslim prayer (before Mecca). The 'al-Aqsa' mosque and the Dome of the Rock were erected on Temple Mount after the Muslim invasion of AD 614 and the capture of Jerusalem in AD 638. Muslims were tolerant of Jews and Christians in Jerusalem until 1009 when many Christian buildings were destroyed. Saladin overthrew the Crusaders, who had captured Jerusalem and respected religious differences.

❖ see JESUS CHRIST p35, CRUSADES p39, HEROD THE GREAT p55

Jesus Christ (c. 6 BC – C. AD 31)

Born in Bethlehem to Mary and Joseph and raised in Nazareth in Galilee (Israel), Jesus was a wandering teacher in the north of Israel who visited Jerusalem only once or twice. Jesus gained a reputation for healing and exorcism and challenging the religious authorities. He appeared to possess insight into the reality and Fatherhood of God. He ate and drank with the outcasts in society and taught forgiveness, compassion and humility, and the nearness of the rule of God to human life. Jesus gathered a group of 12 disciples around him, encouraging them to go and preach that the Kingdom of God was at hand. After a ministry of three years, he came to be regarded as a religious and political troublemaker. He was betrayed by one of his disciples, arrested, deserted by his followers, tried by religious authorities and then Pontius Pilate the Roman governor condemned him to death on a cross in public. He died and was buried. After that, a number of his disciples had visions and experiences that led them to believe that God had raised Jesus, God's son, from the dead. Jesus was the Messiah. It is on this story that the Christian Church and Christianity rest.

❖ see PONTIUS PILATE p36

ABOVE: *An image of Jesus Christ.*

Pontius Pilate

Pilate was the Roman governor of Judea at the time of Jesus of Nazareth's death. The Christian Gospels record Jesus's appearance before Pilate who allowed Jesus to be crucified, a Roman method of executing criminals. The Gospels record Pilate's weakness in giving in to the demands of the religious authorities with regard to Jesus, symbolized by his hand washing. Pilate's main concern would have been to keep the peace at the tense time of the Jewish Passover; Jesus would simply have been another criminal to die.

❖ see BIBLE p34, JESUS CHRIST p35

Ethnic Cleansing

Purging an area of an unwanted ethnic group. Although ethnic cleansing is associated with the former Yugoslavia, in particular Bosnia and Herzegovina, deportation, mass murder and genocide have featured in European history for many centuries. The Jews suffered from ethnic cleansing in Spain, Great Britain and Germany in the 1930s and 1940s. The Armenians suffered at the hands of the Turks at the end of the nineteenth century. Following the break-up of Yugoslavia, Bosnian Muslims suffered at the hands of the Serbs from 1992, forcing the UN to deploy troops to protect six safe areas in the region. To date, many of those responsible for ethnic cleansing have not been brought to trial despite widespread world condemnation of the massacres that claimed the lives of up to 250,000 people and displaced 2.3 million. In 1996, the International Criminal Tribunal for the former Yugoslavia indicted 50 Bosnians for massacring civilians during the war, including Radovan Karadzic, the President of the Bosnian Serb Republic and General Ratko Mladic, his military commander. By 1997, the tribunal had indicted 74 people: 54 Serbs, 17 Croats and three Muslims, the first time an international court has tried someone for war crimes since World War II.

Council of Nicaea (AD 325)

Called by Emperor Constantine to deal with heresy threatening the unity of the Christian Church. Most of the 220–250 bishops present were from the eastern half of the empire, while only six attended from the Western Church. This first ecumenical Council produced a creed (statement of faith), probably based on the baptismal creeds of Antioch and Jerusalem, and calculated the date

WORLD HISTORY

of Easter. The creed, used frequently today, was received and agreed by the majority of bishops present.

❖ see JERUSALEM p34

St Augustine of Hippo (AD 354–430)

A native of North Africa, Augustine was a professor of rhetoric until his conversion at the age of 32 in AD 387. Ordained in AD 391, by AD 394 he was Bishop of Hippo in North Africa. He became one of the most influential thinkers in Christianity, using his considerable intellect to defend the Christian faith and refute heresy. He argued that all humans are born into an inherited state of sin, the penalty for which is death. This was caused by the disobedience of Adam (Genesis 3). His *Confessions* (basically autobiographical, c. AD 400) and *City of God* (AD 413–26) are classics of their kind. His feast day is 28 August.

❖ see BIBLE p34

BELOW LEFT: *The prolonged conflict in Bosnia-Herzegovina, formerly Yugoslavia, resulted in countless 'ethnic cleansing' atrocities.*

BELOW: *A Hindu artesan chisels a statue of Buddha. Buddhism is a faith that has enjoyed an increase in followers in recent years.*

Siddhartha Gautama (the Buddha) (566–483 BC or AD 368–448)

Born Siddhartha Gautama into the Sakya clan of a wealthy family, he was married with a son, Rahula. At the age of 29 he saw an old man, a sick man, a corpse and an ascetic. He renounced his life at home and became an ascetic, and while he was meditating under the Bodhi tree he achieved Enlightenment. He was then 35 years old. He spent 45 years in the company of an order of monks and later nuns teaching his philosophy to the people of North India. He taught the 'Middle Way'; between the life of a householder doomed to countless rebirths, and the celibate life of extreme asceticism, which seeks the right goal, but by the wrong means. The goal is nirvana (a place of indescribable peace); one who attains it is enlightened (buddha) and is no longer reborn or subject to karma. At his death he enters into 'nirvana'. Gautama was one in a long line of Buddhas. His teaching has been developed over the centuries and as a missionary religion often takes on an element of the culture of that it meets.

Prophet Muhammad (AD 570–632)

Muhammad, the last of the Prophets in the Muslim religion, was of the family of Banu Haskim in the tribe of Quraysh. At the age of 25 he married Khadija, his employer, with whom he had two sons and four daughters. In AD 611, he received a message from Jibril insisting he 'recite' (Iqra). Over the next 22 years he received a number of messages, which form the Qur'an. Muhammad's messages were not well received in Mecca where he lived, and in AD 622 he left (called 'the Hijra') for Yathrib (now called 'al-Madina'). In AD 630 Muhammad returned and purged idols and images from Mecca. He died in AD 632.

Called the 'Seal of the Prophets', his message, Muslims believe, is the true, final and uncorrupted Word of God (Allah). Muhammad was unlearned, a human being (not a god) and not without sin. He is, however, a living commentary on the Qur'an. He is not the founder of Islam as Muslims believe Islam has always been; Muhammad is the final revelation.

Qur'an

Islamic religious text. The Prophet Muhammad received the first of many messages from Allah through the Angel Jibril when he was 40 years old. The first message was the first of many surahs (or chapters) now contained in the Qur'an; it was revealed to Muhammad between AD 610 and 632. Muslims believe the Qur'an is Allah's own word, not that of any human being. Muhammad was illiterate and had to learn each revelation (which continued for the next 23 years) by heart; there are 114 surahs of varying lengths. The revelation would be recited ('Qur'an' means 'recite') so it would be remembered. The Arabic of the Qur'an is the finest form of the language and as the Word of God it can never be effectively translated. After Muhammad's death, the Qur'an was compiled and checked for accuracy by the scribe Zayd Ibn Thabit under the authority of Caliph Uthman. The Qur'an lies at the very heart of Islam, it is the Word of God, the fundamental source of guidance for Muslims and is treated with the greatest respect.

❖ see PROPHET MUHAMMAD p38

Benedictine Order (6th century)

Religious order of monks and nuns. St Benedict's (c. 480–c. 550) 'The Rule of St Benedict' became the fundamental rule of Western monasticism. It consisted of 73 chapters dealing with spiritual matters, organization, liturgy and discipline. Known as the Black Monks, the regime is simple but not harshly ascetic. The monks helped preserve scholarship and art in worship and liturgy during the difficult years of the second millennium. The abbot is elected and, in spite of an attempt in 1215 to unify the Order, their houses remain autonomous and self-governing but group together in congregations.

❖ see BIBLE p34

LEFT: *A fifteenth-century Persian manuscript showing the Prophet Muhammad being escorted to Paradise by the angel Jibril.*

ABOVE: *A Benedictine monk offers his missal to his abbot.*

Crusades (1096–1281)

Series of Christian military expeditions to Syria and Palestine in eleventh and thirteenth centuries. Some argue they continued until 1464, so traditionally the number is eight. The aim was, in theory, to secure the Christian sites allowing proper access to them.

The First Crusade (literally meaning 'cross-marked') was instigated by Pope Urban II in 1095 and was the most successful. The Crusaders captured Jerusalem in 1099. Succeeding crusades were less successful. The Third Crusade included the English King Richard I and much folklore has developed around his absence from England and the activities of his brother King John. In truth, the Crusades emphasized the division between Eastern and Western Christianity and reinforced the ideological divide between Islam and Christianity. The Song of Roland captures the spirit: 'Christians are right, pagans are wrong' (or at least Western Christians are right). Western Christianity was to become identified with military force and power; it was Christians who sacked Constantinople. The era, however, remains in the public mind as a glorious period of Renaissance and the Arab civilization and civilizing tendencies were ignored.

❖ see RICHARD I OF ENGLAND p63

ABOVE: *The Knights Templar vowed to protect Christian pilgrims in the Holy Crusades from attacks by Muslim bandits on their way to the Holy Land.*

St Thomas Becket (c.1117–70)

English martyr. Thomas Becket was born in London and educated in Bologna and Auxerre before becoming chancellor in 1155 and Archbishop of Canterbury in 1162. A close friend of King Henry II, he had lived a worldly life, but once appointed archbishop he became a fierce supporter of the rights of the clergy. He objected strongly to the claim that clergy found guilty by a bishop should be handed over to the state for punishment. His close friendship with Henry turned into bitter enmity and he was exiled a number of times. He returned to Canterbury in 1170 and was murdered in his cathedral on 29 December by knights from Henry's court. He was proclaimed a martyr at once and canonized in 1173. His shrine in Canterbury Cathedral is a famous place of pilgrimage for Christians. His feast day is 29 December.

Knights Templar (1119–1314)

Religious military order. A group of knights, led by Hugues de Payens, vowed to devote themselves to the protection of pilgrims at risk from marauding Muslim bandits in the Holy Land. They were supported by Baldwin II, King of Jerusalem, and given the former Jewish Temple as their base. They numbered 20,000 at their height, and had many fortresses in Palestine. They became wealthy and were used as bankers by kings and pilgrims. In 1307, with the help of Pope Clement V, King Philip IV of France imprisoned the Templars in France and their property was confiscated by various states.

❖ see CRUSADES p39

Pope Innocent III (1160–1216)

Italian pope. Born Lotario dei Conti de Segni in Agnoni, Italy, Innocent III was pope from 1198 to 1216. His papacy represented the high point of temporal and spiritual supremacy of the Roman See. He excommunicated King John for refusing to recognize Stephen Langton as Archbishop of Canterbury in 1212. He convened one of the great councils of the Church, the Fourth Vatican Council in 1215. Innocent was the first pope to call himself 'Vicar of Christ'. During his papacy, clerical celibacy became more widespread, the chalice was withheld from the laity at mass, and confession was introduced. Persecution became the duty of Catholic kings.

BELOW: *The murder of St Thomas Becket in Canterbury Cathedral at the hands of killers hired by his former patron, King Henry II.*

St Francis of Assisi (c.1181–1226)

A native of Assisi and born into a wealthy family, Francis was led to a complete change of lifestyle when, after hearing at Mass Jesus's commission (Matthew 10:7-19) in 1209, he founded the Franciscan Order. It was based on joyous worship of Christ and poverty. In 1214 Francis travelled to Palestine to convert the Muslims but failed. The Order was approved by Innocent III and tradition says that on 14 September 1224 he received the stigmata on his hands and feet. Traditionally kind and gentle to animals, he is believed to have created the first 'crib scene' now familiar at Christmas time in Christian homes and churches.

Inquisition (1232)

Roman Catholic tribunal for prosecuting heresy, it was first created on a temporary basis by Pope Gregory IX in France and Germany in the thirteenth century. The Inquisition in general was established by Gregory IX in 1232 with inquisitors being mainly Dominican and Franciscan monks. The office has been redesigned and renamed over the centuries and in 1965 it became the Congregation for the Doctrine of the Faith.

In Spain the Inquisition was centred in Tarragossa in Aragon. This was superseded by the Spanish Inquisition founded by papal bull (1478) and set up in 1480. It was concerned to investigate the orthodoxy of Jews (1492) and Muslims of Castile (1502) who had been forced to accept the Christian faith. Sixteen permanent tribunals were eventually created in Spain between 1500–1640. In the first 10 years it burnt 2,000 people and punished 15,000 others. It played a major role in the extermination of Islam from Spain in the fifteenth to seventeenth centuries. The Inquisition was extended to Portugal, Goa (1560), Brazil, Peru (1570) and Mexico (1571). It was finally abolished in Spain in 1834. The Inquisition represented the end of the easy-going ways of the past and the start of a regime of repression.

Great Schism (1378)

The 'Great Schism' refers to two unrelated events: the first being the excommunication by Rome in 1054 of the Patriarch of Constantinople, and the second being the disputed elections of Urban VI. The doctrinal reason for the excommunication merely set a seal on the rift between the Eastern and Western churches that had lasted for centuries. The papal schism in the Western church (1378–1417) arose from the disputed election of Urban VI. Disaffected cardinals elected Clement VII, a cousin of the French king, who took up residence in Avignon. In 1409, the two sides met, disagreed and created a third pope at Pisa. In 1415 at the Council of Constance, the Pisa pope was deposed; the Roman pope Gregory XII resigned. The Avignon pope took refuge in Spain where his successor finally repudiated claims in 1429.

❖ see POPE CLEMENT VII p44

Pope Paul III (1468–1549)

Italian pope (1534–49). He was born Alessandro Farnese at Canino, Italy, educated in Rome and Florence, where he was taught by humanists. He became a cardinal in 1493, although he was not ordained until 1519. Paul III was a reforming pope who encouraged artists and architects (including the completion of the Sistine Chapel by Michelangelo). A report he commissioned, *Concilium de Emendenda Ecclesia* (1538), formed the basis of the Council of Trent (1545). He recognized the Society of Jesus (1540) and in 1542 created the Holy Office of the Inquisition to combat heresy. He excommunicated Henry VIII of England in 1538.

❖ see HENRY VIII OF ENGLAND p72, INQUISITION p42

Guru Nanak (1469–1539)

First Sikh Guru and founder of the Sikh religion. Nanak married and had two sons, after which he became pre-occupied with a spiritual quest. In 1499, he experienced God's call. He went on to teach that God is 'One and eternal'. One can meditate on God's name to master the impulses and passions of life, but above all one must trust the guru (spiritual teacher). He composed hymns, now contained in the Adi Granth. He also taught irrelevance of caste – inner purity was vital.

RIGHT: *St Francis of Assisi.*

Pope Clement VII (1478–1534)

Born Guilio de Medici in Italy, he was pope from 1523–34. He allied himself with François I of France against the Holy Roman Emperor, Charles V, who sacked Rome in 1527 and took Clement prisoner. Eight thousand people were killed in the Sack of Rome. Clement managed to escape to Orvieto. The sacking of Rome is often regarded as the event that brought the Renaissance to an end. Clement was indecisive and his failure to deal with the English Henry VIII's divorce from Catherine of Aragon hastened the Reformation in England. The antipope, Clement VII (d. 1394) was elected by French cardinals in 1378, so beginning the Great Schism and the Avignon Papacy.
❖ see GREAT SCHISM p42, HENRY VIII OF ENGLAND p72

St Thomas More (1478–1535)

Chancellor to Henry VIII and scholar. A twice-married lawyer, More published *Utopia* in 1516 gaining him a European reputation for scholarship. In 1529 he became Lord Chancellor but was unable to support Henry VIII's drive for a divorce. He resigned, refused to recognize the king as head of the English Church and was imprisoned in the Tower of London where he wrote *Dialogue of Comfort against Tribulation*. After 15 months, he was beheaded in 1535 and his head displayed on Tower Bridge. He was made a saint in 1935.
❖ see HENRY VIII OF ENGLAND p72

Martin Luther (1483–1546)

Born at Eisleben, Luther was the founding father of the German Reformation. Ordained in 1507, he was appointed professor of scripture at Wittenberg in 1512. In 1517 he posted his '95 Theses' on the door of Wittenberg Cathedral, objecting to the selling of indulgences by the Church. After debating his views with Catholic theologians he was censored by the pope in 1520. At the Diet of Worms the Emperor Charles V asked him to recant; Luther refused unless scripture could persuade him. Concerned for Luther's safety, the Elector of Saxony gave him protection.

In 1525 Luther married, and the security of home life became a great strength to him. Luther was not to argue his case in the systematic way of the other great reformer, Jean Calvin. He argued passionately and occasionally paradoxically, with pastoral concerns at the forefront of his mind. His main theological emphasis lay on the importance of scripture and salvation: Through faith alone can a person attain salvation. Faith is the means by which a person can receive all that Christ offered by his death. Lutheranism spread rapidly across Europe, particularly in Scandinavia, Iceland, Prussia and the Baltic States.
❖ see JEAN CALVIN p45, REFORMATION p47

Jean Calvin (1509–64)

Leader of the Protestant Reformation in Europe. Calvin was born in Noyon, Picardy, and studied at Paris, Orleans and Bourges. In Paris he experienced a change in religious outlook. Encouraged by the work of people like Martin Luther, he began to write and teach. He was soon forced to leave Paris. In 1536 he published *Institutes of the Christian Religion* and soon settled in Geneva before having to flee to Strasbourg. In 1541 he returned to Geneva and remained there until his death. In *Ecclesiastical Ordinances* Calvin displays a grasp of the importance of structure and discipline for the Church's survival in difficult conditions. He argued that at the heart of Christian life lies 'union with Christ', salvation being dependent entirely on God's grace. The Bible focused attention on Jesus Christ and was vital in reforming every aspect of the Christian life and faith. Calvin's teaching was hugely influential in Western Christianity.

❖ see BIBLE p34, MARTIN LUTHER p44, REFORMATION p47

BELOW: *Martin Luther (centre) reformed the German Christian Church and became one of the founders of Protestantism in Europe. One of his main objections to the Catholic Church was its sale of indulgences to the devout.*

Huguenots

French Calvinist Protestants whose rivalry with Catholics in the form of the House of Guise led to the French Wars of Religion (1562–98). There had been increasing persecution under Henri II (1547–59). Their leader, Henri of Navarre, succeeded to the throne in 1589. In spite of being a Huguenot, he reportedly said, 'Paris is worth a Mass,' to justify taking control of the capital. He then converted to Catholicism. He did grant important concessions to the Huguenots in the Edict of Nantes (1598). After 1630, there was another Huguenot rebellion and Louis XIV revoked the freedoms agreed in the Edict (1685) with consequent persecution and emigration. On 24 August 1572, the slaughter of Huguenots in Paris was ordered by King Charles IX. This became known as the St Bartholomew's Day Massacre. Two days before, an attempted assassination of the Huguenots' leader, Admiral Coligny, had failed; this led to even more fervent civil war.

❖ see LOUIS XIV OF FRANCE p78

BELOW: *Jean Calvin helped preserve the structure of the Church, troubled by internal schisms, by arguing in favour of its 'union with Christ'.*

George Fox (1624–91)

Founder of the Quakers. Fox preached to an enormous crowd at Pentecost 1652, the date when The Religious Society of Friends is traditionally considered to have begun. Fox had remarkable energy and vision, teaching that the Holy Spirit could come directly to people without the mediation of Church or scripture. The origin of the term 'Quaker' possibly derives from the Spirit of God making people tremble or 'quake'. Originally a term of abuse, it is now a familiar name for the Religious Society of Friends.

Reformation (16th century)

Name given to changes in Western Christianity from the fifteenth century. There were many 'reformations' during this period. It was a time of social and political unrest that fuelled a range of religious protests, from criticism of papal orthodoxy to discontent with the practices of the Church.

The beginning of the Reformation is usually placed when Martin Luther nailed his '95 Theses' to the door of Wittenberg Cathedral in October 1517. Luther's 'protest' was defended by the Elector of Saxony but there were others protesting. It was in 1529 at the Diet of Speyer that the word 'Protestant' emerged, with six German princes protesting at the Emperor's attempt to silence Luther. Ulrich Zwingli (1481–1531) in Switzerland worked with the state to out-manoeuvre the Catholic Church. Jean Calvin also created a theocracy in Geneva. Calvinist revolution became deeply involved with political change across Europe. Geneva rather than Wittenberg became the centre of the Protestant world and the movement spread rapidly to West Germany, France, the Netherlands and Scotland.

In England the development of the Reformation was uneven. Henry VIII severed connections with Rome in 1534 and by the time of his death there was a Bible in every church and the monasteries were dissolved. Scholastic theology took hold and the brief reversion to the Catholic Church under Mary could not halt change. *The Book of Common Prayer* was adopted in 1552; and the Church would be governed under the Queen and parliament. There were other movements – notably the Anabaptists who would wish to abandon all aspects of the medieval Catholic Church and reform a church on New Testament principles.

The Reformation affected every European and forced everyone to make a choice. It transformed the religious map of Europe, with far-reaching consequences.

❖ see JEAN CALVIN p45, HENRY VIII OF ENGLAND p72, MARTIN LUTHER p44

Counter-Reformation (16th to 17th centuries)

Movement for revival and reform in the Catholic Church in the sixteenth and early seventeenth centuries. The reforming elements within the Catholic Church were, generally, not dependent on the Reformation and largely rose from within the Church itself. The religious orders of Augustinians, Carmelites and the Jesuits owed nothing to Protestantism which became the spearhead of the Counter-Reformation in Europe, America and the East (1562–63). The Council of Trent (1545–63) affirmed the supremacy of the pope over those who sought conciliation with Protestants, and the Church emerged with greater vigour and a new liturgy. The Church embarked on a development of architecture, music and ritual and missionary zeal inside and outside Europe. Poland and Germany returned to Rome and in 1622 the Sacred Congregation for the Propagation of the Faith was founded to co-ordinate the missionary enterprise. The movement helped harden the division between Catholic and Protestant that was not resolved until the Treaty of Westphalia in 1648.

❖ see REFORMATION p47

Baha'i (1844)

On 2 May 1844, the Baha'i Faith began. The Bab (1819–50) (meaning 'gate' or 'door') was born in Persia and was a descendant of the Prophet Muhammad. He proclaimed himself the Messenger of God and was executed as a result in 1850, on a charge of heresy against Islam. Three other figures were central to the development of Baha'i: Baha'ullah (1817–92), often considered the founder of Baha'i, Abdu'l-Baha (1844–1921) and Shoghi Effendi (1897–1957). The guiding body of Baha'i is the Universal House of Justice based in Haifa, Israel. Baha'is believe in One God; the common foundation of all faiths; the oneness of humankind; the harmony of science and religion; universal peace; elimination of prejudice; and the equality of the sexes. They are regarded as heretics by Islam and subject to persecution.

❖ see PROPHET MUHAMMAD p38

Haile Selassie (1892–1975)

Emperor of Ethiopia from 1930. Haile Selassie is regarded as the 225th descendant in a line of succession traced back to King Solomon. He took the titles King of Kings, Lord of Lords, and Conquering Lion of the Tribes of Judah. Although now dead, Rastafarians believe his presence can still be felt as Jah (God).

Mother Teresa (1910–97)

Albanian-born founder of the Order of the Missionaries. 'Mother Teresa of Calcutta' joined the Institute of the Blessed Virgin Mary in Ireland in 1928 and then travelled to India to work as a teacher. She studied nursing and founded the Order in 1948, adopting Indian citizenship. In 1963 she was recognized for her services to the people of India and was awarded the first Pope John XXIII Peace Prize in 1971 and the Nobel Peace Prize in 1979. The Order has continued serving the disadvantaged since her death in 1997, numbering 1,000 nuns operating 60 centres in Calcutta and 200 worldwide.

Pope John Paul II (1920–2005)

Polish pope. Born in Wadowice, near Cracow, Poland, Karol Wojtyela moved to Cracow when he was 18 and studied Polish language and literature at university. During World War II he worked in a factory, and in 1946 was ordained, gaining a doctorate at Rome in 1948. He continued to lecture at universities in Poland before becoming a bishop in 1958 and Archbishop of Cracow in 1963. After becoming a cardinal in 1967, he was elected pope in 1978. He travelled extensively throughout the world, the first non-Italian pope for centuries, surviving an assassination attempt in 1981. He had been keen to re-establish and re-affirm traditional Catholic values on social, political and theological matters.

Pope Benedict XVI (b. 1927)

German pope. Born Joseph Alois Ratzinger in Marktl am Inn, Bavaria, Weimar Republic (Germany), he is the reigning Pope, having succeeded Pope John Paul II in 2005. Ratzinger is a well-known Catholic theologian and a prolific author, and is seen as a defender of traditional Catholic doctrine and

values. He served as a professor at several German universities and was a theological consultant at the Second Vatican Council before becoming Archbishop of Munich and Freising, and then Cardinal. During his papacy, Benedict XVI has emphasized what he sees as a need for Europe to return to fundamental Christian values in response to increasing de-Christianization and secularization.

Dalai Lama (b. 1935)

Tibetan religious leader. Born Lhamo Thondup at Takstera in Northern Tibet, Tenzin Gyatso was identified as the 14th Dalai Lama when he was four years old. He assumed temporal power when he was 15 but had to flee Tibet because of the Chinese invasion in 1959. He has lived in Dharamsala, India since then. He has written 40 books teaching a message of love, compassion and non-violence. He was awarded the Nobel Peace Prize in 1989. He is referred to as 'Gyalwa Rinpoche' by Tibetans ('Precious Eminence').

❖ see SIDDHARTHA GAUTAMA p37

BELOW: *Pope Benedict XVI resides at the Vatican in Rome.*

KEY DATES

c. 1766 BC	Shang dynasty established, first Chinese dynasty
1362 BC	Death of pharoah Akhenaten
1333 BC	Death of Tutenkhamen
1050 BC	Chou dynasty established
323 BC	Death of Alexander the Great
AD 14	Death of Augustus Ceasar, the first Roman Emperor
7th century BC	Ch'ing dynasty established
AD 5th or 6th centuries	Rule of Arthur, mythical king of Britain
AD 618	T'ang dynasty founded
AD 768	Carolingian Empire, dynasty of Frankish kings, established
AD 877	Death of Charles II, the first Holy Roman Emperor
AD 899	Death of Alfred the Great
AD 960	Song dynasty established
9th century AD	Holy Roman Empire established
1089	Death of William the Conqueror
1227	Death of Genghis Khan
1273	Habsburg Empire founded
1371	Stuart dynasty founded
1328	Valois dynasty founded

ROYALTY

1368	❖	Ming dynasty founded
1485	❖	Tudor dynasty founded
1547	❖	Death of Henry VIII
1603	❖	Death of Elizabeth I
1715	❖	Death of Louis XIV, the Sun King
1793	❖	Death of Louis XVI of France
1821	❖	Death of Napoleon Bonaparte
1890	❖	Death of Sitting Bull
1901	❖	Death of Queen Victoria
1914	❖	Death of Archduke Franz Ferdinand
1918	❖	Death of tsar Nicholas II
1926	❖	Birth of Elizabeth II
1989	❖	Death of Emperor Hirohito of Japan

Sargon the Great (c. 2371 BC)

Ruler of Mesopotamia. Sargon changed the method of government of conquered empires. Rather than allowing an empire to continue to be governed by its own people, he appointed his own administrators, limiting the chances of rebellion.

Nefertiti (c. 1360–30 BC)

Egyptian queen. As wife of the heretic pharaoh Amenophis IV (Akhenaten), Nefertiti helped lead the religious revolution replacing traditional Egyptian gods with the Sun god, Aten. Nefertiti is best known for the carved reliefs depicting her and her husband with their daughters in intimate settings, and the remarkable portrait bust found in the regime's new capital at Akhenaten. Mystery surrounds her fate, and she has been linked to the obscure figure, Smenkhare, her husband's short-lived successor. Her daughter Ankhesenamun was married to Tutankhamen, owner of the celebrated tomb at Thebes.

❖ see ANCIENT EGYPT p106, TUTANKHAMEN p52

Tutankhamen (c. 1343–1323 BC)

Egyptian pharaoh from c. 1333 BC. The son of the heretic pharaoh Akhenaten, Tutankhamen succeeded as a boy in the aftermath of the regime which sought to establish a new religion based on the sun god, Aten. Tutankhamen's parentage is uncertain and he may have been a cousin, or even a brother, of his wife. The short reign saw the influence of the priests of Amun revived, a return to the capital at Thebes and the suppression of the Aten. The discovery in 1922 of his tomb caused a sensation and provided vast amounts of evidence for the art and culture of the period.

❖ see ANCIENT EGYPT p106, NEFERTITI p 52

RIGHT: *Tutankhamen was Egypt's youngest pharaoh. This golden mask was found in his tomb.*

Rameses II (c. 1310–1224 BC)

Egyptian pharaoh from c. 1290 BC. A great warrior, Rameses II was the third ruler of the nineteenth dynasty which saw Egypt's fortunes reach their last peak. His most famous victory was against the Hittites at Kadesh, though their account suggests Rameses was less successful than he claimed. Rameses built extensively throughout Egypt and usurped the monuments of many of his predecessors. Consequently, more buildings and statues bear his name than any other Egyptian ruler's. His tomb and those of his family survive at Thebes, as does his mummy, found in a cache of royal bodies discovered in the nineteenth century.

❖ see ANCIENT EGYPT p106, HITTITES p108

LEFT: *A stone relief image depicting the Egyptian queen Nefertiti; she is seen here offering libations to the gods.*

Chou Dynasty

The Chou (Zhou) dynasty ruled China from around 1050–255 BC, and defined Chinese society across a period of great advances in writing, philosophy, technology, agriculture and communications. The Chou were rivals of the Shang. A long period of intermittent skirmishing led to an all-out campaign to seize Shang territory. By c. 1050 BC, the Chou had taken control of all China.

To control such a vast territory, a system of feudal states was established which remained effective until the feudal lords began to pursue their own ambitions, at the expense of the emperor's, by the eighth century BC. Thereafter, the empire fragmented further into small units fighting amongst one another and forming alliances.

Art benefited from this diversity, with regional styles being developed. The political chaos led to the development of regional capitals and defences, but also allowed the Ch'ing Dynasty to seize the initiative and wrest supreme control in 221 BC.

❖ see CH'ING DYNASTY p56

Cyrus the Great (d. c. 530 BC)

King of Persia (559–530 BC). Cyrus was renowned as a wise and just ruler who significantly expanded the Persian Empire during his reign. He founded the Achaemenid dynasty and conquered much of Asia Minor, Babylonia, Syria and the Iranian plateau.

❖ see BABYLONIANS p108

BELOW: *A massive stone head portraying the pharaoh Rameses II guards the entrance to a Sun temple in Luxor.*

Alexander the Great (356–323 BC)

Macedonian ruler and conqueror. Son of Philip II of Macedon, Alexander was 19 when he succeeded. By his death 12 years later he had conquered a vast empire stretching from Greece to India, including Egypt, founding cities, of which Alexandria is the most famous. A brilliant general, but a drunkard, he also believed he was a god. His greatest rival was the Persian Empire ruled by Darius, defeating it finally in 331 BC at Gaugamela (in Iraq). In 327 BC Alexander invaded India but his troops were exhausted. In 323 BC he died at Babylon. His empire was immediately divided among his generals.

❖ see PERSIAN WARS p140

LEFT: *Alexander the Great of Macedonia inherited a Greek empire which he expanded to the edges of the Indian subcontinent. Dying childless, his kingdom was eventually divided among his most trusted generals.*

Maharajas (1st century BC)

Title given to the ruler of one of the principal states of India. It is believed that the Kushans first introduced the title during the first century BC, preferring the more elaborate title of 'Great King' to that of simply 'King'. The term 'Maharaja' refers to a Hindu prince ranked above a 'Raja'. Candra Gupta I is said to have been the first ruler to take the title of 'Maharajadhiraja', meaning 'Great King of Kings', during the Gupta period (AD 320–540). Also spelled Maharajaj, nowadays it is used to refer to someone in an administrative rank in India.

Mark Antony (c. 82–30 BC)

Roman politician and Cleopatra's lover. In 44 BC Marcus Antony was consul with Julius Caesar when Caesar was murdered. Antony joined a triumvirate with Lepidus and Octavian (the future Emperor Augustus), fighting a civil war with Caesar's killers, who were defeated at Philippi in 42 BC. Soon after this, Antony met Cleopatra, whose gifts made his loyalty to Rome suspect. In 32 BC a civil war broke out between Antony and Octavian, who defeated him at Actium in 31 BC. The following year, Antony and Cleopatra committed suicide in Egypt.

❖ see BATTLE OF ACTIUM p140, AUGUSTUS CAESAR p56

Asoka (269–232 BC)

King of India. Asoka ruled India for 40 years. At the beginning of his reign he embarked on a military campaign of empire expansion, but he is reputed to have been so shocked at the horror and bloodshed that he turned to Buddhism – then just a small religious sect – and adopted it as the state religion. He is responsible for the spread of Buddhism to Sri Lanka and central Asia.

❖ see SIDDHARTHA GAUTAMA p37

BELOW: *Elizabeth Taylor (Cleopatra) and Richard Burton (Mark Antony) convincingly brought the two ill-fated lovers back to life on the silver screen.*

WORLD HISTORY

Julius Caesar (100–44 BC)

Dictator of Rome and general. Caesar, a senator, loathed the dictator Sulla who wiped out democratic opposition in 82 BC. Caesar wooed the Roman public with handouts, and was made Governor of Spain in 61 BC.

In 60 BC Caesar formed the First Triumvirate with Pompey and Crassus. In 58 BC he began his Gallic war, which secured vast new territories and earned him a spectacular reputation. In 55 and 54 BC he made two brief forays into Britain.

In 49 BC, Caesar returned to Rome, his power at its peak. Hostilities broke out between him and Pompey. In 48 BC, Pompey was defeated at Pharsalus, and then murdered in Egypt. Caesar began a relationship with Cleopatra and had a child, Caesarion. In 46 BC he was made dictator, and in 45 BC defeated Pompey's sons in Spain. Fears that he planned to make himself king led to his murder by Brutus and Cassius in 44 BC in Rome.

❖ see AUGUSTUS CAESAR p56, ROMANS p111

Herod the Great (c. 72–4 BC)

Ruler of Judaea, established as king by Octavian (Augustus) in 31 BC as part of his policy of ruling certain regions through pro-Roman puppet monarchs. Herod restored the cities of the region, and began the reconstruction of the Great Temple in Jerusalem. However, he jealously guarded his power through massacres of rivals, including some of his family, and the entire Hasmonean dynasty. He is attributed with the Massacre of the Innocents in an effort to wipe out Jesus.

❖ see AUGUSTUS CAESAR p56

Cleopatra (c. 70–30 BC)

Queen of Egypt and mistress of Julius Caesar and Mark Antony. Daughter of Ptolemy XII, descended from one of Alexander the Great's generals, Cleopatra became queen in 51 BC with her brother, Ptolemy XIII as king. In 48 BC she was deposed, but when Caesar arrived he restored her. They became lovers, Cleopatra bore him a son, Caesarion, and accompanied him to Rome. She returned to Egypt after his assassination, but in 41 BC she became Antony's mistress and went on to have three sons by him. After the Battle of Actium she fled home, followed by Antony, to commit suicide with a fatal bite from a poisonous snake.

❖ see BATTLE OF ACTIUM p140, MARK ANTONY p54

RIGHT: *Cleopatra, the last queen of Egypt, was romantically linked with both Julius Caesar and Mark Antony, two of Ancient Rome's greatest generals. Her myth has endured throughout history.*

Augustus Caesar (63 BC – AD 14)

First Roman Emperor, and adopted son of Julius Caesar. Augustus won the Battle of Actium and secured absolute power across the Roman world.

Born Gaius Octavius, he married Caesar's niece and became his heir as Gaius Julius Caesar Octavianus. Following Caesar's murder in 44 BC he formed the Second Triumvirate with Mark Antony and Lepidus. Bitter civil war followed as they wiped out their main rivals at Philippi in 42 BC and then fought amongst themselves.

Actium left Octavian the victor in 31 BC. Back in Rome he was awarded the title Augustus (meaning 'majestic') and an exceptional portfolio of positions, leaving him in control of the army and legislation. With support from his friend Agrippa and his wife Livia, he reformed abuses of power, improved public services, erected public buildings and settled frontiers with a system of garrisons, governorships and buffer states. On his death, Augustus's powers passed to his stepson Tiberius.

❖ see BATTLE OF ACTIUM p140, ROMANS p111

Ch'ing Dynasty

In the seventh century BC the Ch'ing (Qin) dynasty became powerful in western China, increasing power by taking western territory. Ch'ing was isolated from eastern power struggles, developed the rules of law and farming reform and exploited diplomacy and subterfuge to divide rivals. In 221 BC Ch'ing unified China under Shih Huang-ti, an absolute ruler who ended feudalism, suppressed knowledge and forced millions to build the Great Wall of China. The Ch'ing dynasty collapsed on his death in 206 BC.

❖ see GREAT WALL OF CHINA p109

Caligula (AD 12-41)

Third Roman Emperor, notorious for cruelty. Succeeding his great-uncle Tiberius in AD 37, Gaius Caesar was initially popular as son of the famous general Germanicus, earning the nickname Caligula as a child for wearing miniature military boots (caligae). His tolerance and liberal behaviour soon gave way to mental instability and his belief in his own divinity. Stories of incest and perversion abounded. In AD 41 he was murdered by the Praetorian Guard.

❖ see ROMANS p111

Nero (AD 37–68)

Roman Emperor from AD 54. Vain and ostentatious, Nero took advantage of the fire of AD 64 to clear space for a vast palace in Rome, covering the expense by fabricating accusations against wealthy men and confiscating their property. Nero performed in public as a musician and charioteer and earned a reputation for perversion and cruelty. He murdered his mother Agrippina in AD 59 and his tutor Seneca in AD 65. In AD 68 he was forced to flee, committing suicide.

❖ see ANCIENT ROME p112

Hadrian, Emperor (AD 76–138)

Roman Emperor from AD 117, succeeding Trajan. Hadrian abandoned Trajan's conquests and fixed the

LEFT: *Augustus Caesar, adopted son of the great Julius Caesar, secured victory at the Battle of Actium and joined forces with Lepidus and Mark Antony to form the Second Triumvirate upon Caesar's death.*

Empire's frontiers, touring the provinces and frontier armies, encouraging discipline and instigating Hadrian's Wall in Britain. A lover of Greek culture, he modelled his villa at Tivoli on architecture from around the Roman world and designed the extant Pantheon in Rome, one of the most celebrated buildings of antiquity.

❖ see ANCIENT ROME p112

RIGHT: *A marble bust of Septimius Severus.*

Septimius Severus (c. AD 146–211)

Roman Emperor from AD 193. Born in Africa, Severus was a senator with a successful career as a provincial governor when he joined in the civil war following the murder of Commodus in AD 192. Playing off his rivals, he defeated them one by one. Recognizing the importance of military support, he increased soldiers' pay and privileges. In AD 208 he embarked on a war in Britain, designed to toughen his sons and heirs, Caracalla and Geta, and win the dynasty prestige. The campaign proved bloody and inconclusive and he died in York in AD 211.

❖ see ANCIENT ROME p112

ABOVE: *Hadrian's Wall was an impressive fortification built to protect the furthest reaches of the Roman Empire from the marauding Barbarians of the North.*

── ROYALTY ──

Gupta Empire (AD 320–550)

India's classical age. From AD 320, Chandragupta I founded the Gupta dynasty after conquering neighbouring states. His grandson Chandragupta II (AD 375–413) expanded the Empire to incorporate all of India north of the Narmada River. The Empire flourished for 160 years as the centre of Hinduism, music, art and literature. Notably, Sanskrit became the universal language of the subcontinent. Whilst Rome was in decline, the great masterpieces of Indian literature, including the epic *Mahabharata*, were being composed. Buddhist monks established magnificent temples along the Silk Road and converted millions of Chinese to the faith. Gupta culture influenced countries as far afield as Cambodia and Vietnam. By the end of the fifth century, reeling under the attacks of the White Huns, who had followed in the footsteps of the Mongol invaders, the Gupta Empire broke up, finally disappearing by the middle of the sixth century. The Empire has been compared to Hellenism in terms of its influence.

King Arthur (AD 5th or 6th century)

Mythical British king enshrined in legends surrounding the sword Excalibur, the castle of Camelot, the Knights of the

Round Table and the search for the Holy Grail, elaborated in more recent times to associate him with Tintagel (Cornwall) and Glastonbury (Somerset). Geoffrey of Monmouth and other twelfth-century writers developed the myths. Arthur may have had a loose basis in historical fact as a fifth- or sixth-century descendant of the Romano-British, leading resistance against the Saxon invasions.

❖ see ANGLO-SAXONS p114

Justinian
(c. AD 482–565)

Eastern Roman (Byzantine) Emperor from AD 527, who succeeded his uncle Justin I. Justinian's ambition was to restore the Roman Empire's territories. Through his generals Belisarius and Narses he recaptured North Africa and parts of Italy and Spain, restored northern frontiers and held back the Persians. He centralized his rule, broke down the power of bureaucrats and sought Christian unity, but most importantly, he revised and collated Roman law. He built many churches, including St Vitale in Ravenna and Santa Sophia in Constantinople.

❖ see ROMANS p111

T'ang Dynasty
(AD 618–907)

Chinese ruling dynasty. Founded by Li Yuan, an official of the Sui dynasty, on whose rule he modelled his own regime. After a power struggle, Li Yuan expanded Chinese control into Asia, Tibet and Korea, creating a vast empire. Avoiding a cumbersome bureaucracy, but improving the Sui policy of recruitment through examination, Li Yuan created an efficient form of government and encouraged small-scale landholdings at the expense of large estates. His descendants continued this trend, controlling aristocrats, improving the bureaucracy and education and expanding Chinese territory. Although regional and aristocratic ambitions brought about the dynasty's downfall, the period saw the invention of printing and a climax of Chinese culture in music, poetry, painting and Buddhist sculpture.

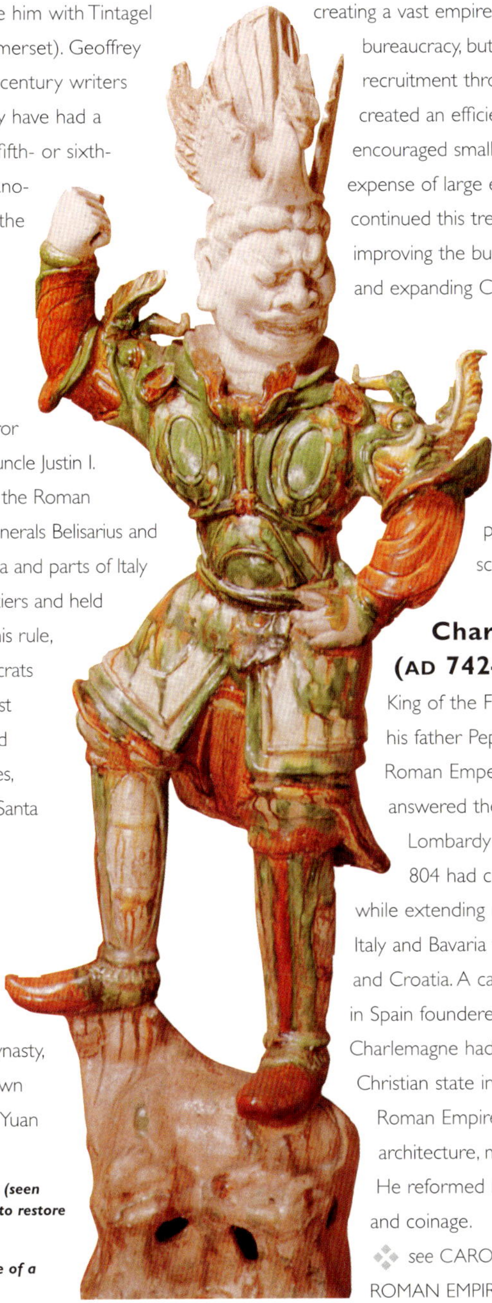

Charlemagne
(AD 742–814)

King of the Franks from AD 768, succeeding his father Pepin the Short, and Holy Roman Emperor from AD 800. He answered the pope's request for help in Lombardy against the Saxons, and by AD 804 had conquered Saxon territory, while extending his control across northern Italy and Bavaria to areas of modern Austria and Croatia. A campaign against the Muslims in Spain foundered in the Pyrenees, but Charlemagne had established the first major Christian state in Western Europe since the Roman Empire, famous for its art, architecture, monasteries and learning. He reformed law, weights and measures and coinage.

❖ see CAROLINGIAN EMPIRE p60, HOLY ROMAN EMPIRE p62

LEFT: *The Byzantine emperor Justinian (seen here in the centre of the image) aimed to restore the Roman Empire's former territories.*

RIGHT: *A Chinese earthenware figurine of a T'ang Dynasty tomb guardian.*

LEFT: *The Carolingian Empire was founded by a dynasty of Frankish rulers and espoused the revival of a Roman style of architecture, literature and the arts. This is the Carolingian Gospels, featuring St Mark.*

Carolingian Empire (AD 768–987)

Dynasty of Frankish kings, characterized by a revival of Roman literacy, architecture, the decorative arts in gold and silver, painting and mosaics. Named after Charles I (Charlemagne).

The Empire extended from western France to the Elbe in Germany, and from Denmark to the Mediterranean. The Empire was the first centralized Christian power in Western Europe, leading to the papal title 'Holy Roman Empire'.

Churches and monasteries were founded and encouraged to improve education and literacy. A new form of standard handwriting ('Carolingian minuscule'), a programme to revise the Bible, and copy and archive surviving classical texts led to the Carolingian Empire becoming a centre of learning, enhancing the prestige of its rulers, preserving the Latin language and attracting scholars, for example Alcuin of York who met Charlemagne in AD 781 and became head of the palace school.

Architecture enjoyed a renaissance. In AD 805, the Palatine chapel at Aachen was consecrated. Based on an octagon and dome, it was modelled on and influenced by surviving monuments of the ancient world. Nothing like this had been built in the West for centuries. Others revived the basilican style, while all the buildings were embellished with mosaics and frescoes.

❖ see CHARLEMAGNE p59, HOLY ROMAN EMPIRE p62

Charles II, Holy Roman Emperor (AD 823–77)

King of France from AD 843 and Holy Roman Emperor from AD 875. Son of Louis I 'the Pious' (d. AD 840), Charles II (known as 'the Bald') and his brothers wrangled over their inheritance until the Carolingian Empire was divided at Verdun (AD 843). Charles ruled western and northern France, constantly buying off Viking raiders. The relative stability of his kingdom led the pope to make Charles Holy Roman Emperor. In AD 877 he died after an unsuccessful war in Italy. His kingdom was split amongst his descendants.

❖ see CAROLINGIAN EMPIRE p60, HOLY ROMAN EMPIRE p62, VIKINGS p114

Alfred the Great (AD 849–99)

Anglo-Saxon King of Wessex (England south of the Thames). Alfred was threatened by the Danes who controlled much of England. They demanded money to buy them off. Alfred paid, but the Danish ruler Guthrum soon returned for more. Alfred had prepared his armies and defeated Guthrum at Edington in AD 878. The Danes left and Guthrum was converted to Christianity. In AD 892, the Danes returned again, but Alfred had organized a cycle of military training for everyone and had built a fleet. By AD 896, the Danes were forced out. Alfred reformed laws to protect poor people, encouraged education and founded monasteries.
❖ see ANGLO-SAXONS p114, VIKINGS p114

Song Dynasty (AD 960–1279)

Chinese dynasty. The Song seized control of China in AD 960. They united the many factions into which the country was divided under one central rule. Early emperors established a good bureaucracy, placing a new class of people – the schola-official – in charge. The dynasty also saw the rise of many cities which became important centres for trade. The rise of Confucianism saw a decline in Buddhism during the dynasty and Confucianism became the state religion.

Canute (c. AD 995–1035)

Viking king of England, Denmark and Norway. In 1013, Sweyn, King of Denmark, invaded England with his son Canute. In 1014 Sweyn died. Canute was forced to leave, returning with a powerful army. In 1016 he defeated Edmund Ironside, son of the English King Ethelred II ('the Unready'). Canute was proclaimed King of England and married Ethelred's widow. He faced opposition but used Anglo-Saxon laws to establish a beneficial reign. In 1018 his brother Harold, King of Denmark, died and Canute took the Crown. In 1027 he forced the Scots to pay him homage and in 1028 he conquered Norway.

BELOW: *Alfred the Great, one of the great Wessex kings, drove out the invading Danes and introduced new legislation from which the poor and the uneducated could benefit.*

Holy Roman Empire (9th century)

Territory ruled by Franks and afterwards Germans from the beginning of the ninth century until 1806. Regarded as the Christian revival of the Roman Empire in the West, it remained one of the most powerful forces throughout medieval Europe. The term 'Holy Roman Empire' dates from the mid-thirteenth century, but the title 'Holy Roman Emperor' is a modern one.

In AD 800 Charlemagne was given the title 'Emperor' by Pope Leo III as a reward for his services to Christian rule. In AD 912 the Frankish title lapsed with the death of Louis IV. In AD 962 the title passed to the German kings through Conrad, Duke of Franconia. Thereafter, the title remained elected by German princes (the electors) until 1806, though in practice the title tended to pass through dynasties, principally the Austrian Habsburgs from the fifteenth century, and became synonymous with that line of descent, though it was always identified with the German nation.

The emperor controlled extensive lands in Central and Northern Europe, stretching from France across Germany to Austria and beyond, and including Switzerland and northern Italy. The papal origins of the title gave way to a conflict over leadership of Christian Europe. The papacy regarded the Empire as its secular form, and saw itself as the basis of imperial authority, while the emperors attributed their power to military strength and political success, for which they were answerable to God.

By the sixteenth century, the effects of the Reformation reduced imperial power and influence when a number of

RIGHT:
Emperor Charlemagne.

German principalities became Protestant. This enhanced the autonomy of the German electors. The Thirty Years' War (1618–48) had a catastrophic effect on Germany, leaving the imperial title little more than a label.

The end came when Napoleon tried to absorb the imperial title into his portfolio. Francis II, the last emperor, changed his title to 'Emperor of the Austrians' to deny it to anyone else, finally bringing it to an end in 1806 to guarantee that no one could usurp it. The concept of German imperial identity was revived with the nineteenth-century 'Second Reich', and then by Hitler's 'Third Reich'.

❖ see CHARLEMAGNE p59, HABSBURG EMPIRE p64, THIRTY YEARS' WAR p146

William I of England (1027–89)

Conqueror and king of England from 1066. The illegitimate son of Robert, Duke of Normandy, William succeeded Robert in 1035. He claimed the English throne on a verbal promise made by Edward the Confessor and an oath of feudal allegiance from Harold, then Earl of Wessex. However, Harold succeeded Edward and William invaded to challenge him, winning the Battle of Hastings in 1066. William was crowned on Christmas Day 1066, but four more years of war followed to secure the north, with Scotland capitulating in 1072.

William's wise feudal rule involved suppressing baronial autonomy. Through his archbishop of Canterbury, Lanfranc, the church hierarchy was replaced with Normans. He granted lands and estates to his own men, and in 1086 ordered the compilation of a complete record of land tenure and population in the Domesday Book. He died after a fall in France.

❖ see DOMESDAY BOOK p116

Richard I of England (1157–99)

King of England from 1189; known as 'the Lionheart'. Richard's mother, Eleanor, incited him and his brothers to rebel against their father, Henry II. Henry died during the revolt, but Richard left soon after accession for the Crusades to recapture Jerusalem from Saladin. The campaign ended in a truce in 1192, and Richard was captured by Leopold, Duke of Austria, on the way home. A vast ransom secured his release, but he left to fight Philip II in France where he was killed. His chivalry and honour earned him the name 'the Lionheart'.

❖ see CRUSADES p39, SALADIN p142

Genghis Khan (1162–1227)

Mongol ruler and conqueror. Born in central Asia near Lake Bailal, inheriting lands controlled by his father, Yesukei, stretching from the River Amur in the west to the Great Wall of China in the east. In 1206 he was awarded the name Genghis Khan ('Mighty Ruler'). China refused him tribute, so in around 1212 he invaded north China, following this with more wars of conquest, which extended his power west and south to northern India. By 1227 his dominions extended from Persia and the Black Sea in the west to Korea and parts of China in the east. He left no permanent form of government, but the Mongol Empire continued to grow, becoming the largest in history.

❖ see MONGOLS p117

Edward I of England (1239–1307)

King of England from 1272; son of Henry III. Nicknamed 'Longshanks' for his height, Edward was influenced by Simon de Montfort who led the barons against Henry III's rule. Edward was reconciled with Henry and fought Simon de Montfort in the Barons War, killing him at Evesham in 1265. He acceded while on crusade. Edward believed in government and taxation by consent, creating the first parliament in 1295 and reforming feudal abuses. He conquered Wales between 1282–84, after Llewellyn's uprising, creating his son Prince of Wales in 1301. Wars in Scotland were indecisive despite removing the coronation stone from Scone to London and defeating William Wallace in 1305.

❖ see CRUSADES p39

Habsburg Empire (1273–1918)

European royal family which dominated European history for five centuries until 1918, named after the family castle Habsburg ('Hawk's Castle') in Switzerland.

Serious power began with Rudolf I, a Habsburg, elected king in Germany in 1273. Rudolf conquered Austria, which thereafter became the most important part of the Habsburg possessions. He and his successors were dukes of Austria, becoming archdukes in the fifteenth century.

Frederick III, a descendant of Rudolf, was created Holy Roman Emperor in 1452. Although the title was elective, under the Habsburgs it became effectively hereditary until the Empire came to an end in 1806. His son, Maximilian I (r. 1493–1519), secured through his marriage in 1477 the Low Countries, Burgundy and later Spain and her possessions, while a treaty in 1491 secured the eventual passing of Hungary and Bohemia to the Habsburgs.

Under the Emperor Charles V (r. 1519–56), Habsburg power was at its peak, but the lands were divided between him and his brother Ferdinand, who took Austria, Hungary and Bohemia.

The Habsburgs struggled to control such vast dominions, especially as nationalist and ethnic consciousness developed during the nineteenth century. This led to the Serbian nationalists assassinating Franz Ferdinand, archduke of Austria-Hungary in 1914.

❖ see HOLY ROMAN EMPIRE p62, ARCHDUKE FRANZ FERDINAND p84

Edward II of England (1312–77)

King of England from 1327, son of Edward I and Isabella. In 1330, Edward executed his mother's lover, Roger Mortimer, securing control for himself. He defeated the Scots at Halidon Hill in 1333, establishing a puppet king, John Balliol. In 1337 he began the Hundred Years' War against France, claiming the French Crown. With his son Edward, the 'Black Prince', he secured great victories at Crécy in 1346 and Poitiers in 1356, exploiting the advantage of English longbowmen over mounted knights. In 1360 he recovered Aquitaine, but after 1369 he lost all French lands except Calais. His financial needs strengthened parliament's control.

❖ see BATTLE OF CRÉCY p144, HUNDRED YEARS' WAR p143

Stuart Dynasty

Scottish ruling family from 1371, and in England from 1603 until 1714, presiding over religious conflict and England's Civil War and Glorious Revolution. Deriving its name from the title 'steward', the dynasty began in 1315 when Walter, sixth hereditary High Steward of Scotland, married Robert Bruce's daughter Marjorie. Their son, Robert II, succeeded in 1371. A continuous male line lasted to James V (r. 1513–42).

James V's heir, Mary, Queen of Scots, was brought up in France, leading to the French spelling, 'Stuart', becoming used. Mary bore a son, James Stuart, afterwards James VI of Scotland (r. 1566–1625) and I of England (r. 1603–25).

Charles I, son of James I, nearly destroyed the family's control of the crown when the English Civil War, and afterwards the Commonwealth, ousted the monarchy. The restoration of Charles II in 1660 faltered with his failure to produce a legitimate heir and fears of Stuart enthusiasm for Catholicism.

In 1685 Charles II's Catholic brother James II succeeded on the understanding his Protestant son-in-law and daughter, William and Mary, would follow. But the birth of a Catholic son, James Stuart (the 'Old Pretender'), by James's second wife, occasioned the Glorious Revolution of 1688, placing William and Mary on the throne. William and Mary (d. 1694) were childless and on William's death in 1702, the Crown passed to Mary's sister Anne, during whose reign England and Scotland were joined in the Act of Union.

Anne died with no living heir in 1714, and the Crown passed to a distant Protestant descendant of James I, George, elector of Hanover, bypassing the Catholic descendants of James II. James Stuart and his son Charles, the 'Young Pretender', continued to pursue Stuart claims on the throne up to 1745. Charles's son, Henry (d. 1807), was the last of the line.

❖ see CHARLES I OF ENGLAND p76, CHARLES II OF ENGLAND p78, RESTORATION p122

LEFT: *King Edward II of England was overthrown by his wife, Isabella and her lover, Roger Mortimer.*

Valois Dynasty (1328–1589)

French ruling house. The Valois kings of France, a junior line of the Capetian house, ruled from 1328–1589. In 1285, Philip III (r. 1270–85) gave the county of Valois to a younger son, Charles, who, on the death of his brother Philip V in 1322, succeeded as Charles IV. In 1328, Charles's son acceded as Philip VI of Valois. The new dynasty was soon preoccupied with the problems of the Hundred Years' War with England and challenges from French barons. Charles VII (1422–61) brought the war to an end, as well as increasing royal power at the expense of the feudal lords.

The Valois kings strengthened royal power through parliaments and control of taxation, allowing France to start competing with the Habsburg Holy Roman Empire for territory. These began with inconclusive wars in Italy lasting into the sixteenth century. In the late sixteenth century, royal control became weakened as religious factionalism came to dominate French affairs. The reign of Charles IX (1550–74) saw the brutal massacre of thousands of Huguenots in 1572. Although his brother Henri III (r. 1574–89) attempted to broker a workable relationship between Catholics and Protestants, he assassinated the Catholic leader, the Duke of Guise, fearing that he might be usurped. Henri was murdered himself the following year.

❖ see HUNDRED YEARS' WAR p143

Charles V of France (1337–80)

Regent from 1356–60, King of France 1364, during the Hundred Years' War with England. Charles V (known as 'the Wise') stuck to the terms of the 1347 Treaty of Calais with England, but challenged the transfer of his rights in Aquitaine. Initially, he concentrated on controlling power struggles with his barons and dealing with mercenary bands ravaging the countryside. When war with England resumed, Charles engaged the English in small-scale skirmishes and started eroding English territory. He regularized taxation, encouraged military training, introduced pay and created a system for maintenance of defences. An alliance with Castile brought naval support and he founded a French navy.

❖ see HUNDRED YEARS' WAR p143

Medici Family

Ruling family of Florence. Medici power began with Giovanni di Medici (1360–1429), a banker. His son, Cosimo (1389–1464), was expelled by the ruling oligarchy. Returning in 1434, he became the model for Machiavelli's *The Prince* through his manipulation of republican government to wield supreme power over the city. Like Cosimo, he patronized art, further embellishing Florence, and was a poet. His great-granddaughter was Catherine di Medici (1519–89), mother and regent of Charles IX of France.

Following Lorenzo's death, Charles VIII of France invaded Italy to seize Naples, and exiled the Medici, damaging their power in Florence even though they came back in 1512. Medici power now lay with Lorenzo's son, the pope Leo X (in office 1513–21), and nephew, the pope Clement VII (in office 1523–34), until a descendant of Giovanni di Medici, Cosimo (1519–74), revived the family fortunes. Granted Siena by the emperor, he was created First Grand Duke of Tuscany in 1569, establishing a dynasty which lasted until 1737.

❖ see CHARLES IX OF FRANCE p76

Ming Dynasty (1368–1644)

Last native Chinese dynasty. Founded by Chu Yuan-Chang, who ruled as Hung-wu, following the fall of the Mongol Yuan dynasty, the Ming dynasty united China for nearly 400 years. The Ming bureaucracy had over 20,000 positions, from ministers to police chiefs. It was a structured society that saw the population rise from 60 to 150 million. Hung-wu's successors extended the empire, but by the sixteenth century they were under pressure from the Mongols and the Japanese.

❖ see MONGOLS p117

Henry V of England (1387–1422)

King of England from 1413, son of Henry IV. Henry fought successfully against Welsh rebels led by Owen Glendower during his father's reign. On accession he immediately acted on his ambition to restore England's power over France. In 1415 he invaded France, winning a devastating victory at Agincourt when English longbowmen decimated French mounted knights. A second expedition in 1417 led to the surrender of Rouen in 1419 and his marriage with Catherine, daughter of Charles VI of France, in 1420. By this, Henry became heir to the French throne. However, the war continued and Henry died on campaign in 1422.

❖ see HUNDRED YEARS' WAR p143, BATTLE OF AGINCOURT p145

ABOVE: *Cosimo di Medici.*

Ivan III of Moscow (1440–1505)

Grand Prince of Muscovy (Moscow) from 1462; known as 'the Great'. Ivan refused to pay tribute to the Tatar leader, Grand Khan Ahmed. He then expelled the Tatars, annexed Novgorod, Yaroslavl and Rostov land, and recaptured Ukrainian territory from Poland and Lithuania. Centralizing control over his possessions gave meaning to Ivan's imperial ambitions, which developed when he married Sophia Palaeologus, niece of Constantine XI, the last emperor of Byzantium. Ivan named himself Tsar of all Russia and introduced the Russian imperial device of the double-headed eagle. He granted life tenure of lands to servants on condition of loyalty to the grand prince. Ivan made Muscovy a significant force on the European stage.

Ferdinand (1452–1516) and Isabella of Spain (1451–1504)

Ferdinand was King of Aragon in his own right from 1479 and King of Castile through his marriage to Isabella, adding Naples by war in 1504. Castile passed to their daughter on Isabella's death, but her husband, Philip of the Netherlands, ruled as regent until his death in 1506, when Ferdinand assumed it, passing an intact inheritance to his grandson Charles V, Holy Roman Emperor, in 1516.

The reign saw the final expulsion of Islam from Spain in 1492, and the unification of Spain as a Catholic nation. Administration was centralized although the regions retained their identities. Feudal power was suppressed, parliamentary influence declined and magistrates appointed by the monarchs replaced local officials. Any Jew or Muslim failing to convert was expelled, costing Spain talent. A Papal Bull established the Inquisition to enforce Catholic orthodoxy.

Ferdinand and Isabella funded Christopher Columbus's 1492 voyage seeking a westerly route to Asia, but the discovery of America led to Spanish power being widely established thanks to the papal allocation of territory in the New World.

❖ see INQUISITION p42

BELOW: *Queen Isabella of Spain.*

Maximilian I (1459–1519)

Holy Roman Emperor and German king from 1493. Through marriage and war he greatly increased imperial possessions. His marriage to Mary, heiress of Charles the Bold of Burgundy in 1477, added the Low Countries. In 1495, at the Imperial Diet at Worms, the imperial princes resisted any attempts by Maximilian to reform the imperial chamber and taxation, forcing Maximilian to introduce commissions of his own to deal with these. In 1496 he married his son Philip I to Joanna, daughter of Ferdinand and Isabella of Spain. Philip and Joanna's son, the emperor Charles V, inherited Spain in 1516.

Maximilian pursued inconclusive wars in France, Switzerland and Italy, in a futile attempt to revive a universal empire in the west and make himself pope, though his war against Hungary in 1506 improved the imperial claim to the throne there.

❖ see FERDINAND AND ISABELLA OF SPAIN p67, HOLY ROMAN EMPIRE p62

Richard III of England (1452–85)

King of England from 1483. Edward IV's death in 1483 left Richard, his brother, protector of his 12 year-old nephew, King Edward V. But the enmity of Edward IV's widow, Elizabeth of York, and her circle towards Richard, a competent ruler, led to his coup. Richard declared Edward V a bastard, and himself king. Edward V and his brother were imprisoned in the Tower of London, dying in mysterious circumstances, probably with Richard's knowledge. This lost Richard support, allowing Henry Tudor a chance to claim the throne, defeating and killing Richard at Bosworth Field, and bringing to an end the Wars of the Roses.

Montezuma II (1466–1520)

Last Aztec emperor of Mexico, from 1503. He regarded the coming of the Spanish warrior and conqueror, Cortés, as the arrival of a god. To please Cortés, Montezuma offered him gifts, which only stimulated the Spaniards' greed. Realizing the truth, Montezuma invited Cortés to his lake capital, Tenochlitlán. Cortés seized Montezuma as a hostage, but his soldiers lost control and embarked on massacring the inhabitants. In the confusion as Aztec forces attacked Cortés and his men, Montezuma was killed.

❖ see AZTECS p119

BELOW: *A modern production portraying King Richard III of England.*

ABOVE: *Montezuma, the last great Aztec emperor, was first tricked and then taken hostage by Hernán Cortés, the Spanish conquistador.*

ABOVE: *Queen Elizabeth I was a member of the ruling Tudor Dynasty.*

RIGHT: *Babar, the first Mogul emperor and a direct descendant of Genghis Khan.*

Emperor Babar (1483–1530)

First Mogul Emperor. Descended from Genghis Khan, Babar (also spelled Babur, and meaning 'tiger') became ruler of Turkestan from 1495, but by 1501 he had lost Turkestan and Samarkand to the Uzbeks. However, Babar retained enough support to enter Afghanistan and seize Kabul in 1504. In 1512 he finally abandoned attempts to regain Samarkand. Seeing potential in the political dissent on the subcontinent, he made several raids, climaxing in 1526 with the defeat of the Afghan emperor of Delhi, and in 1527 the Rajputs. Although further wars followed, by 1530 Babar could bequeath the core of the later Mogul Empire to his descendants, who were left with the task of organizing its control and government.

❖ see EMPEROR AKHBAR p75

Tudor Dynasty (1485–1603)

English ruling house. The Tudor period marked the beginning of England's rise to European prominence, as well as the establishment of the Protestant religion.

Descended from a Welshman, Owen Tudor, married to Henry V's widow Catherine, Henry Tudor's claim came from his mother, a descendant of Edward III. Crowned Henry VII in 1485 after defeating Richard III at Bosworth, Henry's marriage to Elizabeth of York, daughter of Edward IV, resolved the dynastic differences of the Wars of the Roses, and his restoration of a sound administration ended the political chaos, as well as bequeathing sound finances and a solvent Crown.

Henry VIII and Elizabeth I in particular created enduring images of monarchy. However, the dynasty was beset by religious conflict and challenges from the great European powers of France and Spain, as well as problems of succession, and lasted only three generations. Henry's eldest son, Arthur, died in 1501 and the line of succession passed to the second son, afterwards Henry VIII.

The religious revolution of Henry VIII's reign was founded in the failure of his first marriage to produce a male heir, though the celebrated procession of five further wives, two of whom were executed, yielded two daughters, Mary and Elizabeth, and a son, Edward. Edward succeeded as Edward VI but died young. Both Mary and Elizabeth remained childless, Elizabeth not even marrying. However, James VI of Scotland succeeded in 1603 as James I of England and was descended from Henry VII's daughter Margaret.

❖ see ELIZABETH I OF ENGLAND p74, HENRY VIII OF ENGLAND p72

Henry VIII of England (1491–1547)

King of England from 1509, son of Henry VII and Elizabeth of York whose union had ended the Wars of the Roses. The reign was defined by Henry's quest for a male heir, which led to the introduction of the Protestant Church, and the strengthening of England's international influence.

Highly intelligent, Henry was a talented sportsman and musician, becoming heir after his elder brother, Arthur, died in 1502. Henry married Arthur's widow, Catherine of Aragon, who bore him Mary (afterwards Mary I of England). Advised by Thomas, Cardinal Wolsey, Henry played Spain and France off against each other, making and breaking alliances, seeking to increase England's influence. The pope's refusal to annul the marriage to Catherine so Henry could marry Anne Boleyn led Henry, helped by his adviser Thomas Cromwell, to declare himself head of the Church in England. In 1533 he married Anne and proceeded to dissolve monasteries and confiscate their wealth.

Anne bore Henry a daughter (afterwards Elizabeth I), but in 1536 Anne was executed for being unfaithful. Henry married Jane Seymour who died in 1537 after bearing a son (afterwards Edward VI).

To strengthen England's Protestant connections, Cromwell arranged for Henry to marry the German Anne of Cleves in 1539. Revolted by her, Henry divorced Anne and executed Cromwell, marrying Catherine Howard in 1540, and executing her for adultery in 1542. In 1543 he married Catherine Parr who survived him.

❖ see ELIZABETH I OF ENGLAND p74, MARY I OF ENGLAND p73

RIGHT: *King Henry VIII.*

Suleiman the Magnificent (1494–1566)

Turkish sultan from 1520. During Suleiman's reign, the Ottoman Empire reached its climax. At Istanbul (Constantinople), Suleiman (also spelled Sulaiman) built four great mosques, including the Blue Mosque, and he gained a reputation as a poet and law reformer.

In the west, advances began well, but met resistance. In 1522 Suleiman took Rhodes and also advanced into Southern and Eastern Europe by taking Belgrade in 1521 and defeating the Hungarians in 1526 at Mohacz. Although Ferdinand I lost almost all of Hungary, he retained Austria when Suleiman failed to take Vienna in 1529. Suleiman's fleet also failed to take Malta in a severe defeat in 1565.

In the east, Suleiman was more successful, taking Persia and much of North Africa, but at the time of his death he was still waging war in Hungary.

Safavid Dynasty (16th–18th centuries)

Persian clan. In the early sixteenth century the Safavid clan of Persia was at war with the Ottomans in Turkey. Having absorbed some of the western and northern Turkic tribes, they were threatening to expand into Turkey itself. The Ottomans had beaten them back by 1514 and confined them to what is now the Iranian plateau. The best-known king of the Safavid Empire was Abbas I, who encouraged trade with Europeans. The Empire eventually submitted to the Afghans in 1722.

LEFT: *Mary I of England.*

Mary I of England (1516–58)

Queen of England from 1553. The Catholic eldest daughter of Henry VIII, by Catherine of Aragon, Mary succeeded after the early death of Edward VI, suppressing the Protestant attempt to place Lady Jane Grey on the throne. Committed to restoring the Catholic Church, Mary's marriage to Philip II of Spain annihilated support, provoking a Protestant rebellion led by Sir Thomas Wyatt. Persecutions and executions followed, while her loveless and childless marriage foundered. In 1557–58, Mary joined Spain in war against France, only to lose Calais, England's last French possession.

❖ see HENRY VIII OF ENGLAND p72

Philip II of Spain (1527–98)

King of Spain from 1556, succeeding on the abdication of his father, the emperor Charles V. Philip inherited vast dominions in South America, the Low Countries, Naples and Milan, adding Portugal in 1580.

Imports of American bullion caused damaging inflation and England's increasing naval power provided a serious threat to Spain. Philip's childless marriage to Mary I of England ended an attempt to secure England that way. He then resorted to force, a tactic which ended with the Armada's destruction by storms and Elizabeth I's privateers in 1588.

Philip's determination to enforce the Counter-Reformation led to a futile and protracted war with the Netherlands, depriving Spain of Dutch trade and wealth. The Inquisition caused Spain to lose much intellectual and commercial talent.

❖ see ELIZABETH I OF ENGLAND p74, INQUISITION p42, MARY I OF ENGLAND p73, SPANISH ARMADA p146

RIGHT: *Philip II of Spain.*

ROYALTY

LEFT: *Ivan the Terrible, the Grand Duke of Muscovy, brought the borders of his principality to the Urals, the mountain range dividing Europe and Siberia.*

Ivan IV of Moscow (1530–84)

Tsar of Russia from 1547; known as 'the Terrible'. Crowned at the age of 17, Ivan IV was subjected to squabbles amongst the nobility (boyars), and he learned to loathe them. Despite starting his reign by introducing reforms, he degenerated after 1564 into ruthless and suspicious despotism, thereby founding the tsarist style of autocratic rule, for example the sacking of Novgorod. He instituted a secret police force, which operated through summary arrest, torture and execution. He extended his territories to the Caspian Sea and east into Siberia. He instituted trading with England and made overtures of marriage to Elizabeth I. In 1580, Ivan killed his son in a fit of temper. He remained in penance until his death.

❖ see ELIZABETH I OF ENGLAND p74

Elizabeth I of England (1533–1603)

Queen of England from 1558, daughter of Henry VIII by Anne Boleyn. Highly intelligent and fluent in several languages, Elizabeth established an archetype of Protestant monarchic power.

Declared illegitimate after Anne's execution, Henry's will restored Elizabeth to the succession after Edward VI and Mary I. Mary imprisoned her in 1554, believing Elizabeth was involved in plots against her.

Elizabeth's accession was followed by the 1559 Religious Settlement enforcing Protestantism. She depended on William Cecil, later Lord Burghley, chief secretary from 1558–98, but spurned all potential suitors, including her favourite, Robert Dudley, Earl of Leicester. Her heir remained her cousin Mary, Queen of Scots, but Elizabeth's spies uncovered plots by Mary's circle to kill her. In 1587, Elizabeth executed Mary, leaving Mary's son James as heir.

In 1588, the destruction of Philip II's Spanish Armada by weather and English naval commanders was a triumph, but Spain remained a problem, and an Irish rebellion followed in the 1590s. Elizabeth died in 1603, one of the longest-serving and most effective rulers England had known.

❖ see PHILIP II OF SPAIN p73, SPANISH ARMADA p146

BELOW: *Queen Elizabeth I of England.*

Frederick II of Denmark (1534–88)

King of Denmark and Norway from 1559. The reign was defined by the northern Seven Years' War with Sweden, which started in 1563 over competition for supremacy in the Baltic. Frederick's plan was to conquer Sweden and unify all three countries. In this he comprehensively failed and, in 1570, peace secured Sweden's independence. Thereafter, Frederick exploited and improved Denmark's control of access to the Baltic to raise money to rebuild the country. He provided facilities for the astronomer Tycho Brahe.

❖ see SEVEN YEARS' WAR p148

Emperor Akhbar (1542–1605)

Most powerful ruler of the Mogul Empire. Jalal Ed-Din Muhammad Akhbar (meaning 'the Great'), a Muslim, was descended from Genghis Khan. He succeeded in 1556 when India was ravaged by civil war. In 1560, when he was 18, he embarked on a 40-year war at the end of which he controlled all India. He saw that Muslim–Hindu rivalry spelled disaster, so he married a Hindu princess and tried to create a new religion combining the best of all faiths. He ruled India by dividing it into 18 provinces, each administered by an aristocrat. Akhbar reformed the law and taxation and encouraged art.

❖ see GENGHIS KHAN p63, EMPEROR BABAR p71

Mary, Queen of Scots (1542–87)

Queen of Scotland within a week of birth, on the death of her father James V. While Mary was brought up in France for protection, her mother, Mary of Guise, ruled as regent. In 1558, Mary married François, the French dauphin. He became king in 1559, but she returned to Scotland after his death in 1560. Mary then married Henry, Lord Darnley, who fathered her son, the future James VI of Scotland (I of England). Mary married the Earl of Bothwell soon after Darnley's murder, in which Bothwell was implicated, in 1567. Mary's Catholicism and behaviour alienated her from the Protestant nobility in Scotland. Fleeing to England for help, Elizabeth I (her cousin) imprisoned Mary, where she became the centre of Catholic plots against Elizabeth. She was executed in 1586.

❖ see ELIZABETH I OF ENGLAND p74

RIGHT: *Frederick the Great, King of Denmark and Norway, is approached by a petitioner with a letter.*

Charles IX of France (1550–74)

King of France from 1560, son of Henri II. He succeeded his brother François II as king at the age of 10, and his Italian Catholic mother, Catherine de Medici, ruled as regent for a decade. Henri II had persecuted French Protestants (Huguenots), but Charles was influenced by their leader, the French admiral Gaspard de Coligny. Terrified, Catherine made Charles order the St Bartholomew Massacre from 24 August to 3 October 1572. Around 25,000 Huguenots were killed.

❖ see HUGUENOTS p46, MEDICI FAMILY p66

Bourbon Dynasty

One of Europe's most powerful ruling families. Descended from Louis IX, King of France (1226–70), through his grandson Louis I, Duke of Bourbon (1327–42), a title inherited from his mother. Bourbons ruled France (1589–1792, 1814–48), Naples and Sicily (1735–1861), and Spain (1700–1868, 1870–73, 1874–1931, 1975–), and lesser dukedoms such as Lucca and Parma.

Henri IV of France (1553–1610), son of Antoine de Bourbon, inherited the title. His descendants ruled France until 1792 when Louis XVI was executed during the French Revolution. Louis XVIII was restored in 1814, followed by his brother Charles X (1824–30), who was toppled in the Revolution of 1830.

In 1700 Charles II of Spain died childless. The title passed to his great-nephew, Philip of Anjou, succeeding as Philip V. He was grandson of Louis XIV of France, who had married Charles's sister, Marie-Thérèse. In 1713, following the War of the Spanish Succession, the Treaty of Utrecht forced Philip to give up any claims to the French throne.

Philip V's third son, Charles, seized Naples and Sicily in 1735. In 1759 he succeeded to the Spanish throne, handing over Naples and Sicily to his younger son Ferdinand.

❖ see LOUIS XIV OF FRANCE p78

Emperor Shah Jahan (1592–1666)

Mogul emperor from 1628–58, and builder of the Taj Mahal. A failed revolt against his father, Jahangir, in 1622 led to reconciliation and his accession at Agra in 1628. The reign saw territorial expansion into eastern India (the Deccan), and was the high point of the Empire, despite the loss of Kandahar to Persia in 1653. However, the vast costs of campaigning meant that the reign saw the Empire pass its peak.

Shah Jahan's enthusiasm for art and architecture included the erection of mosques and the celebrated mausoleum, the Taj Mahal, at Agra. He removed his capital from Agra to Delhi, rebuilt it as Shjahanabad, and erected the fortified palace, called the 'Red Fort', there. Hinduism was tolerated, painting and literature flourished and the court became renowned for its magnificence.

Gustavus Adolphus of Sweden (1594–1632)

King of Sweden from 1611. A skilled strategist, Gustavus faced war with several countries simultaneously. He reformed and modernized his armies, negotiated peace with Denmark, fought Russia in 1617, and then Poland, securing an advantageous settlement in 1629. His purpose thereafter was to dominate Baltic trade, and he intended to do this by controlling Protestant German states, entering the Thirty Years' War in 1631 to do so, but was killed at the Swedish victory of Lutzen in 1632.

❖ see THIRTY YEARS' WAR p146

Charles I of England (1600–49)

King of England from 1625, executed in 1649. Frustrated by parliament's refusal to grant money, Charles dissolved it in 1629, resorting to taxation of coastal districts. This provoked outrage, fuelled by resentment at his religious policy, regarded as pro-Catholic, and brought to a head when he imposed an English prayer book on Scotland. Parliament was recalled in 1640 but dissolved when it refused money

RIGHT: *Charles I of England (seen here with his queen, Henrietta Maria) was tried and beheaded – an event which sent shock waves through Europe.*

until grievances were settled. The Scots invaded and parliament met again, outlawing Charles's excesses. In August 1642 Charles challenged parliament to war, leading to his final defeat at Naseby in 1645.

Continued plotting led to the trial condemning him to death.

❖ see CHARLES II OF ENGLAND p60

Romanov Dynasty (1613–1917)

Russian rulers for 300 years. This dynasty provided 17 tsars or tsarinas who ruled Russia until the Revolution of 1917. Descended from Andrey Ivanovich Kobyla, a Muscovite living during the reign of Ivan I, the name was derived from Roman Yurev (d. 1543) whose daughter was the first wife of Ivan IV 'the Terrible'. Her brother's children took the surname Romanov and when Fyodor I, the last ruler of the Rurik dynasty, died in 1598, 15 years of chaos ended with Michael Romanov as the new tsar. Notable Romanovs include Catherine the Great (1729–96), who attempted to westernize Russia and succeeded in making her country a major European power. Alexander I (1777–1825) ruled Russia during the Napoleonic Wars. Alexander II (1818–81) ruled during the Crimean War and led Russia against Turkey, and sold Alaska to the United States (1867). Nicholas II (1868–1918) was the last tsar, deposed by the Russian Revolution. He led Russia to defeat in the Russo-Japanese War (1904) and allowed the Russian economy to become paralysed. During World War I, the failures mounted and he was forced to abdicate. The Bolsheviks held him and his family captive until they were executed on 16 July 1918.

❖ see BOLSHEVIKS p18, NICHOLAS II OF RUSSIA p84, RUSSO-JAPANESE WAR p162, WORLD WAR I p164

Aurangzeb, Emperor (1618–1707)

Most powerful Mogul Emperor. In 1658 Aurangzeb organized a palace revolution, becoming Mogul Emperor of northern India. A Muslim fanatic, his despotic rule provoked opposition. He continued the work of his father, Shah Jahan, fighting to extend the Empire into southern India, reaching Bijapur and Golconda, but overstretched Mogul resources.

❖ see SHAH JAHAN p76

Charles II of England (1630–85)

King of England, son of Charles I, restored in 1660 after being recalled from exile. Charles made a triumphant entry to London, but spent much of his reign secretly planning to establish himself as a Catholic absolute monarch, accepting French money in support of his naval wars with the Dutch. Parliament forced Charles to back down. In 1678 fears of a 'popish plot' led to further legal restrictions on Catholics. His marriage to Catherine of Braganza was childless, but Charles was notorious for his numerous mistresses and illegitimate children. He was a great supporter of the arts and scientific discovery.

❖ see RESTORATION p122

Louis XIV of France (1638–1715)

King of France from 1643, also known as the Sun King. During his minority, power was wielded by Cardinal Mazarin who faced Spanish-backed opposition from the nobility for his exclusion of them from office. Louis's marriage to Maria Theresa of Spain in 1660 brought peace.

Louis took firm control of government in 1661, choosing effective ministers to reform finances and the armed forces. These enhanced his territorial ambitions, but William III of England led European resistance against him in the War of the League of Augsburg (1689–97). Louis saw the importance of image, creating a performance of monarchical grandeur and sophistication at Versailles. The latter part of his reign was beset by defeats in the War of the Spanish Succession (1702–13).

❖ see WAR OF SPANISH SUCCESSION p147

LEFT: Charles II of England was proclaimed King of England during the Restoration.

Peter I of Russia (1672–1725)

Tsar of Russia from 1682, known as 'the Great'. Determined to modernize Russia, Peter, a ruthless man of action, took great interest in developments in industry and science in Western Europe.

From 1696–98, Peter travelled to Holland and England, working as a labourer in the dockyards to master shipbuilding. Back in Russia, he promoted education, hired instructors from the West, started a newspaper and brought religion under state control. However, the building of the beautiful new capital at St Petersburg was achieved by forced labour. A protracted war against Sweden finally yielded a victory in 1709, winning Russia territory in Finland, Estonia and Lithuania and increasing control of the Baltic. Peter died with no heir.

RIGHT: *Peter the Great, one of Russia's tsars, exploited the skills of craftsmen and engineers to modernize Russia and build the city of St Petersburg, named after him.*

Charles VI, Holy Roman Emperor (1685–1740)

Holy Roman Emperor from 1711. Charles claimed the Spanish throne in 1700. In 1711 he succeeded to his brother's titles in Austria, costing him support in the War of the Spanish Succession. From 1716–18 Charles seized territory in Eastern Europe from the Ottoman Empire, but by 1740 he had lost most gains. Hopes that his daughter Maria Theresa could succeed him as Empress of Austria were compromised by the War of the Austrian Succession.

❖ see WAR OF AUSTRIAN SUCCESSION p148, WAR OF SPANISH SUCCESSION p147

LEFT: *Louis XIV of France.*

ABOVE: *Catherine the Great became Empress of Russia after her husband's life was claimed in a military coup. During her rule, Russia's empire extended its boundaries considerably.*

Catherine the Great (1729–96)

Russian empress. A German princess, Catherine's husband Peter succeeded in 1762, but was quickly deposed and murdered for his insanity and despotism. Catherine was made ruler in his place and was very popular throughout her reign. However, she depended on aristocratic support, which prevented reforms for peasants and led to a series of revolts.

Catherine extended Russia's territories by partitioning Poland and, in the Crimea during wars with the Turks, establishing a base on the Black Sea. Catherine always encouraged an interest in European culture; she wrote a history of Russia, collected art, painted, and corresponded with Voltaire. Her affairs were notorious.

George III of England (1738–1820)

King of Great Britain and Ireland from 1760. Grandson and successor of George II, following the death of his father, Frederick. George sought supportive prime ministers, initially depending on his old tutor, the Earl of Bute, who was forced to resign after ending the Seven Years' War on unfavourable terms. Lord North's pro-George administration of 1770–82 foundered on the loss of the American colonies in the Revolution. George's appointment of Pitt the Younger led to the erosion of royal power over government. Later years were taken up with the French Revolutionary and Napoleonic Wars, and the regency of the future George IV during George III's later periods of dementia.

❖ see AMERICAN REVOLUTION p150, REGENCY p82, SEVEN YEARS' WAR p148

RIGHT: *George III of England.*

ABOVE: *Louis XVI.*

Louis XVI of France (1754–93)

King of France from 1774, and married to Marie Antoinette. Attempts to tax nobles were wrecked by Marie Antoinette's support of aristocrats, leading to dismissal of ministers like Necker. France backed the American War of Independence, causing further financial trouble and popularizing liberty. In 1788 Necker was reinstated, demanding the recall of the estates-general (parliament: nobles, clergy and commons) in 1789 for the first time since 1614. The commons declared themselves the National Assembly, a revolutionary act followed by the storming of the Bastille.

Louis and his family were brought to Paris but they escaped. Recaptured, they lost control as the new government took France into the Revolutionary Wars with Prussia and Austria. Louis sought aid from other monarchs but was executed on 21 January 1793.

❖ see STORMING OF THE BASTILLE p127, FRENCH REVOLUTION p150

Marie Antoinette of France (1755–93)

Queen of France and daughter of Maria Theresa of Austria. Marie Antoinette was married to Louis XVI at the age of 15. The marriage was happy, but Marie Antoinette's frivolity damaged the French monarchy in the face of demands for liberty. She supported nobles in their resistance to taxation. During the Revolution, her steadfastness kept the royal family together, but her scheming and attempts to secure intervention by her brother, the emperor Leopold II, ended chances of a settlement. In October 1793, she followed her husband to the guillotine.

❖ see FRENCH REVOLUTION p150

Nawab

Name given to a ruling prince of India. In 1756 Siraj-ud-Dawlah, the nawab or viceroy of Bengal, seized Calcutta and imprisoned several British in a dungeon called the Black Hole of Calcutta. In January 1757 Robert Clive recaptured Calcutta, and in June decisively defeated the nawab at Plassey, thus securing British power in India.

❖ see BLACK HOLE OF CALCUTTA p148, BATTLE OF PLASSEY p148

Napoleon Bonaparte (1769–1821)

Emperor of France (1804–14 and 1815). Napoleon Bonaparte was born in Corsica. He was commissioned into the army in 1785, but he welcomed the French Revolution in 1789. Bonaparte fought in the Revolutionary Wars, to great acclaim at Toulon in 1793, but was forced into retirement. Recalled to crush a Royalist rebellion in 1795, he was made a general in 1796 and fought against the Austrians in Italy. He carried the war to Egypt, hoping to conquer India, but his fleet was defeated at the Battle of the Nile by Horatio Nelson. Spotting his chance in domestic political turmoil, Bonaparte returned home in 1799 and toppled the ruling Directory, making himself dictator. Bonaparte reformed French government, law and finances. In 1804 he was created Emperor, but in 1803 began the Napoleonic Wars. In 1814 he abdicated after the Battle of Leipzig, returning in 1815 to be defeated finally at Waterloo.

❖ see NAPOLEONIC WARS p152, ADMIRAL HORATIO NELSON p148, BATTLE OF WATERLOO p152, DUKE OF WELLINGTON p148

RIGHT: *Napoleon Bonaparte, Emperor of France and skilled military commander, disrupted European political infrastructure with his nationalist ideas.*

Napoleon III (1808–73)

Last Emperor of France, from 1851–70. Nephew of Napoleon I, Napoleon III grew up with a romantic interest in liberal causes. In 1836, he led a revolt against the French monarchy. In 1848 he was created president of the new French Republic, but in 1851 declared himself emperor. He encouraged industrial and financial modernization, built railways, allied France with Britain, and supported Italian unification. He compromised popularity by supporting the pope and sending an army to Mexico to collect debts. Leading France into the Franco-Prussian War was unpopular and a republic was declared when Napoleon was captured at Sedan in 1870. He died in England.

ABOVE: *Napoleon III.*

Regency (1811–30)

Latter period of George III's reign. George III was intermittently incapacitated by porphyria, called then his 'madness'. After 1811 he became afflicted with blindness and dementia. His son George (after 1820, George IV), a personal and political enemy of his father, became regent. The period was characterized by the introduction of the Prince Regent's love of art and dissolute behaviour, and his friendships with educated and gifted men of the age like Sheridan. The period has given its name to the art and architecture of the late eighteenth and early nineteenth centuries, of which elegance and revived styles of Ancient Greece are principal features.

❖ see GEORGE III OF ENGLAND p80

RIGHT: *Queen Victoria, in the first few years of her reign.*

Victoria, Queen of England (1819–1901)

Queen of England from 1837. Victoria's reign saw the climax of Britain's imperial power and an unprecedented pace of scientific discovery and industrial growth.

Failure of the legitimate direct male line from George III passed the Crown to Victoria, daughter of George's fourth son Edward, Duke of Kent, on the death of her uncle William IV. Initial advice and support from the prime minister, Lord Melbourne, were followed by Victoria's marriage to Albert of Saxe-Coburg in 1840. Victoria's lover, confidant and adviser, Albert became the main influence on the middle years of the reign, contributing to friction with her ministers over foreign policy.

Albert's death in 1861 was followed by the Queen's virtual withdrawal from public life until Benjamin Disraeli persuaded her of the value of being proclaimed Empress of India in 1877. Victoria delighted in Disraeli's flattery, but was irritated by the manner of the other great prime minister of the period, William Gladstone. Despite holding strong personal opinions, the reign was strictly constitutional and Victoria acted according to the advice of her ministers.

The Great Exhibition of 1851 marked the aspirations of the time. The Jubilees of 1887 and 1897 were symbolic milestones in Victoria's personal identification with the age, marked by colossal advances in science, industry, communications and learning, as well as styles of art and architecture. The reign elevated royal prestige to its zenith, enhanced by the proliferation of her own descendants amongst the royal houses of Europe.

❖ see BRITISH EMPIRE p124

Victor Emmanuel II (1820–78)

King of Sardinia from 1849, and King of Italy from 1861. He fought Austria unsuccessfully between 1848–49, in pursuit of Italian unity. After his father's abdication, Victor Emmanuel turned to politics and diplomacy for the cause. Securing French support by handing Napoleon III the province of Savoy, he was provided with enough resources to defeat Austria at Magenta and Solferino in 1859.

With the grudging support of the nationalist leader Giuseppe Garibaldi, Victor Emmanuel was declared the first king of a unified Italy and maintained a constitutional monarchy. In 1866 a treaty with Prussia secured Venice. The withdrawal of the French papal garrison in 1871 allowed the establishment of a national capital at Rome.

❖ see NAPOLEON III p82

RIGHT: *Victor Emmanuel II.*

ABOVE: *The great Sioux chief, Sitting Bull.*

Sitting Bull (1831–90)

Sioux Indian chief (Teton Dakota). For his fearlessness during invasions, he was made principal chief of the Sioux nation in 1867. When the Second Treaty of Fort Laramie (1868) was broken, beginning the Battle of Little Bighorn, Sitting Bull and the Sioux tribes wiped out Lieutenant Colonel George Custer and his armies. Forced out of Canada (1877), Sitting Bull joined Buffalo Bill's Wild West Show. He was killed at Grand River during the Ghost Dance uprising.

❖ see BATTLE OF LITTLE BIGHORN p158

Nicholas II of Russia (1868–1918)

Last tsar of Russia, from 1894. His rule saw Russia ravaged by World War I and Russian society turned upside down by Communist revolutions.

Nicholas II was happily married to the Tsarina Alexandra who dominated him, and who bore him four daughters and one son. Alexandra was heavily influenced by the religious fraud Rasputin.

Nicholas rejected liberal movements in Russia and supported the suppression of any suggestion of socialist revolution or reform. He preferred the support of old-fashioned conservative advisers and politicians. Russia was defeated by Japan in the war of 1904–05, a humiliation leading to the formation of a parliament (duma), but it was soon rendered impotent, which Nicholas encouraged.

The outbreak of World War I allowed these problems to be shelved but setbacks and government mismanagement exposed them once more, leading to the Revolution in 1917. Nicholas abdicated, and the family were imprisoned and executed in July 1918.

❖ see BOLSHEVIKS p18, RASPUTIN p12, RUSSIAN REVOLUTION p168, WORLD WAR I p164

Archduke Franz Ferdinand (1863–1914)

Heir to the Habsburg Crowns of Austria and Hungary, through his uncle, Emperor Franz Josef I, after the suicide of his cousin Rudolf in 1889, and his father's death in 1896. Highly committed to the monarchy, he acted against the nobility who challenged imperial authority, but he was also prepared to consider reform. He was profoundly opposed to Serbian nationalism and visited Sarajevo in Bosnia on 28 June 1914, the anniversary of the end of Serbian independence. He and his wife, Sophia, were assassinated there by Serbian nationalists, 'The Black Hand', triggering events leading to the outbreak of World War I.

❖ see WORLD WAR I p164

RIGHT: *Tsar Nicholas II of Russia.*

Hirohito (1901–89)

Emperor of Japan from 1926. Hirohito ruled Japan throughout its wars of aggression in Manchuria, China, and then World War II from 1941. Real power lay with Hideki Tojo, general and premier between 1941–44, with Hirohito playing only a reluctant role. By the end of the war, Hirohito favoured unconditional surrender. After the dropping of atomic bombs on Hiroshima and Nagasaki in August 1945 he made the first public address by a Japanese emperor, announcing the surrender. The US-controlled post-war reconstruction of Japan retained Hirohito as a figurehead.

❖ see HIROSHIMA p176, NAGASAKI p176

Pu Yi (1906–67)

Last emperor of China, of the Ch'ing dynasty. Pu Yi, or P'u-i, succeeded as emperor with the name Hsuan Tung in 1908. He was deposed in 1912, ending two millennia of imperial rule (267 years by the Ch'ing). He was briefly restored in 1917, but throughout continued to live in the palace at Beijing. During the Japanese occupation of Manchuria from 1931–45 he was installed as their puppet emperor of Manchukuo. After World War II he was imprisoned as a war criminal from 1950. Released in 1959, he then worked in a botanical garden.

❖ see CH'ING DYNASTY p56, WORLD WAR II p172

Elizabeth II of England (b. 1926)

Queen of the United Kingdom since 1952, and Head of the Commonwealth. Daughter of George VI and Elizabeth, the late Queen Mother. Elizabeth served during World War II in the ATS. In 1947 she married her cousin Philip Mountbatten, created Duke of Edinburgh, and succeeded to the throne while on a tour of Kenya. They have four children: Charles, Prince of Wales (b. 1948), Anne (b. 1950), Andrew (b. 1960) and Edward (b. 1964). The reign has been characterized by great changes in the image of the monarchy, while the Queen has remained fervently committed to the duties of her position, despite the marital problems of her children.

ABOVE: *Following unconditional surrender by the Japanese at the end of World War II, Emperor Hirohito was the first Japanese monarch to renounce his divinity. He is seen here standing underneath the Japanese flag.*

BELOW: *Pu Yi, the last emperor of China, became a puppet king in the hands of the Japanese.*

KEY DATES

322 BC	Death of Aristotle
1543	Death of Nicolaus Copernicus
1600	British East India Company founded
1642	Death of Galileo Galilei
1682	Halley's Comet first sighted
1698	Steam engine invented
18th & 19th centuries	Industrial Revolution in Britain
1790	James Watt's steam engine widely adopted
1720	South Sea Bubble
1823	Death of Edward Jenner, the vaccination pioneer
1825	First railway line opened, UK
1848	Death of George Stephenson,
1871	Death of Charles Barbage, father of the computer
1872	Death of Samuel Morse, inventor of the telegraph
1882	Death of Charles Darwin
1895	Death of Louis Pasteur
1922	Death of Alexander Graham Bell, inventor of the telephone
1848	Beginning of the Gold Rush, USA
1859	Suez Canal begun
1903	First controlled aeroplane flight

SCIENCE AND INDUSTRY

1912	❖	Sinking of the Titanic
1929	❖	Wall Street Crash
1945	❖	Start of the Cold War
1946	❖	Death of John Logie Baird
1947	❖	Death of Henry Ford
1957	❖	First space satellite launched
1969	❖	First man on the Moon
1955	❖	Death of Albert Einstein
1955	❖	Death of Alexander Fleming
1976	❖	First Concorde flight
1986	❖	Chernobyl disaster
1994	❖	Channel Tunnel opened

LEFT: *The great Greek philosopher Aristotle.*

Aristotle (384–322 BC)

Ancient Greek philosopher. Long before scientists began to properly understand chemistry and the elements, Aristotle came up with his own theory to explain the way things are made. For Aristotle there were just four 'elements': Earth, Air, Fire and Water. He believed that all earthly matter comprised these elements in different proportions. He claimed that a fifth element called aether made the celestial bodies seen in the sky. Interestingly, Aristotle was the first to consider the Earth to be spherical, although he did mistakenly think it was the centre of the Universe as well.

❖ see ANCIENT GREECE p110

Archimedes (c. 287–212 BC)

Ancient Greek scientist. Ancient Greece was where science and civilization merged. One of the greatest scientific or natural philosophers from that world was Archimedes. He is described as a mathematician and engineer, because he used mathematical principles in explaining how things worked and in designing things to work. Archimedes's principles of fluid displacement are probably his best-documented achievement. They demonstrate that the water displaced by a vessel weighs the same as the vessel.

❖ see ANCIENT GREECE p110

Nicolaus Copernicus (1473–1543)

Polish astronomer. Anthropocentrism had led people to believe that the Earth must be at the centre of the Universe ever since the Ancient Greeks first suggested it. Nicolaus Copernicus was the first to suggest that the Earth and other planets actually revolved around the Sun. Copernicus was still slightly wrong, as he believed that the Sun was the centre of the Universe, but his theory introduced the idea of the Solar System.

Paracelsus (1493–1541)

Swiss medical reformer. Switzerland became a hotbed of medical contention in the sixteenth century due to the rise of Philippus Bombastus von Hohenheim, known as Paracelsus. He advocated a new approach to medicine. Dismissing traditional notions of bodily humours, he asserted that ailments had specific causes that required treatment with specific chemicals.

Galileo Galilei (1564–1642)

Italian scientist. Galileo Galilei pioneered the modern method of scientific investigation by experimentation. He is thought to have been the

RIGHT: *Galileo Galilei perfected the lens of the refracting telescope and exploited the phenomenon of the pendulum as a time-keeping device.*

first to notice that a pendulum swings at a constant frequency even though its arc decreases with gradual loss of momentum, and therefore noted its value for timekeeping. Galileo showed Aristotle was wrong by demonstrating that objects of different weight but the same density will fall at equal rates (allowing for air resistance) by dropping objects from the tower at Pisa. He also discovered the parabolic flight paths of projectiles, which was of practical importance in ballistics warfare.

❖ see ISAAC NEWTON p90

British East India Company (1600)

English commercial company chartered by Queen Elizabeth I in 1600 and given the monopoly of trade between England and India. Its first trading posts were established in India in Mumbai and Madras provinces. It competed with the Dutch, French and Portuguese. Under Charles II the Company acquired sovereign rights in addition to its trading privileges and the Company became in effect the ruler of much of India. In 1813 the Company's monopoly of Indian trade was abolished, however, and in 1858, following the Indian Mutiny, its powers and possessions were assumed by the Crown. The Company was dissolved in 1874.

❖ see DUTCH EAST INDIA COMPANY p89

Dutch East India Company (1602)

Commercial company incorporated in 1602. Its monopoly extended from the Cape of Good Hope to the Strait of Magellan, with sovereign rights in whatever territory it acquired. The Company's headquarters was Batavia (now Jakarta, Indonesia). Through war with Spain (1605–65), the Company gained control of Indonesia, the Malay Peninsula, Japan, Ceylon (Sri Lanka) and the Malabar coast of India. It drove the English from the Malay Archipelago and the Moluccas, and established the first European settlement in southern Africa. At its greatest power in 1669 the Company deployed 10,000 soldiers and 40 warships. The Company went into liquidation in 1799.

❖ see BRITISH EAST INDIA COMPANY p89

Christiaan Huygens (1629–95)

Dutch physicist and astronomer. Huygens built the first pendulum clock, based on the principle observed by Galileo. He was also the first person to suggest that light might be thought of as waves, rather than particles; although it has since been shown to behave as both. As an astronomer Huygens did much to improve the telescope, invented by Hans Lippershey (1570–1619), and discovered the rings of the planet Saturn.

❖ see GALILEO GALILEI p88

ABOVE: *Christiaan Huygens.*

ABOVE: *Isaac Newton discovers the refraction of light.*

Isaac Newton (1642–1727)

English physicist. Newton worked on a theory of gravitation. It was fundamental to a new way of looking at the Universe, where counter-intuitive forces had to be taken into account. Newton realized that every object must possess its own gravitational pull, which is proportional to its mass. He also showed that white light comprises a spectrum of colours by using a glass prism.

❖ see ALBERT EINSTEIN p98

Hudson's Bay Company (1670)

English corporation formed in 1670. It enjoyed a monopoly in fur trade throughout the Hudson's Bay region. The Company also had the power to establish laws, erect forts and maintain warships. A clash with the French over the fur trade was finally settled when the British conquered Canada in 1763. In 1821 the company merged with its great rival, the North West Fur Company of Montreal. It lost its monopoly in 1859 but remained the most important Canadian fur company.

RIGHT: *The Hudson's Bay Company was set up to monopolize fur trade in the region around the Hudson River.*

Halley's Comet (1682)

Comet first sighted in 1682 by British astronomer Edmund Halley (1656–1742). Halley's Comet completes its eccentric orbit once every 76 years. Halley correctly predicted that it would return in 1758, having deduced that earlier sightings in 1531 and 1607 had been the same comet.

Industrial Revolution (18th–19th centuries)

Term applied to the economic developments that, from c. 1760 to 1830, transformed Britain from a primarily agricultural country to a primarily industrial one. It also denotes the social effects of this great change and its worldwide impact.

The Industrial Revolution was made possible by a series of inventions, especially in the textile industries, such as the flying shuttle, spinning jenny, spinning frame and power loom. Increasing mechanization had several consequences: domestic industry based on human labour gave way to the factory system; productivity was increased; further invention was encouraged; a division of labour occurred; management became more specialized; and marketing required new flair.

A common factor in industrialization everywhere was the advent of new sources of power other than water – first steam, then electricity – to drive machines and later also for

LEFT: *Edmund Halley sighted Halley's Comet in 1682 and extensively studied the movements of astronomical bodies, compiling catalogues of stars.*

locomotion. In Britain roads were improved, a network of canals was built and in 1825 the first railway was opened. The iron industry was transformed by the substitution of coke for charcoal in smelting. Existing materials such as iron and glass acquired new uses and further materials were discovered or created, particularly chemicals.

A sense prevailed that nature had finally been conquered. Work in factories attracted innumerable people to towns, where for at least a generation many suffered hard and unhealthy conditions, owing to overcrowding and lack of sanitary facilities.

Social change also revolutionized political life – the industrialists replaced the great landowners as the dominant class, and an independent labour movement was created.

Agrarian Revolution (18th century)

Term applied to the changes in agricultural practice that began in the late eighteenth century. In Britain almost all traces of the ancient 'open-field' system of arable farming vanished. Wealthier landowners gained title to huge enclosed tracts of land. Farmers now began experimenting with livestock breeding. Extra fodder could be grown to feed animals year-round. Similarly, crop rotation meant all fields could be used fully each year. Improvements in crop production derived from inventions such as new types of agricultural machinery. Mechanization reduced the need for human labour, causing unemployment, hardship, the eviction of peasant farmers, riots and revolts and even mass emigration. However, wherever the Agrarian Revolution impacted, people on the land were able to produce more food for the growing urban population, partly thanks to artificial fertilizers and the cultivation of high-yielding, reliable crops. The term Green Revolution is sometimes applied to the movement to increase yields and diversify crops in developing countries.

❖ see INDUSTRIAL REVOLUTION p90

Franklin, Benjamin (1706–90)

American scientist. Franklin was a man of many talents. He played an active role in the American Revolution by enlisting the help of the French on the colonial side, and became president of Pennsylvania in the post-war years, championing anti-slavery sentiments. He was also a scientist; fascinated by electricity, he showed that lightning is electrical by using a wet kite line to conduct lightning into an electrical cell. He invented the lightning conductor as a result, and explained electrical flow by distinguishing between negative and positive electricity.

LEFT: *After repairing a faulty steam engine, James Watt invented a better model using only a fraction of the coal used by earlier versions.*

James Watt (1736–1819)

Scottish inventor. While repairing a model of a Newcomen steam engine in 1764 Watt devised an exterior condenser, which would allow the working cylinder to remain permanently hot, increasing the efficiency of Newcomen's engine. Watt also invented a pumping engine and a rotative engine and with Matthew Boulton went into production near Birmingham.

❖ see RAIL TRAVEL p94

Edward Jenner (1749–1823)

British physician. Jenner established the principle of vaccination by demonstrating that someone inoculated with cowpox would become immune to smallpox. Cowpox is related to smallpox but far less virulent, so the lesser disease can be used to stimulate the body into producing the right antibodies.

ABOVE: *Richard Trevithick ran the first steam-powered locomotive on the Penydarren railway in Wales in 1804.*

Richard Trevithick (1771–1833)

British engineer, often considered the real inventor of the steam locomotive. His high-pressure steam engines were more efficient than James Watt's low-pressure engines. In 1801 he constructed the first passenger-carrying steam-propelled road locomotive and in 1804 the first steam engine to run on rails. This locomotive carried 10 tons of iron 15 km (9.5 miles) from Merthyr Tydfil to Abercynon, Wales. Trevithick's success encouraged him to build further steam-operated locomotives.

❖ see JAMES WATT p92

Humphry Davy (1778–1829)

English inventor. Davy discovered six of the elements in the periodic table. He isolated four of the six alkaline earth metals in group II – barium, calcium, magnesium and strontium – and two of the six alkali metals from group I – potassium and sodium. He used electrolysis to obtain samples. Davy also invented a miners' lamp that used a gauze to prevent ignition of firedamp: a mixture of methane and air.

LEFT: *English chemist, Humphry Davy, responsible for the isolation of six of the chemical elements named in the periodic table. He was also responsible for the invention of the eponymous safety lamp.*

ABOVE: *Michael Faraday proved the connection between magnetism and electricity by moving a compass needle along an electrical current.*

Michael Faraday (1791–1867)

British physicist and chemist. Initially an assistant to Humphry Davy, Michael Faraday was a pioneer of electromagnetic investigation. He was the first to show that electrical energy can be translated into motive force, by building a prototype electric motor. Conversely, he demonstrated that motive force could be converted into electricity – magnetic induction – by inventing the dynamo. Faraday also pioneered scientific understanding of electrolysis by enunciating the appropriate laws.

Charles Babbage (1791–1871)

British mathematician. Charles Babbage is considered the father of the computer. He was interested in developing mechanical calculating machines that could automatically solve complex mathematical problems. Two of his brain children were the 'difference engine' and the 'analytical engine': theoretical computing machines that were eventually built after his death.

Samuel Morse (1791–1872)

US inventor. The telegraph was invented by Samuel Morse in 1838. It was an electrical system that transmitted on/off signals along a wire, from one location to the next. To make his invention practicable, Morse adopted Alfred Vail's (1807–59) system of long and short signals that coded the letters of the alphabet, which became known as Morse code. A short signal was called a 'dot' and a long one a 'dash'.

Charles Darwin (1809–82)

English naturalist, evolutionist and writer, known for 'Darwinism'. The son of Dr Robert Darwin and the grandson of Erasmus Darwin, author of *Zoonomia, or the Laws of Organic Life*, Charles Darwin set off on HMS Beagle in 1831 as a naturalist studying evolution, to the west coast of South America on a five-year voyage. On his return in 1836 he began working on his books and is renowned for his writings on evolution and for his evolutionary theories. Two major works, *On the Origin of Species by Means of Natural Selection* (1859) and *The Descent of Man, and Selection in Relation to Sex* (1871) subsequently had a huge impact on the thoughts of future scientists, as well as on future developments. Darwin was also interested in the natural phenomena and wrote *Variation in Animals and Plants under Domestication* (1868) which, amongst other things, was a study of the role of earthworms in the fertility of soil.

ABOVE: *Samuel Morse, inventor of the Morse code, was also credited with building the first electric telegraph in 1835.*

SCIENCE AND INDUSTRY

Louis Pasteur (1822–95)

French chemist. Pasteur discovered that micro-organisms can be destroyed by heat. He published his 'germ theory' in 1865, which put forward the idea that micro-organisms are responsible for fermentation. He demonstrated that the application of heat prevents the fermentation process because it sterilizes the sample. Pasteur also made the important discovery that vaccines for serious diseases, such as rabies, can be produced by weakening the bacterium or virus that causes the illness. This is very useful when a secondary disease, such as cowpox or smallpox, is not available for inoculation.

Rail Travel

Rails, first of stone or wood, then of iron, have long been used to reduce friction in locomotion. The first public railway was the Surrey Iron Railway (south of London) utilizing animal power. Early experiments produced locomotives, but the first railway line, Stockton to Darlington, opened in 1825 thanks to George Stephenson, whose engine reached a speed of 24 km/h (15 mph). The Rocket locomotive followed in 1829, drawing a coach at 50 km/h (30 mph) on the Liverpool–Manchester line.

This was the general signal for widespread building of railways. In 1846 a British Act of Parliament established a standard gauge for all new railways. In 1948 the various rail companies were nationalized as British Railways. The construction of world railways followed quickly. Electric and diesel traction was developed in the late nineteenth century. In the 1960s Britain's main lines were electrified. High-speed trains such as the Japanese 'Bullet' and the French TGV have reached speeds of over 500 km/h (350 mph). London has the world's largest underground rail system. The top rail-freight countries are the USA, China and Russia. Despite ageing stock and congestion on lines, rail provides fast, efficient and relatively safe travel.

Joseph Lister (1827–1912)

English surgeon. Joseph Lister was the first person to introduce sterilization procedures into his operating room. He sprayed phenol (carbolic acid) on to wounds and heated instruments before use so that the environment was as antiseptic as possible. He was influenced by the work of Louis Pasteur.
❖ see LOUIS PASTEUR p94

James Clerk Maxwell (1831–79)

Scottish mathematician. James Clerk Maxwell studied the phenomenon of electromagnetic radiation. Maxwell devised equations that demonstrated the relationship between electricity, magnetism and light. He went on to study the nature of colour vision and, in 1861, produced the first colour photograph that used a three-colour process in the same way that the human eye receives and interprets visual images on the retina.

Dmitri Mendeleyev (1834–1907)

Inventor of the periodic table of chemical elements. In 1869, Dmitri Mendeleyev published the periodic table he had devised for the chemical elements. Chemically similar elements were grouped in vertical rows, yet the elements appeared in order of relative atomic mass (RAM) in periods. Mendeleyev correctly predicted the discovery of elements to fill the vacant spaces.

Alexander Graham Bell (1847–1922)

Scottish inventor. Alexander Graham Bell demonstrated the telephone for the first time in 1876 in the United States. The inventor was Scottish-born, but moved across the Atlantic to Canada in 1870 with his family. He invented the telephone by assembling and perfecting various devices invented by others.

Thomas Alva Edison (1847–1931)

American inventor. Edison first made his fortune by selling a machine he had invented in 1869 that used a paper 'ticker' tape for sending electrical information on stocks and shares. With the proceeds, Edison established his industrial research laboratory that served him for the rest of his life. In the laboratory he had a team of dedicated technicians who would try things out time and time again until an idea was perfected into a working prototype. His most celebrated invention was the electric light bulb.

ABOVE: *Thomas Edison invented the first commercially viable electric bulb.*

(Antoine) Henri Becquerel (1852–1908)

French physicist. Although Marie and Pierre Curie are popularly regarded as the parents of radioactivity, there was another scientist who was making similar discoveries contemporaneously. Antoine Henri Becquerel had discovered that radiation was emitted from uranium salts and it was, partly, his work that inspired the Curies. The three of them shared the Nobel Prize for Physics in 1903.

❖ see MARIE AND PIERRE CURIE p96

Max Planck (1858–1947)

German theoretical physicist. Modern physics is largely based on the principles of quantum theory – the brainchild of Max Planck – and Einstein's theories of relativity. Quantum theory concerns itself with the relationship between matter and energy at the subatomic or nano scale. Planck suggested that matter and energy were the same within atoms and come in tiny 'packets' called quanta. The theory revolutionized our understanding of subatomic physics.

❖ see ALBERT EINSTEIN p98

Suez Canal (1859–69)

Artificial waterway connecting the Mediterranean Sea with the Gulf of Suez, providing a short cut for ships operating between Europe or America and the East. The Suez Canal is about 163 km (101 miles) long and can accommodate ships up to 150,000 dwt (deadweight tonnage) fully loaded. It was built between 1859 and 1869.

Henry Ford (1863–1947)

American industrialist and automobile pioneer. In 1903 he founded the Ford Motor Company, and in 1908–09 developed the famous Model T vehicle (discontinued after sales of 15 million in 1927). In 1913 he began using standardized interchangeable parts and assembly-line methods of manufacture, which became widespread practices throughout American industry, greatly increasing productivity. A pacifist, Ford visited Europe in 1915–16 to try to end the war. During World War II, the Ford Company manufactured 8,000 bombers.

❖ see WORLD WAR II p172

Marie (1867–1934) and Pierre (1859–1906) Curie

French scientists; pioneers in the study of radiation. In fact, they shared the Nobel Prize for Physics with Henri Becquerel, in 1903, for the discovery of radiation. They discovered the radioactive elements polonium and radium in pieces of pitchblende, managing to isolate samples in 1902. Marie went on to win the Nobel Prize for Chemistry in 1911 for her continued work in the field.

❖ see HENRI BECQUEREL p96

ABOVE: *The US automobile manufacturer Henry Ford sitting in his first prototype model of a car.*

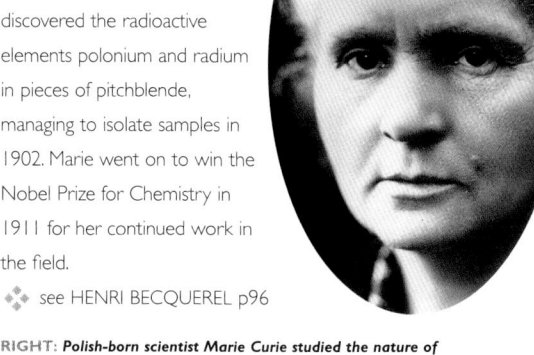

RIGHT: *Polish-born scientist Marie Curie studied the nature of uranium rays and discovered the elements polonium and radium.*

ABOVE: *Louis Blériot perfected the powered monoplane, which he used to make the first Channel crossing in 1909.*

Wright Brothers

American brothers Wilbur (1867–1912) and Orville (1871–1948), pioneers of flying. While running a bicycle repair business, they experimented with gliders and the effects of air pressure on wing surfaces. From their own calculations they built propellers, a wind tunnel and finally a machine with a 12-horsepower motor, which they called the Flyer. On 17 December 1903 they made the first controlled powered-aeroplane flights. They made hundreds of flights in the succeeding years, the longest lasting some 38 minutes.

Louis Blériot (1872–1936)

French aviator. Louis Blériot was the first person to fly across the English Channel or La Manche ('The Sleeve') as the French call it. He did so in 1909 in a machine designed and built by himself. Blériot was a skilled aviation designer and he did much to hasten the evolution of the aeroplane. He pioneered the monoplane shape and devised means of operating ailerons by cable and pulley.

Guglielmo Marconi (1874–1937)

Italian physicist. In the late 1890s Guglielmo Marconi developed radio communications, or the 'wireless' as it became known. He perfected the system by 1897 and was able to raise the funds to establish a communications company which was transmitting between England and France by 1899. Transatlantic transmissions were possible by 1901 and the wireless would soon become a vital piece of kit in shipping and warfare communications.

RIGHT: *Guglielmo Marconi produced the precursor of the radio, a type of wireless telegraph. He had been much influenced by Hertz's theories of electromagnetic waves.*

SCIENCE AND INDUSTRY

Albert Einstein (1879–1955)

German mathematician. Albert Einstein's work in mathematical physics astounded the world. Prior to Einstein's theories, human understanding of gravity and other physical phenomena had been based on Newtonian laws.

Einstein published his own theories, based on mathematical formulae, that demonstrated relationships between time, light, mass, gravity and space. Unlike Newton's laws, however, they could not be easily proven by experimentation, even though they worked on paper. Other scientists, such as Arthur Eddington, eventually began to show that Einstein was correct in his assertions.

Einstein's best-known theory is his theory of general relativity, published in 1905. It shows that motion and mass have relative, rather than absolute, characters, because of interdependence between matter, time and space. His famous formula $E = mc^2$ demonstrates that mass and energy are equivalent.

❖ see ARTHUR EDDINGTON p98, ISAAC NEWTON p90

ABOVE: *Albert Einstein formulated theories about the nature and structure of the Universe which permanently changed our view of cosmology.*

Alexander Fleming (1881–1955)

Scottish scientist. In 1941, during World War II, commercial production of penicillin began. The theatre of war was the perfect setting to show how remarkable this antibiotic was at combating bacterially infected wounds. Alexander Fleming was the man behind the discovery of penicillin. He had been researching pathogenic Staphylococci bacteria and noticed that a mould called Penicillium notatum secreted a substance that inhibited growth in the bacteria. He won the Nobel Prize for Medicine in 1945.

Arthur Eddington (1882–1944)

English astronomer and physicist. Einstein's theory of relativity was published in 1905, but it required some tangible proof to become popularly accepted. Arthur Eddington conducted pioneering work on atomic theory. In 1919 he obtained proof that Einstein was right. Einstein had argued that light should be attracted by gravity and Eddington was able to show that light passing the Sun was indeed pulled off course by its gravity.

❖ see ALBERT EINSTEIN p98

John Logie Baird (1888–1946)

Scottish inventor. The television started life as the brainchild of John Logie Baird. The first working prototype was demonstrated in 1926. It was primitive, but showed that the idea worked. Eventually the familiar television, using a cathode-ray tube, became the preferred format. The design has gone on to be used for computer monitors. By 1928 Baird had also perfected the workings of colour television.

Werner Heisenberg (1901–76)

German physicist. In 1927 Heisenberg drew up the 'Uncertainty Principle' of quantum mechanics, which states that an atomic particle cannot have a measurable position and momentum simultaneously, because at nanoscale the very act of measuring will disturb the particle so as to nullify the measurement.

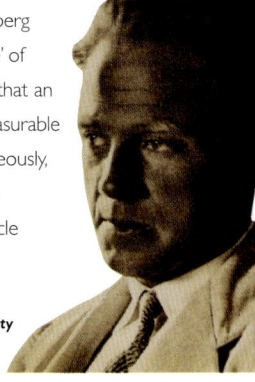

RIGHT: *Werner Heisenberg's Uncertainty Principle has become fundamental to understanding quantum physics.*

Titanic (1912)

British luxury liner that suffered one of the worst maritime disasters in history. The Titanic (46,000 gross tonnes) was a White Star liner, which, on her maiden voyage from Southampton to New York, struck an iceberg about 153 km (96 miles) south of Newfoundland in April 1912. The Titanic had been declared unsinkable, having 16 watertight compartments, but five of these were punctured and the ship sank in under three hours. Of some 2,220 people aboard, more than 1,500 died, partly owing to an inadequacy of lifeboat space. The wreck was found in 1985 and some of its contents subsequently salvaged and exhibited.

Alan Turing (1912–54)

During World War II the British made concerted efforts to break the communications codes being used by the German forces. Alan Turing was at the forefront of these developments. He designed a digital tape machine that could decipher code extremely rapidly. He also helped break the Enigma code.

❖ see WORLD WAR II p172

Wall Street Crash (1929)

Stockmarket crash in the USA in 1929. The growth in the US economy encouraged excessive buying in the domestic market, which pushed prices up drastically. Some professionals then decided to take profits and sell short. Other investors also switched to selling and prices plummeted. On one day, 'Black Tuesday' – 29 October – 16 million shares were traded and $10 billion wiped off share values. The crash caused innumerable bankruptcies and unemployment rose by two million within six months. Elsewhere in the world, banks closed, unable to pay depositors. The crash started the worldwide economic slump called the Great Depression.

❖ see GREAT DEPRESSION p134

ABOVE: *Hearing news of the crash, worried investors pour out on to Wall Street in New York. Millions lost jobs, businesses, savings and homes.*

SCIENCE AND INDUSTRY

Cold War (1945–89)

Term given to the political and economic struggle between the capitalist, democratic Western powers and the Soviet Union. The Cold War began after World War II and continued (with a brief respite during détente) until the break-up of the USSR.

The first stand-off came during the post-war division of Germany. With 20 million dead and having suffered two German invasions in 30 years, the Soviet Union was determined to crush Germany's ability to start another war. US President Truman was equally bent on rebuilding a capitalist Europe with a healthy German economy at its centre. After a number of incidents, the Iron Curtain descended and communications virtually ceased between the two sides. The US pumped huge sums of money into Europe through the Marshall Plan and rallied the Western powers into strategic alliances such as NATO (North Atlantic Treaty Organization). Stalin retaliated by tightening Soviet control over the Communist bloc and signing an alliance with the new Communist China in 1950.

'Hot wars' broke out in Korea and Vietnam as the US tried to stop the spread of Communism in Southeast Asia in the 1950s and 1960s. The nuclear stand-off reached its peak during the Cuban Missile Crisis. There were various flashpoints during the 1970s and 1980s, such as the Soviet invasion of Afghanistan, but the world had outgrown the superpower clash. The Cold War had proved costly to both the Soviet and US economies and Mikhail Gorbachev's huge concessions on arms reduction, the withdrawal of Soviet troops from Afghanistan and the demise of Communism in the Soviet Union signalled its end.

❖ see CUBAN MISSILE CRISIS p29, IRON CURTAIN p24, KOREAN WAR p176, JOSEPH STALIN p14, VIETNAM WAR p178

LEFT: *Two iconic figureheads of the Cold War in the 1960s: US President John F. Kennedy and Russian prime minister Nikita Kruschchev.*

Space Race (1950s–1960s)

Term used to describe the activity of and rivalry between the then USSR and the USA in the exploration of space. From the mid-1950s the two nations successfully launched over 5,000 satellites and space, lunar and planetary probes, as well as manned space flights.

It began with the launch by the Soviet Union of the first artificial satellite, Sputnik 1, on 4 October 1957. On 31 January 1958 the United States followed with Explorer 1. The manned space programme marked an acceleration of the space race. On 12 April 1961 the Soviet cosmonaut Yuri Gagarin, in Vostok 1, made the first successful orbit of the Earth. The Soviets led also in the achievement of true space flight: Luna 1, launched in 1959, became the first man-made body to escape the Earth's gravitational field and fly past the Moon. Luna 2 crashed on the Moon, but Luna 3 (October 1959) photographed the far side of the Moon. By the time the Soviets landed Luna 9 on the Moon (1966), the USA had also sent up several craft and received from them countless close-range photographs and information about the Moon's surface. On 20 July 1969 the USA landed two men on the Moon, and a further five landings were made before the programme was curtailed in 1972.

Other ventures in space have looked to the possibilities of planetary exploration, beginning with Mariner 2 (USA 1962), which passed by Venus, and continuing with Venera 3 and Venera 4 (USSR, 1966 and 1967). From 1981 the USA concentrated mainly on the reusable space-shuttle manned research vehicle, but its flights were halted immediately after an explosion that destroyed Challenger and its seven crew in 1986. The Russian space station Mir finally came to Earth in 2001 after 15 years in space.

Genetic Engineering

When James Watson (b. 1828) and Francis Crick (b. 1916) discovered the chemical structure of DNA (deoxyribonucleic acid) in 1953, the way was opened for genetic engineering to become a part of progress in the biological sciences. Genetic engineering is done by a technique known as gene splicing, which involves the cutting and rejoining of genes, just like lengths of film. As all living things use the same basic molecule – DNA – for coding, this means that sections of gene can be transplanted from one species to another totally unrelated species, thereby arriving at new species with unique traits.

Concorde (1976)

Supersonic Anglo-French aircraft, which entered passenger service in 1976. Famed for its stylish elegance, it had a maximum cruising speed of 2,179 km/h (1,176 knots), twice that of any other long haul aircraft. A Concorde tragically crashed soon after take-off near Paris in July 2000, killing over 200 people.

Chernobyl (1986)

Nuclear disaster. In April 1986 two explosions at a nuclear power station in Chernobyl, Ukraine, destroyed the central reactor and removed a protective roof weighing some 1,000 tonnes. Thirty-one people died immediately, but it is reckoned that tens of thousands will die from cancers as a result of exposure to radiation contamination over the following few decades.

Channel Tunnel (1994)

Rail connection beneath the English Channel, connecting England with France. The tunnel is 50 km (31 miles) long and runs between Folkestone and Sangatte (near Calais), with a journey time of 35 minutes. There are three tunnels, two for rail traffic and one for services and security. It accommodates coaches and cars.

BELOW: *The launch of Russian cosmonaut Yuri Gagarin into orbit in 1961 sparked the space race between the USA and Russia.*

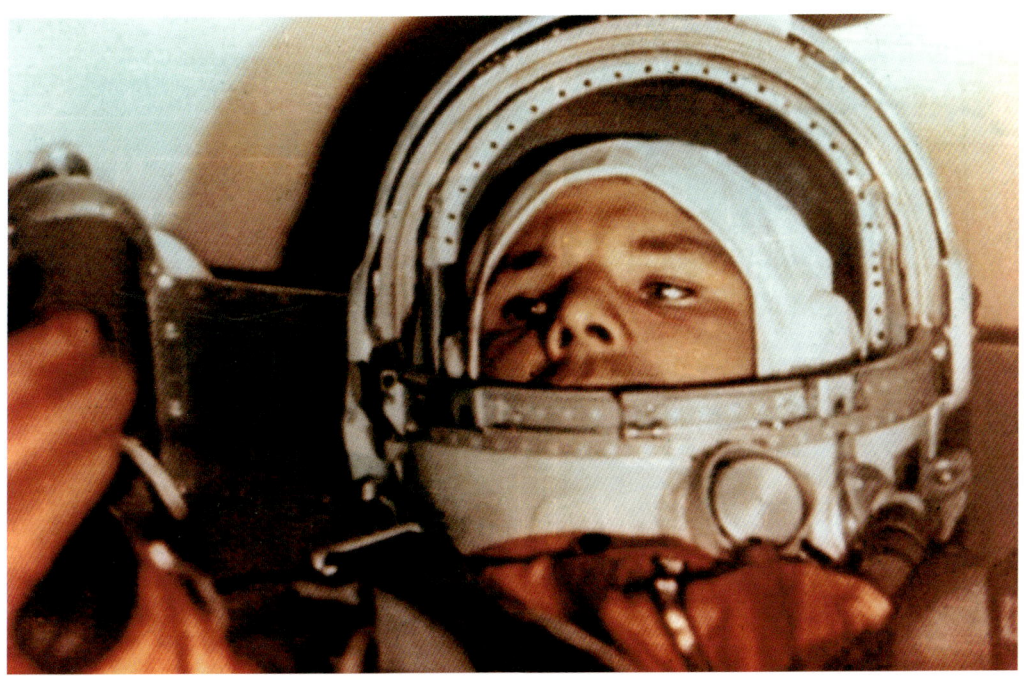

KEY DATES

3000 BC	❖	Construction of walled citadels in Mediteranean Europe
2686 BC	❖	Old Kingdom established in Ancient Egypt
2500 BC	❖	Rise of the Phoenicians
2300 BC	❖	Beginning of the full European Bronze Age
2000 BC	❖	Rise of the Hittite civilization in Mesopotamia
1991 BC	❖	Middle Kingdom established in Ancient Egypt
1792 BC	❖	Rise of the Babylonian civilization in Mesopotamia
1766 BC	❖	Rise of the Shang dynasty in China
1554 BC	❖	New Kingdom established in Ancient Egypt
1500 BC	❖	Rise of the Mayan civilization in central America
1500 BC	❖	Rise of the Olmec civilization in central America

SOCIETY AND CULTURE

1050 BC	❖	Rise of the Chou dynasty in China
900 BC	❖	Assyrian civilization of the Ancient Near East
800 BC	❖	Rise of the Etruscan civilization in Italy
206 BC	❖	Collapse of the Ch'ing dynasty and establishment of the Han
AD 117	❖	Roman Empire at its height
AD 320	❖	Rise of the Gupta Empire in India
AD 395	❖	Rise of the Byzantine Empire
AD 410	❖	Sack of Rome and the collapse of the Western Roman Empire

Maoris

Polynesian people of New Zealand. The Maoris arrived in New Zealand from other Pacific islands over a period of 500 years to 1350. Maori culture was well developed before the arrival of the Europeans in the late eighteenth century. In 1840 Great Britain and Maori Chiefs signed the Treaty of Waitangi that established British rule. Conflicts arose between the Maoris and Europeans, after which most Maori land was confiscated. As a result of the wars and European diseases, the Maori population rapidly declined. However, in the twentieth century the Maori population recovered and their arts, culture and politics continue to flourish.

❖ see MAORI WARS p154

Native American Indians

Indigenous people of America. Prior to the arrival of the Europeans, 90 million people inhabited the Americas, with 10 million north of Mexico. It is believed that these peoples came from Siberia during the Paleolithic period. By the seventeenth century the Americas had been infiltrated by Europeans in their thousands. Systematically, the Native Americans were dislocated, driven off their native lands, slaughtered and, on rare occasions, absorbed into the new European society.

For the fledgling United States, the Native Americans were considered a danger to human life and an inhibition to the expansion of their country. By 1830 the Indian Removal Act had been passed and their removal from areas designated for settlers had become commonplace. The Allotment or Dawes Act (1887) attempted to parcel out communally-owned reservation land to individual Indians, but many found themselves landless as speculators snapped up the 160-acre allotments. As far as the settlers and frontiersmen were concerned, the indigenous people needed to be slaughtered in self-defence. By the mid-nineteenth century Indian territories, or reservations, had been set aside in some of the least habitable parts of the country, inciting the Plains Indian Wars, which eventually saw the slaughter of the Sioux tribe. By the 1890s settlers had reached the Pacific Ocean and as far as the government was concerned Native Americans were now wards of the USA.

By the 1990s Native Americans accounted for less than one per cent of the US population. They still have 56 million acres of reservation land. Notable Native American leaders include Tecumseh (d. 1813), leader of the Shawnee; Geronimo (d. 1909), Apache chief; and Sitting Bull (d. 1890), Sioux chief.

❖ see BATTLE OF LITTLE BIGHORN p158, SITTING BULL p84

Slavery

Involuntary human servitude. Slavery was an essential feature of ancient civilizations, including the Indian, Chinese and Roman ones. During the Middle Ages, despite the spread of Christianity, slavery was not eliminated. Islam recognized slavery from the seventh century and the Prophet Muhammad encouraged his faithful followers to be kind to their slaves.

During the exploration of Africa and the invasion of the Americas, the modern slave trade gained impetus. Colonists forced the native population to work their land. African slaves were taken to the Americas and the Caribbean to work on

LEFT: *Native American Indians lost their lands and culture to European settlers. Nowadays they account for less than one per cent of the entire US population.*

the newly formed plantations. Slavery became an essential element of the English colonies in America. Denmark was the first European country to abolish slavery (1792) followed by Great Britain (1807). Despite the United States abolishing slavery in 1808, there were still nearly four million slaves by the year 1860. Slaves did have some legal rights, but their masters were not bound to respect them. Mutilation, chaining, branding, rape and murder were widespread despite being prohibited by law. The American Civil War (1861–65) brought about the freedom of four million slaves upon whom the southern economy had depended.

During the late nineteenth century the Arabs were particularly active in the slave trade in North Africa which was gradually brought to an end as states fell under the power of European countries such as Great Britain and France. In 1926 the International Slavery Convention abolished slavery in all forms. Nevertheless, slavery still continues across the world, notably in West Africa.

❖ see AMERICAN CIVIL WAR p156

Aboriginals

The most famous Aboriginals are the Australian Aborigines who had settled there and in Tasmania when the Europeans reached there in the eighteenth century. It is believed that the Aboriginals made their way to Australia via a land shelf connecting it to New Guinea and that 500 tribes originally settled there, amounting to a population of some 300,000. It is estimated that 230,000 still exist in Australia alone. Factors such as changes in culture and marriage between different tribes and different cultures have affected the way the Aboriginals live, as well as their physical appearance.

ABOVE: *Australian Aboriginals: anthropologists believe these indigenous tribes did not migrate but settled in a particular place.*

SOCIETY AND CULTURE

Sumerians

Civilization of the Ancient Near East. The Sumerians were the first peoples to inhabit Mesopotamia. The civilization grew up around the Tigris and Euphrates rivers. The Sumerians became an advanced people, building rivers and dykes to control the rivers and harness their properties for their own uses. They built ziggurats, or temple towers, and developed the form of writing that has become known as cuneiform.

❖ see ASSYRIANS p109, BABYLONIANS p108

Ancient Egypt

The civilization of Ancient Egypt began about 3100 BC and flourished for over 2,000 years. It was one of the earliest and greatest civilizations, remarkable for its richness and sophistication and its lasting achievements.

In 3100 BC the kingdoms of Lower Egypt, on the Nile delta, and Upper Egypt south of the delta were unified by the legendary King Menes, who ruled from Memphis. The first major phase of the civilization was the Old Kingdom established in 2686 BC. During this period the great pyramids at Giza were built and hieroglyphics, or picture writing, developed. This script covers clay tablets, manuscripts and the walls of buildings, describing every aspect of life in Ancient Egypt. In the Middle Kingdom (1991–1786 BC) Nubia was conquered and became part of the Egyptian kingdom. Trade links with Asia were established and the kingdom prospered. The Egyptian Empire reached its largest extent and Egyptian civilization its greatest heights during the New Kingdom (1554–1196 BC), when the capital was also moved to Thebes. After the eleventh century BC Egypt was often divided and sometimes subjugated to Assyria and Persia and ultimately to Alexander the Great. The empire survived until Cleopatra's death in 30 BC.

To Ancient Egypt is owed not only the construction of the pyramids and other monuments such as the rock temple at Abu Simbel (built by Rameses II in the thirteenth century BC), but also the invention of irrigation, early discoveries in astronomy, mathematics and medicine and the legacy of a rich pantheon of deities and totemic animals. The arid climate

BELOW: *The funerary mask of Tutankhamen, part of a vast treasure unearthed inside the Valley of the Kings.*

has preserved a wealth of treasures and other objects. The most famous find was that of the tomb of Tutankhamen (r. 1358–53 BC), the young pharaoh who succeeded Akhenaten and reversed his monotheistic policy.

❖ see ALEXANDER THE GREAT p54, CLEOPATRA p55, GREAT PYRAMID OF GIZA p106, RAMESES II p52, TUTANKHAMEN p52

Great Pyramid of Giza (2600 BC)

Egyptian monument. One of a cluster of monuments at Giza which includes the slightly smaller (and younger) pyramids of Khafre and Menkaure as well as the figure of the Sphinx, the Great Pyramid was one of the Wonders of the Ancient World. Built around 2600 BC as a tomb for the Pharaoh Khufu, it still seems extraordinarily imposing today, possibly the most massive single building ever constructed. Standing at just under 150 m (492 ft) in height, and measuring over 200 m (656 ft) on each side at the base, it has been calculated to contain some 2.3 m (7.5 ft) blocks of stone.

❖ see ANCIENT EGYPT p106

Phoenicians (2500–64 BC)

Ancient culture on the east coast of the Mediterranean. Originally a group of city-states, the Phoenicians found themselves under Sumerian and Akkadian control for many years until 1800 BC when Egypt took over the eastern Mediterranean. When the Hittites revolted, this gave the Phoenicians the opportunity to take their independence in 1100 BC. From then on their fleets and traders founded many colonies, including Carthage, Rhodes and Cyprus. They traded in wood, linen, cloth, embroidery, wine, metalwork, glass, salt and fish, and it is believed that they invented glass-blowing in the first century BC. Phoenician religion comprised a variety of gods dominated by the father of the gods, El, and the goddess Astarte. The Phoenician alphabet was later adopted by the Greeks and, later still, the Romans.

They were conquered by the Assyrians in the late seventh century BC and became part of the Persian Empire in 539 BC. The leading Phoenician city of Tyre fell to Alexander the Great in 332 BC and they became much more Hellenized, as they were absorbed into the Greco-Macedonian empire. The name Phoenicia disappeared in 64 BC when the country became part of the Roman province of Syria.

❖ see ALEXANDER THE GREAT p54, HITTITES p108, SUMERIANS p106

BELOW: *Egypt's ancestral glory is evident from monuments like the Sphinx and the Pyramids of Giza, the last of the world's ancient wonders.*

SOCIETY AND CULTURE

Indus Valley Civilization (2400–1500 BC)

Ancient civilization of northern India resulting from waves of migration by Aryan peoples who settled in the Indus Valley and created great cities. The magnificence of their remains suggests a high degree of culture. The petty kingdoms were eventually subjugated by the Persians under Darius.

Hittites (2000–1200 BC)

Ancient people who dominated Syria and Asia Minor 2000–1200 BC, the Hittites rank after the Egyptians and Assyrians in importance among the civilizations of the Middle East. According to Genesis, they were the followers of Heth, son of Canaan. They are best remembered for their hieroglyphics and cuneiform script.

❖ see ASSYRIANS p109

Babylonians (c. 1792 BC)

Peoples of the Ancient Near East. The Babylonian Empire became significant in Mesopotamia c. 1792 BC under Hammurabi. Babylon is renowned for its decadence, but also its advanced technology. Most famously Nebuchadnezzar II captured Jerusalem in 586 BC and exiled the Jews to Babylon for 70 years to help on the Babylonians' hydraulically irrigated Hanging Gardens. Astronomical and mathematical developments included the establishment of an hour of 60 minutes and 360 degrees in a circle. In 539 BC Babylon itself fell to Cyrus the Great.

From then on the civilization was in decline, but from the palace at Mari, which had 12-m (40-ft) thick walls, clay tablets survive with extensive information.

❖ see ASSYRIANS p109, CYRUS THE GREAT p53, SUMERIANS p106

Maya (1500 BC–AD 1519)

Meso-American civilization. The Mayans settled in present-day Mexico, Guatemala, Honduras and El Salvador. Before AD 200 they had been an agricultural people but began to build

temples, palaces and pyramids and develop writing and astronomy. They made paper and were great sculptors and architects. At the height of the Mayan civilization the population had reached two million across their 40 cities. Whether war or the exhaustion of the land was to blame, by AD 900 the civilization was in decline. The Mayans abandoned most of their temples and returned to their agricultural life. During the tenth century the Toltecs had taken over the most important city of the Mayans, Chichén Itzá. When the Spanish arrived in the sixteenth century, they easily overcame the remnants of the Mayan civilization but independent communities still existed until 1901. Their writing was not deciphered until the mid-twentieth century, shedding light on their religion, rituals, mathematics and astronomy.

Olmec (1500–600 BC)

Pre-Columbian culture of central America. These indigenous peoples lived on the Gulf of Mexico and extended their influence into the Valley of Mexico and south-east into Central America. Their probable capital, San Lorenzo, was destroyed in 900 BC and replaced by La Venta. They were the first people to use stone in architecture and sculpture, creating massive stone heads to adorn their temples and plazas. Olmec writing was the foundation of all South American languages and their culture influenced the whole region for many centuries. Their society was complex and their culture gradually changed over a period of years and at some stage, probably around 600 BC, they ceased to be the dominant influence in the region. They created vast urban pyramids about 30 m (100 ft) high at the centres of their civilization and traded widely. They are particularly remembered for their remarkable art forms, as can be seen at Villahermosa.

LEFT: *This colossal stone head representing an Olmec ruler was found at La Venta, Tabasco, Mexico.*

RIGHT: *Chinese tourists walk along the Great Wall of China, the only man-made construction visible from outer space.*

Assyrians (c. 900 BC)

Civilization of the Ancient Near East. The Assyrians replaced the Babylonians in the area of Ancient Mesopotamia (present-day Iraq). They were a warlike people and the first to form a military state, which assisted in the successful conquest of other civilizations and the expansion of their empire. The Assyrians are also noted for their love of learning; they took care to preserve the libraries of the states they conquered. The most famous of these is that of King Ashurbanipal, discovered at the Assyrian capital Nineveh.

❖ see BABYLONIANS p108, HITTITES p108

Great Wall of China (7th century BC)

The only human-built construction able to be seen from orbit. The defensive construction began on the 'Square Wall' in the northern part of the kingdom, from earth and stone, terminating at the shores of the Yellow Sea. The Great Wall, through several centuries and different leaders, was constructed from castles and fortifications of the several different Chinese kingdoms, mainly to protect them from threats of invasion. The first Ch'ing Emperor, Shih Huang-ti, saw the unification of China.

❖ see CH'ING DYNASTY p56

SOCIETY AND CULTURE

Classical Period (c. 500 BC–AD 400)

Much more than an age of history, the Classical Period is now seen as the basis for the consciousness and culture of modernity, influencing the way the Western world has thought in recent times. Beginning with the rise of democratic Athens, in the fifth century BC, the period continues with the emergence of imperial Rome, which developed the civilization it found in the conquered Greek cities. The 'classic' principles of balance, order and restraint find their ultimate expression in Athens's Parthenon – though they can be discerned in everything from poetry to sculpture. Although later Greek artists sacrificed these principles in pursuit of more complex forms, the Romans spurned such 'effeminacies' in favour of a return to severer symmetries. Essentially a humanistic approach, emphasizing man's ability to impose regular forms on unco-operative nature, classicism was out of kilter with the religious values of the Middle Ages. Its rediscovery between the fourteenth and fifteenth centuries would be the key to the European Renaissance; it has underpinned our tastes and attitudes ever since.

❖ see ACROPOLIS p113, RENAISSANCE p118

Ancient Greece (c. 800–300 BC)

The civilization of Ancient Greece lasted from c. 800 to 300 BC. More than any other civilization except that of the Jews, it bequeathed ideas about politics, society, philosophy and culture to modern Western civilization. The first Greek civilization, the Mycenaean (c. 1600–1200 BC), probably spread by the marriage of Greek-speaking invaders with indigenous inhabitants. At the two great centres of this era, Knossos on Crete and Mycenae on the mainland, royal dynasties developed palace societies in which writing evolved and art (notably frescoes) and architecture flourished.

Between the fourteenth and twelfth centuries BC, Greece and Crete were invaded by the Achaeans and the Dorians, who founded Sparta. Between 1100 and 800 BC the great city-states arose. The mountainous terrain of Greece prevented the cities from attaining any national unity and compelled them to take to the sea. Thus from 750 to 550 BC

ABOVE: *A high-relief stone carving of life in Ancient Greece shows the wealth and sophistication enjoyed by this advanced civilization.*

the Greeks became great traders and founded colonies around the coasts of the Mediterranean and the Black Sea. These wealthy ports became the main centres of Greek culture, where philosophy, science and lyric poetry originated.

In the fifth century BC the focus of the Greek world shifted to Athens, and here tragedy, comedy, sculpture and architecture reached their glorious height. Ultimately, Athens was surpassed by Alexandria and then by Rome. Homer, Hesiod and the lyric poet Pindar were the three greatest names of Ancient Greek literature. Socrates, Plato and Aristotle laid the foundations of moral philosophy. The city-states, poleis, which included both rural and urban areas, passed from monarchy to the rule of landowners or merchants and then to democratic communities of citizens. For the first time in known history, ideas of freedom and autonomy emerged and the art of politics was practised. Greek religion included many gods, who were honoured with animal sacrifices, gifts and offerings.

❖ see ARISTOTLE p88, TROJAN WAR p140

Etruscans (800–283 BC)

Ancient Italian civilization. It is unknown whether the Etruscans were descended from migrants of Asia Minor or were native Iron Age people. By the middle of the seventh

ABOVE: *The ruins of a Roman ampitheatre provide a glimpse into the incredible heritage left us by this fascinating civilization.*

century BC, the Etruscans had begun to settle in Italy, from the Alps to the Tiber River. The aristocracy controlled Etruscan society and most of their cities had an independent status, forging links through marriage. By the fifth century BC their expansion had been stopped as the Greeks, Romans and Carthaginians united against them. The Romans captured the city of Veii in 396 BC, marking the beginning of Rome's conquest. The Romans captured most of central and southern Italy and then turned their attention to the northern cities of Caere Tarquinia and Vulci. All attempts to ally with the Gauls against the Romans failed. At their height they had immense military strength but it was not well co-ordinated due to the independence of the city-states. Little is known about religion, but it is believed that they worshipped animal gods and many of their deilies became the well-known Roman ones, such as Venus and Apollo. Etruscan art was similar to that of the Greeks and many of their buildings were constructed of wood and brick.

❖ see ROMANS p111

LEFT: *A bronze Etruscan head.*

Romans (753 BC – AD 476)

Rome was founded in 753 BC and gradually the cities of Latium fell under Roman control. The Etruscans were defeated in the fifth to fourth centuries BC and the Samnites in 343–290 BC. The Greek cities to the south were conquered (280–272 BC) as was Cisalpine Gaul (226–222 BC). Rome fought two Punic Wars against Carthage for the possession of Sicily, Sardinia, Spain and North Africa. By 148 BC Macedon had become a province and Greece was added in 146. By AD 117, after having added Gaul, Egypt, Great Britain, Dacia and Mesopotamia, the Empire had reached its greatest expansion, stretching from the Persian Gulf to the Iberian Peninsula.

Gradually the frontiers came under pressure from the Franks, Goths and Parthians. Ultimately, the Empire was divided between two emperors in Rome and Constantinople. By AD 410 the Goths had overrun Greece and Italy and sacked Rome, and the Vandals had conquered Italy itself. Britain was abandoned in AD 407 and when the Huns raided Gaul and Italy (AD 451–52), the Empire was virtually unable to defend itself. Each time the Empire contracted, Barbarians filled the vacuum. The last emperor was deposed in AD 476 and a Western Roman Empire ceased to exist.

❖ see ANCIENT ROME p112, AUGUSTUS CAESAR p56, EMPEROR HADRIAN p56, PUNIC WARS p140

SOCIETY AND CULTURE

Ancient Rome

The centre of the Roman Empire, which became the greatest of the ancient world and for its duration was the predominant world culture. According to tradition, Rome was founded in 753 BC on seven hills and ruled in succession by seven kings. A republic was established in 510 BC, governed by two consuls (chief magistrates), elected by a popular assembly, and by the Senate, a council of elders. One of Rome's arch opponents was the North African port of Carthage with which Rome fought between 264 and 146 BC. In the first Punic War with Carthage the Roman navy was founded. Roman conquests became provinces ruled by Roman governors.

Civil wars, unrest and revolution marked the transition of Rome from a republic to an empire. Julius Caesar took over Rome as its dictator. Assassinated in 44 BC, he was succeeded by a triumvirate of rulers. Under Augustus, the first Roman emperor, Rome began to prosper again. At its greatest expansion, in AD 117, the Empire stretched from England to Egypt and Spain to Mesopotamia, and had a population of over a million. The last emperor was deposed in AD 476, completing the fall of Rome.

The Romans were essentially pragmatic, militaristic people, remembered especially for the efficiency and discipline of their army. They imitated the best of Greek culture, including its coinage, units of measure and fine arts. Roman law was codified in the sixth century. Roman roads were unmatched in the ancient world and Roman city planners and engineers excelled in the building of houses, temples, monuments, aqueducts and dams. The Colosseum and the Forum are testimony to their architectural skill. Roman religion, like the Greek, was pantheistic. Latin, the language of the Romans, was the medium for a multitude of brilliant and enduring literary works.

❖ see AUGUSTUS CAESAR p56, PUNIC WARS p140

LEFT: *In its heyday, the Roman Empire was a nexus for world culture and commerce. The discovery of Roman coins is a testament to the wide-ranging trade network established by the Romans.*

Pompeii (600 BC–AD 79)

Ancient Roman city. Founded by the Oscans and Samnites, Pompeii became a Roman colony (80 BC) with a population of 20,000. It was a favoured resort for wealthy Romans. An earthquake damaged the city in AD 63, but when Mount Vesuvius erupted on 24 August AD 79 it buried the city in ash and pumice to a depth of 7 m (23 ft). The heated gas asphyxiated the residents, but the city has endured for 17 centuries.

❖ see ANCIENT ROME p112

BELOW: *A mural fresco discovered at Pompeii, just outside Naples.*

Acropolis

Rocky outcrop overlooking Athens, Greece. A natural stronghold housing the citadel of Athens's first aristocratic rulers, the Acropolis might have been rendered redundant by the advent of democracy had the statesman Pericles not seen the opportunities it afforded both to promote the state's prestige and create employment. It was on this site that, from 449 BC onwards, an ambitious programme of public works was undertaken. The great temple to Athene, now known as the Parthenon, is merely the most celebrated of the monuments built at that time, a lasting symbol of the enterprise and achievement of the Ancient Greeks.

❖ see ANCIENT GREECE p110

Boudicca (c. AD 30-62)

Queen of the Iceni tribe of Britons. Married to King Prasutagus of the Iceni tribe, Boudicca is the most famous of

ABOVE: *Queen Boudicca of the Iceni and her daughters were raped and tortured by the Romans before leading a vicious military campaign against their oppressors which resulted in the sacking of major cities like Colchester, London and St Albans.*

the Celtic queens. Prasutagus died (AD 61); Boudicca and her daughters were flogged and raped by Roman soldiers. She led the Icenis against the Romans, sacking Colchester, St Albans and London, killing 70,000. She was only stopped when reinforcements were called from Wales to assist the Romans. Boudicca was said to have poisoned herself rather than be captured.

Dark Ages (AD 476–800)

Early Middle Ages in Western Europe. After the fall of Rome a collapse in the trade and communication infrastructure across Europe emerged. Barter replaced money, towns and cities declined, and roads became overgrown. Feudalism emerged with lords ruling a small state by force of arms. Self-sufficiency replaced trade and the more ambitious warlords carved out larger kingdoms, but these often collapsed when the leader died. Many historians suggest that the period AD 500–1000, marked by a lack of written records, is a more accurate measure of the Dark Ages because little is known of this time. Europe at this time was comparatively primitive. Eventually loose confederations became kingdoms, but government was weak. The Church was fragmented but, by the ninth century, European unity began to re-emerge, based on the Roman legacy. The period drew to a close with the coming of the Vikings and Magyars in the tenth century.

❖ see FEUDALISM p116, VIKINGS p114

Anglo-Saxons (AD 597–1066)

Germanic rulers of England. The Roman army left Britain (AD 410) and to help the Picts, Scots and Vikings defend themselves against raiding parties, mercenary Angles and Saxons were employed from northern Germany. They brought their families and were paid in land. They colonized the Celts' kingdoms; by AD 850 Mercia, Northumbria and Wessex were Anglo-Saxon. The Vikings invaded (AD 865) and overran Mercia and Northumbria. Alfred the Great, King of Wessex, counter-attacked (AD 878) and drove the Vikings to the sea. By AD 955 Edred, Alfred's grandson, ruled a united England. During Ethelred the Unready's rule, the Vikings returned and on his death (1016), the Viking Canute ruled England. When he died, Edward the Confessor became king, dying in 1066 without a male heir. Harold, the Earl of East Anglia, claimed the throne, but his reign was abruptly brought to an end by the Norman invasion, culminating in William I's coronation (Christmas Day 1066), ending Anglo-Saxon rule of England.

❖ see ALFRED THE GREAT p61, CANUTE p61, WILLIAM I OF ENGLAND p63

ABOVE: *After the Romans' departure from England, the Anglo-Saxons were employed as mercenaries by local tribes to defend themselves against invaders.*

Vikings (AD 800–1100)

Nordic raiders and settlers. The Vikings began raiding around AD 800, gradually becoming more determined to settle in the lands. They had conquered much of England by the ninth century and had penetrated as far as Paris in their raids. To begin with, Christian Europe could do little to prevent them apart from paying ransoms, but larger Viking armies appeared in the early eleventh century and the system of paying tribute to the Vikings, or Danegeld, became the strategy. In AD 911 Charles III of France gave the Vikings Normandy and it was these Vikings, now called Normans, that invaded England in 1066. Elsewhere, the Vikings had settled in Greenland and North America and had penetrated Russia to reach Constantinople and Baghdad. Swedish Vikings fought for the Byzantines. The Viking impact was not simply destructive; they became a part of the settled European community. Vikings were great storytellers, sailors and warriors.

Árpád (AD 840–97)

Chief Magyar and national hero of the Hungarians. Árpád led the Magyars from Asia to the Avars-occupied region of what is now Hungary in AD 890 and founded the Árpád dynasty and line of Hungarian kings. The Holy Roman Emperor Otto I defeated the Árpád dynasty at Lechfeld in AD 955.

Middle Ages (5th–15th centuries)

European history from the collapse of Rome to the Renaissance. Italian Humanists describing the 1,000 years between the fifth and fifteenth centuries introduced the term. After Alaric had sacked Rome in AD 410, the early Middle Ages, or Dark Ages, saw a period of fragmentation and incessant war. By the tenth century the era of migrating Barbarians had ended and trade and commerce began to revive. Strong cultural and economic forces shifted power

ABOVE: *The Middle Ages was a violent period in history, but it also cultivated gentler pursuits like the art of courtly love.*

from the eastern Mediterranean to Western Europe. Agriculture had developed and the population expanded rapidly. By the thirteenth century gothic architecture and sculpture, politics and religion dominated society, including the works of Thomas Aquinas. In this century medieval society saw the growth of the Secular State and the emergence of the monarchies of Spain, France and England. After the Black Death in the 1340s, the expansion of trade and finance transformed the European economy and paved the way for the Renaissance period.

❖ see DARK AGES p113

Toltecs (AD 650–12th century)

Indigenous Meso-American people. These people left the city of Teotihuacán and established their own empire in Mexico. They used their army to conquer neighbouring rivals. The Toltecs built their capital at Tula, which has three pyramidal temples dedicated to Quetzalcoatl. According to Toltec legend, the rival god Tezcatlipoca, god of the night sky, drove Quetzalcoatl, the plumed or feathered servant, the god of the morning and evening star, out of Tula in around AD 1000. The Toltecs' art and architecture were a major influence on the Mayans and particularly their city of Chichén Itzá. Like the Aztecs, the Toltecs believed in human sacrifice.

❖ see AZTECS p119

SOCIETY AND CULTURE

ABOVE: *The rise of feudalism in the Middle Ages involved landowners granting land to their serfs in return for their loyalty and service.*

Moors (7th century)

After the Arab conquest of the Berbers, a period of intermarriage and development created a new group of peoples who settled in North Africa and conquered Spain. After settling here they were gradually expelled by the Christians between the eleventh and seventeenth centuries. The Umayyad dynasty ruled Muslim Spain for three centuries. Particularly notable was its greatest ruler, Abd-ar-Rahman III. They returned to inhabit Morocco, Algeria and Mauritania. Historians also describe the Arabic-speaking Berbers who lived in towns in North Africa as Moors and, more generally, the inhabitants of the Turkish Barbary States.

Feudalism (8th–14th centuries)

Political and military system in Western Europe. Feudalism represented the granting of fiefs (land) by a lord to a vassal in return for his personal loyalty. The early Frankish kingdoms in the eighth century established the practice and it spread with the Frankish conquests into northern Italy, Spain, Germany and the Slavic kingdoms. After the Normans conquered England in 1066 it was adopted there and in Scotland and Ireland. Crusader knights brought it to the Near East. Military service was central to feudalism but, by the thirteenth century, payments had replaced this. By the fourteenth century it was no longer a political or social force. The feudal system was also used to describe the triangular social hierarchy adopted in the Middle Ages, in which the monarch stood at the top and the serfs at the bottom, little more than slaves.

Domesday Book (1086)

William the Conqueror's survey of England. Despite much public resentment, William carried out his survey of England using seven or eight teams of commissioners, each of whom covered all of England, with the exception of the northern

ABOVE: **The Domesday Book.**

areas. The survey resulted in 'Great Domesday' covering all counties with the exception of Norfolk, Suffolk and Essex, which were covered in 'Little Domesday'. The survey contained information about the estates of the king and his tenants, gathered from formal sessions held with sheriffs, barons and representatives from each of the villages. The Domesday Book is kept in The National Archives in London.

❖ see WILLIAM I OF ENGLAND p63

Samurai (12th century–1868)

Japanese warrior caste. Originally the term was used to describe aristocratic warriors in Japan. They dominated Japanese government for over 600 years. Samurai culture incorporated their military skills and codes of conduct or Bushido and Zen Buddhism. They were superseded by a more vibrant merchant economy and lost their privileges finally in 1871 when feudalism was abolished. The end of the Samurai is usually considered to be when the Meiji Restoration took place (1868) following a Samurai revolt.

❖ see SATSUMA REBELLION p158

Incas (1100–1572)

Native South American Andean Empire. Originally from Peru, they settled in the Valley of Cuzco. The tribe's eighth ruler enlarged the Empire in the early fifteenth century. In the next 30 years successive rulers extended it 4,000 km (2,500 miles) north to south and 800 km (500 miles) east to west, the population rising to 16 million. In 1525 the Empire was divided between the emperors Huáscar and Atahualpa, who prevailed in 1532, but the Spanish under Francisco Pizarro arrived. The Incas viewed them as demi-gods and Pizarro, through political skills and treachery, captured Atahualpa. In return for a room of gold, the Spaniards promised his release, but on 29 August 1533 Atahualpa was strangled after converting to Christianity. Manco Capac, brother of Huáscar, took the throne, revolted against the Spaniards, was defeated and assassinated. The Spaniards, bringing an end to the Inca Empire, beheaded the last heir to the Inca throne, Tupac Amaru, son of Manco Capac.

Mongols (1196)

Tribal people. By 1196 Temujin had eliminated most of his rivals among the Mongols and become Genghis Khan. Under his leadership, the Mongols would carve out one of the largest land empires in history, from the Caspian Sea to the South China Seas. In 1214 he crossed the Great Wall of

RIGHT: *Japanese Samurai, members of a proud and fierce warrior caste, were virtually wiped out following the Meiji Restoration of 1868.*

SOCIETY AND CULTURE

China and defeated the Manchus. After Peking had surrendered, he razed it to the ground and turned westward to conquer Afghanistan and Persia. He died in 1227 but the Mongols continued their conquests. Mongol rule in China continued as the Yuan dynasty, despite the rest of the Empire fragmenting.

❖ see GENGHIS KHAN p63

Renaissance (14th–17th centuries)

Movement in art, architecture, literature and philosophy. Widely held to have started in the city-state of Florence in the fourteenth century, the Renaissance would, in the course of the next 200 years, diffuse throughout the length and breadth of Europe. While the roots of the Renaissance may well have lain in a mercantile boom that saw the European states both increase their consumption of luxuries and extend their commercial horizons through that period, it is to the cultural consequences of the economic revolution that the term is taken to refer.

A new mood of intellectual and artistic confidence meant intellectuals felt more enterprising than they had under the authority of the medieval Church. Renaissance humanism found its inspiration not in the slavish scholarship of the Middle Ages, but in the philosophical ferment of classical Greece. Poets, painters and architects too looked to the classical past to find a way forward. Drawing on the great traditions of ancient epic poetry, the *Divine Comedy* of Dante Alighieri (1265–1321) was not only a magnificent work of literature in its own right: the first major poem to be written in Italian, it broke the intellectual stranglehold of Latin, language of the Church. Architects like Giovanni Brunelleschi (1377–1446) also reinterpreted classical rules for a modern age, while men like Michelangelo, Leonardo and Raphael did the same for the visual arts.

Yet Italy was only the starting point: the great engraver and painter Albrecht Dürer (1471–1528) took on the task of spreading the Renaissance in his native Germany; Lucas van

BELOW: The Birth of Venus *by Alessandro Botticelli at the Uffizi museum in Florence is emblematic of the vigour and love of beauty celebrated by Renaissance artists.*

Leyden (c. 1494–1533) came to prominence in the Netherlands. The literature of the period was every bit as exciting, with great humanists like Michel de Montaigne (1533–92), the passionate poetry of Petrarch and his followers, and great comic writing ranging from the work of the riotously scatological Frenchman François Rabelais (c. 1490–1553) to Miguel de Cervantes' (1547–1616) mock-epic *Don Quixote*. The unrivalled English writer William Shakespeare belongs unmistakeably to the late Renaissance, as crucial in the history of Western culture as any artist.

❖ see CLASSICAL PERIOD p110

elaborate collection of deities, including Quetzalcoatl. In 1519 with the Aztec Empire still developing, Spanish explorers arrived in the area. Montezuma II, the ninth Aztec Emperor, had been on the throne for 17 years. He was captured by Hernán Cortés and, whether by design or accident, died whilst being held captive. Cuitláhuac and Cuauhtémoc, Montezuma's successors, waged an unsuccessful war against the Spanish but when Tenochtitlán was captured and sacked by the Spanish in 1521, the Aztec Empire collapsed.

❖ see MONTEZUMA p68

Aztecs (1325–1521)

Mexican Indian Empire. Originally hunters and gatherers in Northern Mexico, the Aztecs established their city Tenochtitlán in 1325. Through the cultivation of all land, including swamps, within 100 years they had become dominant in the area. By 1519, with an empire covering over 200 sq km (125 sq miles) and a population of six million, the Aztec empire had absorbed about 500 smaller states. War was a part of Aztec culture and human sacrifice played a role in their rituals and ceremonies. When the Great Pyramid Temple in Tenochtitlán was dedicated, 20,000 human beings captured in battle had their hearts removed. The Aztecs were occasional cannibals, believing that by eating the flesh of victims they could absorb their virtues. The Aztecs worshipped an

ABOVE: *This striking Aztec skull artefact bears witness to the ferocity of these warrior Mexican-Indian people.*

Printing

Technological process for reproducing text. Though seals and signet rings had been used to make impressions in hot wax for many centuries, the first use of printing for making multiple copies of text seems to have taken place in ancient China. By the ninth century AD, Buddhist scriptures were routinely being produced this way. The pages for these scripts were, however, permanently fixed, being carved out of single blocks of wood. By the Middle Ages European printers were using similar blocks for printing holy pictures and simple prayers. The idea of a system for setting movable type, whose components could be shuffled and recast in a different order to produce different texts seems to have come to both Eastern and Western printers at quite an early stage: the difficulty lay in finding a viable way of putting it into practice. Though several printers both in Asia and Europe seem to

ABOVE: *Nostradamus made cryptic predictions about world events up to the year 3797, including that there would be a third world war.*

LEFT: *Bartholomew Diaz was the first to sail around the Cape of Good Hope.*

Bartholomew Diaz (c. 1450–1500)

Portuguese navigator. Diaz was the first European to sail round the Cape of Good Hope in 1487. In command of an expedition to explore the west coast of Africa, he sailed to the south of the continent and made landfall at Mosselbaai about 320 km (200 miles) east of the Cape. His voyage opened up the sea route from Europe to the Far East, although it fell to Vasco da Gama to complete the first successful passage to India.

Bartolomé de la Casas (1474–1566)

Spanish missionary and historian. Ordained a priest in 1510, he worked throughout his life to improve living conditions in South America and abolish slavery. The New Laws (for humanitarian treatment of indigenous peoples in Spanish colonies) were adopted in 1542. He became bishop of Chiapas in 1544, working again for the abolition of slavery and among the natives of Guatemala. Bartolomé de la Casas also wrote *Historia de las Indias*.

❖ see SLAVERY p104

Nostradamus (1503–66)

French astrologer and self-styled prophet. Born Michel de Notredame in St Rémy, Provence, Nostradamus qualified conventionally enough as a physician in 1519; not until 1547 did he start his second career as foreteller of the future. Two collections of cryptic pronouncements, the *Centuries*, published in 1555 and 1558 respectively, brought him to the admiring attention of King Charles IX of France. He has had his adherents right up to the present day.

Cossacks (15 and 16th centuries)

Russian fighters and farmers. Forming semi-independent states these people fled from serfdom, fighting off the troops of the

have tried before him, the first man to have succeeded in perfecting a method of making type this way appears to have been the German Johann Gutenberg, who invented not only a movable metal type, but a press suitable for printing it and an ink that could be used on both sides of a single page. All the conditions were thus in place for a proper printed book to be produced: hence the appearance in the 1460s of the Gutenberg Bible.

Other books followed from the presses of printing entrepreneurs like Englishman William Caxton (1422–91), leading to a significant democratization of literature and learning. Like other handicrafts, printing was industrialized in the nineteenth century, with implications not only for news media but literature: the nineteenth-century novelist reached readerships of many thousands, where a sixteenth-century poet might have been read at the most by dozens. Now, thanks to new technologies, the death of the book is widely prophesied: for the moment, however, modern presses, derived from Gutenberg's original invention, are still going strong.

tsars. They formed villages and farmed their lands, paying few taxes and providing additional cavalry resources for the Russian armies. During World War I the Cossacks lost their privileged existence in the Russian Revolution and turned solely to farming. During World War II they assisted the Russians in pushing back the Nazi forces, mostly serving as cavalry.

❖ see RUSSIAN REVOLUTION p168, WORLD WAR I p164, WORLD WAR II p172

Oda Nobunaga (1534–82)

Japanese feudal warlord. From humble beginnings in the Japanese province of Owari, Nobunaga gradually gained control of the whole region and occupied Kyoto in 1568. By 1580 he was in control of all of central Japan but was assassinated by a vassal before he could unite the whole country.

❖ see WARLORDS p167

René Descartes (1596–1650)

French philosopher. Born at Les Hayes near Poitiers in France Descartes attended a Jesuit college, then (probably) the University of Poitiers. He joined the army and served in France and the Netherlands. He settled in Paris (1613) then moved to the Netherlands in 1628 where he remained until 1649 when he went to teach in Sweden, where he lived for the rest of his life. He wrote *Discourse on Method* (1637) in Part IV of which is his famous dictum 'Cogito, ergo sum' ('I think, therefore I am'). He argued that if God is perfect then God must exist, otherwise God would not be perfect (ontological argument). His other works include *Meditations on First Philosophy* (1641) and *Principles of Philosophy* (1644).

Restoration (1660)

Re-establishment of the British monarchy with Charles II. Following the control of London by General Monck (1659), the Royalists' Convention Parliament called for the restoration of Charles II. Charles issued the Declaration of Breda and returned to England (1660), assuming authority for the nation. This period in history saw the Puritans during the Protectorate; the Cavalier Parliament; the rise of anti-Catholic sentiment; the Whig and Tory factions; the Plague (1665); The Great Fire of London (1666) and the Second Dutch War (1664–67). The Restoration period ended with the Glorious Revolution (1688).

❖ see CHARLES II OF ENGLAND p78, GREAT FIRE OF LONDON p122, PLAGUE p122

Plague (1664–66)

Epidemic that raged through London, killing approximately 70,000. This epidemic began in the St Giles in the Fields area of London and soon spread to the poorer and densely populated areas of Clerkenwell, Cripplegate, Shoreditch, Stepney and Westminster. Because of the lack of quarantine (not established until 1720), this was the worst epidemic in history. The King and his court left London and parliament transferred sessions to Oxford. The Great Fire of London (September 1666) is believed to have assisted in the elimination of the plague from London, although it ceased in other parts of the country without such aid.

❖ see GREAT FIRE OF LONDON p122

Great Fire of London (1666)

Worst fire in the history of London. The fire began in a baker's premises in Pudding Lane and an easterly wind exacerbated the flames, causing it to rage for two days. It was extinguished at one point but then it enflamed itself again at the Temple, causing some houses to be blown up by gunpowder. The fire destroyed most of the civic buildings of London, including 13,000 houses, 87 churches and St Paul's Cathedral. Many of the refugees, made homeless by the fire, fled the city by boat on the River Thames, travelling to Hampstead, Highgate and Moorfields.

❖ see PLAGUE p122

RIGHT: *The seventeenth-century French philosopher Descartes conducts a demonstration at the court of Queen Christine of Sweden.*

British Empire (1670–1997)

Phrase used to describe the worldwide colonies, protectorates and territories administered by the British government. Wanting to compete commercially and militarily with France, British colonies were established in the Americas and the West Indies by 1670. The Hudson Bay Company was active in Canada and the East India Company established trading posts in India in 1600. The first British settlement in Africa was made (1661) at James Island on the Gambia River. Although the slave trade was abolished over the period 1807–33, this was one of the driving forces behind colonizing the Caribbean and the Americas. The Seven Years' War that ended in the Treaty of Paris (1763) left Britain dominant in India and Canada. Although Britain finally lost its 13 colonies in America in 1783, new settlements were established in Australia (1788) and there was considerable growth in Canada.

Following the Napoleonic Wars Britain acquired Trinidad, Ceylon, Tobago, Mauritius, St Lucia and Malta. Singapore was acquired in 1819. New Zealand became British (1840), followed by Fiji, Tonga and Papua. Following the Indian Mutiny the British Crown replaced the East India Company and acquired Burma (1886) and the Punjab (1849). The Suez Canal was completed in 1869 allowing British influence to be extended in Arabia and the Persian Gulf. Cyprus was occupied (1878), as were the Malay States (1880s) and Hong Kong (1841). In Africa Britain acquired Egypt (1882), Sudan (1899) and South Africa (1910).

Limited self-government was encouraged, particularly in Canada, Australia, New Zealand and Natal. At the outbreak of World War I, Britain declared war on Germany on behalf of the whole empire, but in 1918 many of the dominions signed independent peace treaties and joined the League of Nations as equals. In 1931 the Statute of Westminster recognized many of them as independent countries within the British Empire. In 1939 they made their own Declarations of War. After World War II independence was granted; India (1947), Sri Lanka and Burma (1948), and Ghana became the first African colony to be independent in 1957. After the 1960s the majority of the former colonies had been granted self-government. The last British colony, Hong Kong, was returned to the Chinese in 1997.

❖ see INDIAN INDEPENDENCE p26

Jacobites (1688–1745)

Supporters of the exiled House of Stuart. William of Orange dethroned James II of England in the Glorious Revolution of 1688. In the next 60 years Jacobites made five attempts to restore the Stuarts to the throne. James II (March 1689) landed in Ireland, but his Irish/French army was defeated by William at the Battle of the Boyne (July 1690). A second French invasion failed (1708). The final rebellion (1745) found Charles Edward Stuart temporarily victorious until he met the Duke of Cumberland at the Battle of Culloden. He was defeated; the revolt and the Stuart cause ended for ever.

Salem Witch Hunts (1692)

American witchcraft investigations leading to 19 hangings. In Salem Village, Essex County, in the province of Massachusetts Bay, New England, hysteria broke out after the claims of three girls that they were possessed by the devil. A West Indian slave, Tituba, Sarah Good and a woman named Osborne were arrested and committed for trial. They incriminated others in false confessions; a total of 150 were awaiting trial. A special court was set up: 19 were found guilty and hanged. Governor Phips dissolved the court, ordering the remaining accused be released and indemnities paid to the families of those executed.

Enlightenment (c. 1700)

Intellectual movement. Breaking the hold of a religious authority already weakened by the two-fold traumas of Renaissance and Reformation, a new spirit of free enquiry can be seen to have arisen from around 1700 onwards. Though its origins lay earlier, in the philosophy of René Descartes and in the scientific discoveries of Sir Isaac Newton, the Enlightenment was very much an eighteenth-century phenomenon. For it was then that, emboldened by these advances, French philosophers like Voltaire (1694–1778) began berating the Church for its 'superstition', and Jean-Jacques Rousseau began denouncing the enslavement of individuals by laws and governments. The prototypical Enlightenment project was the great Encyclopédie (1751–80), edited by Denis Diderot (1713–84) and Jean d'Alembert (1717–83), which attempted to set down and summarize all human knowledge. None of its contents was new: what was truly radical was the implication that it was possible for an individual to apprehend everything on a rational basis – henceforth there would be no ineffable mysteries, the preserve of priests; no God-given authority, the traditional justification for monarchs. While the Enlightenment's values of intellectual and political freedom would find their ultimate expression in the French Revolution of 1789, conservatives would see the ensuing Terror as confirming their most nightmarish fears.

❖ see RENÉ DESCARTES p122, ISAAC NEWTON p90

David Hume (1711–76)

Scottish historian and philosopher. Hume developed the notion that people can know nothing outside of their own experiences and perceptions, arguing that we cannot be certain of cause and effect even if we have experienced it before. He rejected scientific laws, argued that the concept of right or wrong was not rational and contributed to economic theory that influenced fellow philosopher Adam Smith. His History of England described the intellectual and economic forces that played a part in history.

Immanuel Kant (1724–1804)

Famous German philosopher in the theory of knowledge, ethics and aesthetics. In 1740 he studied at the University of Königsberg, working as a

BELOW: *The philosopher David Hume argued that human beings cannot be certain of anything outside of their own experiences and senses.*

private tutor until 1755 when he became a university lecturer. Famous works were Critique of Pure Reason (1781) and Critique of Practical Reason (1788). His main philosophical studies were centred on the 'idealists' and the 'materialists' and the relationship of mind and matter, thus bringing forth a new development in philosophical thought.

LEFT: *Immanuel Kant emphasized the critique of knowledge as the way to get to the bottom of philosophical conclusions.*

SOCIETY AND CULTURE

Declaration of Independence (1776)

Document proclaiming the independence of 13 North American British colonies from Great Britain. On 19 April 1775 war broke out between Britain and her colonies in North America. The Declaration of Independence was the culmination of a conflict that had begun as a protest against restrictions imposed on the states by Britain. The Declaration states the grievances that the colonies had and is the foundation of the Bill of Rights of the US Constitution. On 7 June 1776 Richard Henry Lee, a Virginian delegate of the Continental Congress, proposed a motion of independence. A committee that included Thomas Jefferson and Benjamin Franklin was appointed to prepare a declaration in line with Lee's suggestions. It was unanimously adopted on 4 July and officially endorsed by Congress on 2 August. It resolved that 'these united colonies are, and of Right ought to be Free and Independent States'.

❖ see AMERICAN REVOLUTION p150, BENJAMIN FRANKLIN p91, UNITED STATES CONSTITUTION p126

ABOVE: *Tourists view the original Declaration of Independence in the National Archives.*

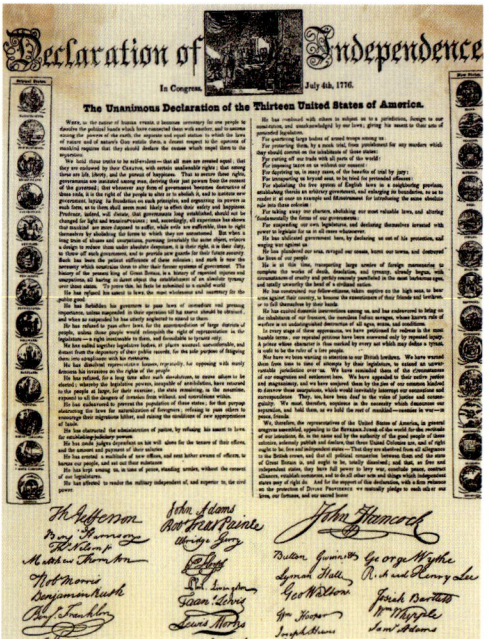

ABOVE: *The signed American Declaration of Independence document.*

United States Constitution (1787)

Oldest written national constitution. The American Constitution defines government, its jurisdictions and the basic rights of US citizens. It was designed to retain the independence of the states whilst establishing central government. It placed legislative powers in the hands of Congress and executive power in the president's hands. Judicial power was the role of the courts and the privileges of citizens enshrined as Civil Rights which encompassed the Bill of Rights and the First Amendment.

❖ see DECLARATION OF INDEPENDENCE p126

Brandenburg Gate (1788)

Monumental gateway in Berlin, Germany. Built between 1788 and 1791, the Brandenburg Gate was designed by Carl Gotthard von Langhans and topped with Gottfried

Schadow's famous Quadriga statue, depicting a winged woman – Victory – in a chariot drawn by four charging horses. This was stolen by Napoleon's troops in 1806, but recaptured and replaced in 1814. International politics intervened again during the Cold War: when the Berlin Wall went up in 1961, the gate was left marooned in the no-man's-land between the city's eastern and western sectors. Its reopening in 1989 resonated profoundly throughout Germany and beyond.

❖❖ see BERLIN WALL p28, NAPOLEON BONAPARTE p81, COLD WAR p100

Storming of the Bastille (1789)

The Bastille, a fortress and prison in Paris, was built by Charles V (1370) and was used to detain prisoners throughout the seventeenth and eighteenth centuries. In 1789 Louis XVI caused unrest by sacking his minister Necker, and fears began to grow that the king might disband the National Assembly. Rioting began on 12 July and the Paris Commune was formed the following day, as was the National Guard, commanded by the Marquis de Lafayette. The Bastille was stormed on 14 July by a mob that freed prisoners and killed officers before razing it to the ground.

❖❖ see FRENCH REVOLUTION p150

BELOW: *The Brandenburg Gate, Berlin's landmark monument. The statue crowning the gate was temporarily stolen by Napoleon Bonaparte before being returned to the German people in 1814. During the Cold War years, the gate remained uneasily located between the city's eastern and western sectors.*

SOCIETY AND CULTURE

Louisiana Purchase (1803)

The province of Louisiana was colonized by the French in the early eighteenth century; it was ceded to the Spanish in 1762 and returned to France in 1800. President Thomas Jefferson, through his minister, James Monroe, negotiated the purchase of the 2.1 million sq km (1.3 million sq miles) of land from France for $11,250,00. The Louisiana Purchase was intended to provide growing room and ease tensions between settlers and France. The US doubled in size.

Missouri Compromise (1820)

Agreement for regulating slavery in the USA. In 1818, Missouri applied for statehood. As a slave-owning state, this would have tipped the balance between the 11 slave and 11 free states. The Compromise allowed them statehood provided that no slaves would be allowed to enter Missouri and that those already there would be gradually freed.

❖ see SLAVERY p104

Florence Nightingale (1820–1910)

English hospital reformer; known as the Lady with the Lamp. During the Crimean War, she was based in the military hospitals of Turkey, managing to cope with severe overcrowding and the lack of basic necessities. In 1856, the Royal Commission on the Health of the Army was formed, leading to the foundation of the Army Medical School. She established, at St Thomas's Hospital, the Nightingale School for Nurses, and in 1907 was the first woman to be awarded the Order of Merit.

❖ see CRIMEAN WAR p155

Friedrich Nietzsche (1844–1900)

German classical scholar and great thinker. Nietzsche attended Bonn and Leipzig

RIGHT: *Florence Nightingale.*

universities, studying classical literature and language. Between 1869–79 he was a professor at the University of Basel, and whilst there wrote *The Birth of Tragedy* (1872), *Thoughts out of Season* (1873–76) and *Human, All Too Human* (1878). A prolific writer, he continued after his retirement, producing works such as *Thus Spake Zarathustra*, *Beyond Good and Evil*, *On the Genealogy of Morals*, *Twilight of the Idols* and *The Antichrist*.

Sigmund Freud (1856–1939)

Austrian neurologist and founder of psychoanalysis. In 1873, he graduated from Sperl Gymnasium and joined the University of Vienna. In 1882, he trained with the psychiatrists Theodor Meynert and Hermann Nothnagel at the General Hospital in Vienna and was appointed lecturer in neuropathology in 1885. Freud opened a clinical practice in neuropsychology in Vienna and continued this work for almost 50 years, studying hysteria, psychological disorders, human bisexuality, erotogenic zones, free association, resistance and unconscious thoughts. In 1895, he wrote *Project for a Scientific Psychology* (published in 1950, 11 years after his death). Freud has been called 'the most influential intellectual legislator of his age'.

❖ see CARL JUNG p130

Communist Revolution

Overthrow of capitalism by a workers' uprising. For hundreds of years, forms of Communism, such as sharing common land, existed in many societies. It was the Industrial Revolution in the nineteenth century that created the new 'working' classes. They often lived and worked in terrible conditions and great poverty, while the industrialists enjoyed great wealth. A number of socialists and revolutionaries of the day advocated a communal solution to this misery.

It was German philosopher and writer Karl Marx who first wrote about Communist revolution in his *Communist Manifesto* (1848). In it he claimed that the overthrow of the property-owning class by the working class was a natural progression of history. Marx believed that the proletariat must seize control of the economy in order to achieve a classless society. In the twentieth century Marxist thinking was behind the Communist Revolutions in Russia, China, Vietnam and Yugoslavia, among others.

❖ see MARXISM p10

ABOVE: *Sigmund Freud, father of psychoanalysis.*

Emmeline Pankhurst (1858–1928)

Militant woman suffragette. Pankhurst founded the Women's Franchise League (1894), and the Women's Social and Political Union (1903), two members of which (one her daughter Christabel) were imprisoned for assaulting police officers. She was jailed (1908–09), and in the following years was imprisoned 12 times before World War I. She returned to England from campaigns in America in 1926. In 1928, the year of her death, equal votes for men and women were established.

LEFT: *A suffragette medal (c. 1908), containing the photograph of Emmeline Pankhurst. It is decorated with the multi-coloured ribbons associated with the movement.*

Billy 'the Kid' Garrat (1859–81)

Notorious gunfighter. Reputedly killing 27 men, he led a life of theft and lawlessness, often with gangs of men. In 1880, he stood trial for murder and was sentenced to hang, but escaped, killing two men, and remained at large for three months, when he was finally shot dead, aged 21.

Carl Jung (1875–1961)

Swiss psychologist and psychiatrist. Forming an alternative school to that of Sigmund Freud, Jung had studied at the University of Basel and in Paris. He worked at the University of Zurich as a physician and lecturer from 1900–13, becoming Professor of Psychology at the Federal Polytechnical University of Zurich (1933–41) and University of Basel (1943). He developed the theories of introverts, extroverts and the unconscious mind, and wrote *Modern Man in Search of a Soul* (1933) and *Memories, Dreams, Reflections* (1962).

❖ see SIGMUND FREUD p129

Ho Chi Minh (1890–1969)

President of North Vietnam (1954–69). Minh was the leader of the Vietnamese nationalist movement for nearly three decades. After spending time in Moscow, he returned to Vietnam during World War II to found the Communist Viet Minh (1941), the Vietnamese independence movement. His army fought the Japanese when they invaded the country, and drove out the French colonial regime in the Indochina War (1946–54). The Geneva Conference in 1954 divided Vietnam in half, and Minh became the first president of North Vietnam. Peace did not last and he lived to see the start of war against the US-backed government of South Vietnam.

❖ see VIETNAM WAR p178

Olympic Games (1896)

Classical Greek – and today international – sporting tournament. In ancient times, it was a competition attended by youths from all the cities of Greece, who offered up to Zeus their strength and skills in running, jumping, boxing and throwing. More recently, the idea was revived in a more secular internationalist spirit by the Frenchman Pierre Coubertin: the first modern games took place in Athens in 1896. Since then, they have taken place four-yearly, the number of events rising from 43 to around 300, while the number of participating countries has reached almost 200. Since 1924, there has been a Winter Olympics in intervening years.

Panama Canal (1903–79)

By the Hay-Bunau-Varilla Treaty of 1903, Panama granted the USA control of the Panama Canal and five miles of land on either side. The Panama Canal Company was responsible for operating the canal and the land, together with the Canal Zone government, with Balboa Heights as the administrative headquarters for both. Following a treaty in 1977, the Zone was abolished (1979) with ownership remaining joint American-Panamanian until 2000, when Panama resumed control.

LEFT: *Carl Jung.*

ABOVE: *The instantly recognizable symbols which today represent the Olympic Games, derived from classical Greek sporting tournaments.*

Oskar Schindler (1908–1974)

Rescuer of Jews during the Nazi Holocaust. Oskar Schindler was recruited by the German Intelligence Agency to collect information about the Polish. In Cracow he set up a factory, Deutsch Emailwaren Fabrik, but as the Nazi plan for the extermination of Jews escalated, he began protecting those working in his factory. He smuggled food and medicines into the labour camp of Plaszow and did everything in his power to keep the Jews out of the concentration camps.

❖ see NAZI PARTY p22, WORLD WAR II p172

Nelson Mandela (b. 1918)

South African nationalist and statesman. Mandela joined the African National Congress in 1944, becoming one of its leaders in 1949. He was tried for treason, but acquitted in 1961, but was jailed again in 1962 for five years. Whilst imprisoned, he was tried for sabotage, treason and violent conspiracy, and in 1964 was sentenced to life imprisonment, incarcerated at Robben Island Prison until February 1990. In March 1990, he was made Deputy President of the ANC, replacing President Tambo in July. For his work to end apartheid, he was awarded the Nobel Peace Prize in 1993, and the following year won South Africa's first all-race elections and established the Truth and Reconciliation Commission. He retired from politics in 1999.

❖ see APARTHEID p135

LEFT: *Liam Neeson as Oskar Schindler in Stephen Spielberg's Oscar-winning film,* Schindler's List.

Prohibition (1919–33)

US ban on the manufacture and sale of alcohol. Although many other countries, including Iceland, Finland, Norway, Sweden and Russia attempted to prohibit the manufacture, sale or transportation of alcohol, it was the American Volstead Act, ratified on 29 January 1919, that is the best-remembered experiment. During Prohibition, bootleggers such as Al Capone saw annual earnings of up to $60 million. By 1932, the Democratic Party had adopted the call for a repeal in order to combat criminal activities and the restriction on individual freedoms. On 5 December 1933, the repeal was achieved, and by 1966 all states had abandoned Prohibition.

❖ see GREAT DEPRESSION p134, WALL STREET CRASH p99

Malcolm X (1925–65)

Black American militant leader, born Malcolm Little. Whilst imprisoned in 1946, he was converted to the Black Muslim faith, and on his release in 1952 changed his name to Malcolm X. He became an effective speaker for the Nation of Islam and founded 'Muhammad Speaks' (1961). He rejected integration and racial equality; left the organization (1964) to form his own religious organization and reaffirmed his conversion to orthodox Islam. He was shot dead by three Black Muslims.

❖ see CIVIL RIGHTS MOVEMENT p137, MARTIN LUTHER KING p134

LEFT: *Nelson Mandela, one of the leaders of the African National Congress (ANC).*

ABOVE: *During Prohibition in the 1920s and 1930s America, all manufacture and sale of alcohol was deemed illegal. Speaksies, or black-market drinking dens, became very popular and were frequently raided by the police.*

Great Depression (1929–39)

Severest economic depression. It began in the USA, but spread to become a worldwide economic slump, hitting European countries most indebted to the USA, including Great Britain and Germany. Germany had six million unemployed. In the USA, 11,000 banks failed and unemployment rose to between 12 and 15 million. Manufacturing output by 1932 was 54 per cent of 1929 levels and world trade had fallen by half. Countries were imposing tariffs and quotas on foreign imports. It led directly to the rise of Adolf Hitler in Germany, who ended the depression by public work projects and the expansion of the munitions industry.

❖ see PROHIBITION p132

Martin Luther King (1929–68)

US non-violent black leader. Son of an Ebenezer Baptist Church pastor, King was ordained in 1947, became pastor of the Dexter Avenue Baptist Church in Montgomery (1954) and received a PhD in theology (1955), as well as heading the Montgomery Improvement Association, formed to boycott the segregation of the city's buses. In 1957, he was awarded the Spingarn Medal by the National Association for the Advancement of Coloured People, and was voted President of the Southern Christian Leadership Conference in 1958. He visited India the following year to study Gandhi's non-violent protest techniques, holding a non-violent protest against discrimination in 1961. He was arrested in 1963 during

LEFT: *A 1930s cartoon conveys the misery and poverty experienced by Americans during the Great Depression, their most severe economic slump.*

campaigns for desegregation in Alabama. He received the Nobel Peace Prize in 1964, being the youngest ever recipient, and he regarded it as a tribute to the Civil Rights Movement. Making a stand against the Vietnam War, believing the money could have been used to combat poverty, and condemning the violence of war, he planned the Poor People's Campaign, marching on Washington (1968). His influence led to the Civil Rights Act (1964) and the Voting Rights Act (1965).

❖ see CIVIL RIGHTS MOVEMENT p137

New Deal (1933–39)

Roosevelt's economic reforms. After becoming president of the US in 1932, Roosevelt enacted a series of reforms in industry, agriculture, labour, finance and housing aimed at ensuring that the USA never suffered again from the ravages of an economic depression. The New Deal for the 'forgotten man' greatly extended the government's involvement in the economy. The sweeping changes were achieved by a series of Acts over the years, meeting opposition from big business and other sections at times due to their 'socialist' tendencies. Nevertheless, the New Deal gathered support and was followed by Truman's 'Fair Deal' policies (1945–53).

❖ see FRANKLIN D. ROOSEVELT p14

Nuremberg Trials (1945–46)

Series of trials in Germany. Under the authority of The London Agreement (8 August 1945), the International Military Tribunal held trials against former Nazi leaders for 'crimes against peace', 'crimes against humanity', 'war crimes' and 'a common plan or conspiracy to commit' the first three counts. At the first session, under General I. T. Nikitchenko, held in Berlin, 24 former Nazi leaders had been charged with the perpetration of war crimes. From 30 November, all trials were held in Nuremberg under Lord Justice Geoffrey Lawrence. After 216 sessions, three were acquitted, seven imprisoned and 12 sentenced to death by hanging.

❖ see WORLD WAR II p172

Apartheid (1948–94)

South Africa's racial segregation and separate development policies. Before the National Party came to power (1948), racial segregation had been sanctioned by law. The Land Acts (1950, 1954 and 1955) set aside over 80 per cent of land for exclusive use by the white minority. Non-whites carried documents authorizing their presence in restricted areas and further laws established separate education, banned non-white unions, access to government and use of public facilities. The Bantu Self-Government Act (1959) created 10 black African homelands and the Bantu Homeland Citizenship Act (1970) made all black South Africans homelands residents, thus excluding them from South African society. Without participation in politics, strikes, demonstrations, protests, assassinations and sabotage became widespread. Condemnation of apartheid led to South Africa's withdrawal from the Commonwealth in 1961 and economic sanctions in 1985. President F. W. de Klerk repealed the apartheid legislation throughout the 1990s and a new constitution was established in 1993. The first all-race elections were held in 1994.

❖ see NELSON MANDELA p132

Geneva Convention (1949)

International treaties protecting civilians sick and wounded in war. Henri Dunant, founder of the Red Cross, established the Convention for the Amelioration of the Wounded in Time of War (1864). It stated that places dealing with the wounded should not be captured or destroyed, the wounded of all sides should be treated equally, civilians aiding the wounded should be protected and the Red Cross symbol should be recognized. Adopted by most great European powers and other states, it was extended (1906). During World War II, many conventions were abused, leading to four new conventions, approved in Geneva on 12 August 1949.

❖ see WORLD WAR II p172

ABOVE: In the 1960s, TIME magazine dedicated its front cover to Martin Luther King, one of the brightest stars of the Civil Rights Movement.

Civil Rights Movement (1955–63)

American social reform movement that secured legal rights for black Americans. Following the American Civil War and the freedom of black slaves, the Jim Crow Laws created separate white and black societies in America. Although the Supreme Court in 1896 established the principle of separate but equal rights, it was not until the 1950s that this was seriously challenged. In 1954, the Supreme Court banned school segregation, and in 1955 the Civil Rights Movement began after Rosa Parks, a black woman in Alabama, refused to move to the back of a bus. Several civil protest movements were created, notably the Reverend Dr Martin Luther King's Southern Christian Leadership Conference, the Student Non-Violent Co-ordinating Committee and the Congress of Racial Equality. Non-violent protests came to a head in 1963 with the March on Washington. This led John F. Kennedy and Lyndon Johnson to push through many civil rights laws. As a result of their protests, the Civil Rights Act of 1964 banned discrimination in many areas. The Voting Rights Act 1965 guaranteed black citizens the right to vote and the Housing Bill 1968 banned discrimination in housing. By the time King was assassinated (4 April 1968), black militants, such as the Black Panthers, had moved away from non-violent action and were behind rioting in many major cities. This period marked the end of the Civil Rights Movement but continuing anti-discrimination policies, supported by the courts, have established many of the rights that lay at the heart of the movement.

❖ see MARTIN LUTHER KING p134

Cultural Revolution (1966–76)

Great Proletarian revolution in China. Mao Zedong favoured more Communist ideals than his contemporaries. Wishing to remake Chinese society, he found that factions opposed him in the Party and army. Unpractised as a ruler or economist, his early policies failed. He proposed the Cultural Revolution to drive opponents out of government and the army. The Red Guards started rebellions and demonstrations targeting Mao's rivals. The Cultural Revolution had dire consequences within China and on foreign affairs. Tension mounted with the USSR, as Mao denounced their invasion of Czechoslovakia. By April 1969, the Maoists appeared to have gained control of the Party and the country, but many of the influential figures were moderates. Mao remained distrustful of bureaucracy and Confucianism, but brought China back on to the world stage with membership of the United Nations, and diplomatic relations were re-established with America and Japan. Mao died in 1976 and the struggle between moderates and radicals re-emerged.

❖ see MAO ZEDONG p16

AIDS (1981)

Acquired Immunodeficiency Syndrome. There are several forms of the AIDS virus (Human Immunodeficiency Virus, or HIV) that can be passed from one person to another and attack the body's immune system by destroying white blood cells. The virus can be spread through unprotected sexual intercourse, transfusion of contaminated blood or sharing of contaminated intravenous needles. The first outbreak in the West occurred in the US in 1981, but the virus is believed to have originated in Africa.

BELOW: *An AIDS patient at the Lighthouse Hospital in London. The number of people with the disease is on the rise worldwide despite the millions of pounds that are continuously invested in research.*

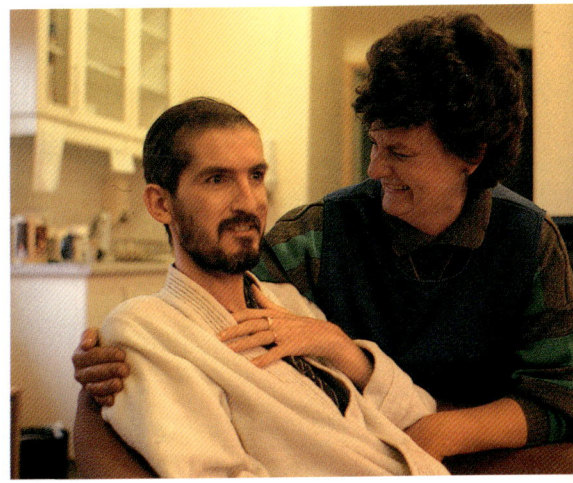

KEY DATES

264 BC ❖ Outbreak of the First Punic War	1845 ❖ First Maori War begins
499 BC ❖ Persian Wars begin	1853 ❖ War breaks out in the Crimea
1066 ❖ Battle of Hastings	1861 ❖ American Civil War begins
1337 ❖ Hundred Years' War begins	1870 ❖ Franco-Prussian War begins
1588 ❖ Spanish Armada	1877 ❖ Russo-Turkish War breaks out
1618 ❖ Thirty Years' War breaks out	1879 ❖ Beginning of the Zulu Wars
1756 ❖ Seven Years' War begins	1899 ❖ Boer War breaks out in South Africa
1775 ❖ American Revolution begins	1904 ❖ Russo-Japanese War breaks out
1789 ❖ Revolution breaks out in France	1914 ❖ Battle of the Mons; Ypres campaign begins
1803 ❖ Outbreak of the Napoleonic Wars	1917 ❖ Revolution breaks out in Russia
1839 ❖ First Afghan War breaks out	1936 ❖ Spanish Civil War
	1939 ❖ Germany invades Poland, triggering WWII

WAR

1940	❖	Battle of Britain; the Blitz
1941	❖	Japanese attack Pearl Harbor; US enter WWII
1941	❖	Siege of Leningrad begins
1944	❖	Battle of Arnhem; D-Day landings
1950	❖	Korean War breaks out
1956	❖	Arab-Israeli War breaks out
1963	❖	Vietnam War breaks out
1965	❖	Indo-Pakistan War
1973	❖	Yom Kippur War
1982	❖	Falklands War
1991	❖	Gulf War
2003	❖	War in Iraq

Trojan War

The Trojan War is an event steeped in myth and legend, because it happened so long ago. So much so in fact that historians disagree on many points. The city of Troy, otherwise known as Ilium, lay on the west coast of Turkey, during the time of Ancient Greece. According to Homer's *Iliad*, legend has it that the Greeks laid siege to Troy to recover Helen, who had eloped with Paris, the prince of Troy. The Greeks finally gained entry by the use of trickery, with a wooden horse, and stole Helen back to Sparta, c. 1184 BC.

Persian Wars (499–479 BC)

Military campaign between the Greeks and Persians. Until 499 BC, the Persians had been expanding their empire into the eastern Mediterranean, and the Greeks prepared to reclaim their Aegean territory. The Persians made two invasion attempts on the Greek mainland (490 BC and 480 BC) which saw the Greeks succeed in defence. From then the Greeks had the upper hand, pushing the Persians back towards Asia Minor (now Turkey) and ending their heyday. When Persia fought back in 480 BC, intending to take part of the Greek mainland, Greek dominance at sea crushed the Persian fleet. The Persian navy and part of its army withdrew. The remainder of the Persian army wintered in Greece but was eventually defeated by a coalition of Athenians, Spartans and their allies in 479 BC.

❖ see ANCIENT GREECE p110

Battle of Thermopylae (480 BC)

Battle in the Persian Wars. The Battle of Thermopylae saw Leonidas, King of Sparta – part of Greece – defend a pass against a greater force of Persian troops.

❖ see PERSIAN WARS p140

Punic Wars (264–241 BC, 218–210 BC, 149–146 BC)

Three wars between the Romans and Phoenicians. Before the heyday of the Empire, the Romans had to assert their dominance in the Mediterranean. The Phoenicians were their main enemy; particularly those of Carthage on the coast of North Africa.

The First Punic War saw victory for the Romans over the Carthaginians and the annexation of Sicily as part of the Roman Empire when the Carthaginian garrison on the island was forced to surrender by starvation. The war ended under the terms of the Treaty of Catulus. The Second Punic War was a far more significant campaign, fought in Italy, Spain and Africa. The war involved the Carthaginian leader Hannibal and the Roman general Publius Cornelius Scipio (185–129 BC). The Third Punic War, saw Carthage invaded by the Romans. The city was razed to the ground and the population sold into slavery.

❖ see PHOENICIANS p107, ROMANS p111

Hannibal (247–c. 182 BC)

Carthaginian general in the three Punic Wars fought between Rome and the Phoenicians of Carthage, North Africa. The Second Punic War was precipitated by the siege of the Roman town of Sagantum (Sagunto), Spain, by Hannibal. Hannibal took his army overland to Italy in 218 BC, and won a series of campaign battles, but failed to take Rome. He poisoned himself following a Roman victory in Carthage.

❖ see PHOENICIANS p107, PUNIC WARS p140

Battle of Actium (31 BC)

Naval confrontation at Akri in western Greece. The members of the second triumvirate of Ancient Rome were Mark Antony, Lepidus and Octavian. Having sought out and killed those who had murdered Julius Caesar, they began quarrelling among themselves. Mark Antony and Cleopatra were eventually defeated by Octavian in the Battle of Actium. Octavian became Emperor Augustus, while Antony and Cleopatra fled to Egypt and ended their lives.

❖ see MARK ANTONY p54, CLEOPATRA p55

RIGHT: *During the Persian Wars, the Greeks defended themselves and tried to reclaim their Aegean territory from the invading Persians.*

Attila the Hun (c. AD 406–453)

King of the Huns from AD 434. During the closing period of Roman rule in Europe the Romans became increasingly troubled by tribes from the north. Attila the Hun became king when he murdered his own brother. He attacked the eastern Roman Empire (AD 441–443), to increase his tribute payments. He did so again between AD 447–449. Then, in AD 450, Attila turned his attentions to the western Roman Empire. He entered Italy but was persuaded to withdraw in AD 452 by Pope Leo I (c. AD 390–461).

Battle of Hastings (1066)

Decisive battle in the Norman Conquest of England, 14 October 1066. Immortalized in the Bayeux Tapestry, the Battle of Hastings marked the end of the Anglo-Saxon era and the beginning of the Norman era in England. William I, Duke of Normandy, took his army across the Channel and met the army of King Harold II (c. 1020–66) at Senlac, just north of Hastings. The Norman army won and William ('The Conqueror') became king of England. Harold was killed in the battle.

❖ see WILLIAM I OF ENGLAND p63

Saladin (d. 1193)

Sultan of Egypt. Saladin was renowned as an intelligent and just ruler. He began a campaign against the Crusades in 1197 after the Christians attacked a travelling party which included his sister. He declared war on Jerusalem, which by this time was a Christian kingdom. Although Saladin succeeded in capturing the city, he did not allow his army to destroy it, and loss of life in the skirmish was minimal. Despite this, European forces combined to recapture the city in what became the Third Crusade. They failed to retake Jerusalem, but captured the city of Acre. Peace was reached in 1192, the year before Saladin's death.

❖ see CRUSADES p39, HOLY ROMAN EMPIRE p62

Tamerlane (1336–1405)

Tamerlane ('Timur the Lame') was a descendant of the great Genghis Khan and was himself a Mongol ruler – Samarkand in Uzbekistan – from 1369. In turn, he was the great-grandfather of Babar (Arabic for 'lion'), who founded the Mogul Empire of India in 1526. Tamerlane conquered Armenia, Azerbaijan, Georgia and Persia. Between 1395 and 1402 he was busy warring in and around the Middle East. He eventually died on a campaign invading China.

❖ see AKHBAR p75, BABAR p71, GENGHIS KHAN p63

LEFT: *Attila the Hun.*

Hundred Years' War (1337–1453)

Series of conflicts fought over the sovereignty of Gascony, now in south-west France. At the time it was part of the kingdom of England, according to the English, but the French had other ideas. Rivalry between kingdoms had existed for many years, so the fighting was more an extension of past disagreement than something new. The war began when England feared that France might assist the Scottish, with whom England had been in conflict. Edward III claimed the Crown of France.

BELOW: *A Mogul miniature painting showing Emperor Tamerlane and three army leaders being lowered into battle in the Kar mountains.*

WAR

Initially fighting went in favour of the English. The naval Battle of Sluys (1340) and the land battles of Crécy and Poitiers were all English victories. But the balance of power began to shift and from 1369 the French had the advantage.

By the time Edward III died in 1377, England was holding only Calais, Bordeaux and Bayonne in the north. A stalemate situation remained while both sides half-heartedly fought one another until 1415. Henry V invaded France and won the Battle of Agincourt on 25 October. Henry gained France and married French princess Catherine of Valois.

Joan of Arc launched the French counteroffensive with the siege of Orléans (1429). It continued following her execution, until France had regained all of her territory – including Gascony – by 1453, except Calais.

❖ see BATTLE OF AGINCOURT p145, BATTLE OF CRÉCY p144, HENRY V OF ENGLAND p66, JOAN OF ARC p145

Battle of Crécy (1346)

First battle in the Hundred Years' War. On 26 August 1346 Edward III of England skilfully defeated Philip VI of France, at Crécy-en-Ponthieu in northern France, by attacking cavalry with his infantrymen.

❖ see BATTLE OF AGINCOURT p145, HUNDRED YEARS' WAR p143

Joan of Arc (1412–31)

French heroine. Seventy-two years into the Hundred Years' War between England and France there came a French heroine named Joan of Arc to the rescue of a France largely held by English forces. In 1429 she met the dauphin, Charles VII of France (1403–61), at Chinon and convinced him that she was on a divine mission to save France. He gave her permission to go to battle, and with her army she managed to raise the Siege of Orléans. Her army defeated the English at the Battle of Patay, and her victory led to the coronation of Charles on 17 October.

Joan's efforts marked the turning point in the war, eventually leading to a French victory in 1453. In 1430, in an attempt to take Paris, Joan was captured by the enemy. She was tried and found guilty of witchcraft and heresy. Her sentence was death by burning and her execution took place in Rouen marketplace on 30 May 1431. She was canonized in 1920.

Battle of Agincourt (1415)

Battle fought during the Hundred Years' War. In the 78th year of the longest-running campaign in history a battle was fought at Agincourt, northern France. On 25 October 1415 English troops under the command of Henry V managed to defeat a considerably larger French army, thereby conquering Normandy. The French had a divided command and this proved their downfall. Some 6,000 French died as Henry took the initiative with only a quarter of the manpower. English losses were minimal.

❖ see HENRY V OF ENGLAND p66

Khair-ed-din (Barbarossa) (c. 1483–1546)

Arabian pirate. In the late medieval period the Barbary Coast – the Mediterranean coast of Africa from Morocco to Egypt – was home to Arab populations who saw Christians as their enemies. Two notorious pirates who emanated from there were Horuk and his brother Khair-ed-din, otherwise known as Barbarossa, 'Red Beard'. They both had great success attacking Christian vessels in the eastern Mediterranean sea, looting them of their valuable cargoes and killing their crews. Horuk was eventually run down and killed by the Spaniards in 1518. Barbarossa and his band of cut-throats took Tunis in 1534 and he eventually died in Constantinople (Istanbul).

LEFT: *The Battle of Agincourt demonstrated the superiority of English longbowmen over French knights.*

RIGHT: *The medieval Arab pirate Khair-ed-din, also known as Barbarossa because of his trademark fiery red beard.*

Spanish Armada (1588)

In 1588, a fleet of 130 ships sailed from Lisbon, Portugal, around the north-west corner of Spain, up the west coast of France and into the English Channel. The fleet was the Spanish Armada sent by Philip II of Spain against England. The Spanish Armada had a running engagement with an English fleet of 197 ships, which were under the command of Howard of Effingham and Francis Drake. The Spaniards then weighed anchor off Calais. The English used fire ships to force the Armada to put to sea, and a battle was fought off Gravelines. Half the Armada was lost to gales on its journey home.

❖ see ELIZABETH I OF ENGLAND p74

Thirty Years' War (1618–48)

In the early seventeenth century Germany was divided over religion. Europe was largely Catholic, but there had been a growth in Protestantism or Lutheranism, which had started under Martin Luther (1483–1546). Mid-northern Europe became the hotspot for Protestantism and conflict with Catholicism finally began in 1618. The Thirty Years' War lasted until 1648. Another Christian faith akin to Protestantism, Calvinism, had also been founded in Switzerland by Jean Calvin (1509–64), so the Catholics had their work cut out in the war. The Austrian Habsburg family

RIGHT: *The battle of Fleurus in the Thirty Years' War.*
BELOW: *The defeat of the Spanish Armada.*

were the principal players on the Catholic side and attempted to control all of Germany. On the Protestant side were the Bohemians, Danes and Swedes. Politics soon took over from religion. After 1634, France's help was enlisted in defeating the Spanish, who were allied with Austria. The Westphalia Treaty saw the German states granted their sovereignty and autonomy.

❖ see JEAN CALVIN p45, MARTIN LUTHER p44

Anglo-Dutch Wars (1652–54, 1665–67, 1672–74)

Three wars between England and Holland in the seventeenth century. This was a period of intense rivalry between Britain and Holland – both nations had vested interests in newly discovered parts of the world where they had established colonies and set up trade links. With vast profits to be had from these colonies, it was only a matter of time before both countries went to war.

In 1600 Elizabeth I of England had chartered the British East India Company. The Dutch East India Company was established in 1602. Both countries used their companies for founding new colonies in the East and West Indies, and by 1652 rivalries had initiated the First Anglo-Dutch War, which lasted until 1654 and culminated in English control of the seas. Tensions remained throughout the 'Golden Age' and war broke out again in 1665 in which the Stadtholderless Republic regained control. The Dutch became preoccupied by war with France in 1672 and the Third Anglo-Dutch War contributed to the Netherlands' eventual fall from power.

❖ see BRITISH EAST INDIA COMPANY p89, DUTCH EAST INDIA COMPANY p89

War of Spanish Succession (1701–14)

Campaign fought over rights to the Spanish throne. Louis XIV of France claimed the Spanish throne on behalf of his grandson Philip V in 1700. This was in defiance of the Partition Treaty which had the Crown of Spain reserved for Charles of Austria (later Holy Roman Emperor, Charles VI). France, Spain and Bavaria fought against an Allied side, comprising Austria, Britain, Denmark, the Netherlands and Portugal. The Duke of Marlborough, John Churchill (1650–1722) played a key military role throughout the war. In 1704 came the Battle of Blenheim. The French had marched on Vienna in an attempt to end the war, but the Allies under the Duke of Marlborough and Eugene of Savoy intercepted and defeated them. Marlborough was again successful at Ramillies in 1706, Oudenaarde in 1708 and Malplaquet in 1709. Treaties were signed in 1713 and 1714.

❖ see LOUIS XIV OF FRANCE p78

War of Austrian Succession (1740–48)

War between European states over the right to succession of the Holy Roman Empire. When the Holy Roman Emperor Charles VI died in 1740, his daughter Maria Theresa assumed succession to the throne of Austria. This was supported by England and Holland, but disputed by Prussia, France and Spain. The result was the War of the Austrian Succession, principally between Austria and Prussia, and thus sometimes described as the Austro-Prussian War.

The first act of aggression came from Frederick the Great of Prussia who seized an area of Austria called Silesia. The Battle of Dettingen (1743) saw an army comprising Britons, Austrians and Hanoverians, under King George II, victorious over the French. The Battle of Fontenoy (1745) saw an Anglo-Austrian army beaten.

The war was not solely confined to land: action was also seen at sea. Eventually British naval superiority began to tell, particularly around America and India. Eventually, after eight years of fighting, the war came to an end. The Treaty of Aix-la-Chapelle (1748) was the official end to hostilities. Maria Theresa's husband subsequently became the new emperor of Austria until 1765.

❖ see HOLY ROMAN EMPIRE p62

Black Hole of Calcutta (1756)

In 1756 the Nawab of Bengal attacked the East India Company's operations centre. He took 146 British prisoners in the process. On 19 June he chose to incarcerate them all in the dungeon at Fort William, which measured just 90 sq m (300 sq ft). Unfortunately, due to neglect rather than intent, between 43 and 123 prisoners (history has it somewhat confused) failed to survive the ordeal, and the incident became known as the Black Hole of Calcutta.

❖ see BRITISH EAST INDIA COMPANY p89, SEVEN YEARS' WAR p148

Seven Years' War (1756–63)

International struggle for colonial supremacy. The Seven Years' War arose from conflict between European nations including Austria, Britain, France, Prussia, Spain and Russia. Allegiance between these nations was complex, but Britain fared well, gaining control of India and many French colonies, including Canada. Florida was handed to Britain by Spain, who received Cuba in exchange. Prussia emerged as a great European power through its considerable military success against unlikely odds. The 1763 Treaty of Paris, marking the end of the war, was signed by Britain, France and Spain.

Battle of Plassey (1757)

Battle between the British and Indians. In 1756 the Nawab of Bengal, Suraja Dowla, captured Calcutta in defiance of the British. Robert Clive led the army of the East India Company against the Nawab and defeated them at Plassey. Clive was made governor of the area as a result and received many honours for his heroism there.

❖ see BLACK HOLE OF CALCUTTA p148

Admiral Horatio Nelson (1758–1805)

British hero of the Napoleonic Wars. Horatio Nelson joined the navy at the age of 12. He fought in the Revolutionary Wars against France, losing his arm in action. During that time, he climbed the ranks and had considerable military success. His greatest moment came with victory against the Napoleonic fleet at Trafalgar in 1805, by which time he was serving as Admiral. He was hit by sniper fire and died on board HMS Victory.

❖ see NAPOLEONIC WARS p152, BATTLE OF TRAFALGAR p152

Duke of Wellington (1769–1852)

British military leader. Arthur Wellesley became a national hero with his victories in the Peninsula Wars of 1808–14. He became the first Duke of Wellington, and was dubbed the 'Iron Duke' by his troops, because he had a fearsome reputation for discipline. His greatest moment came when he defeated Napoleon at the Battle of Waterloo, 18 June 1815.

❖ see BATTLE OF WATERLOO p152

Boston Massacre (1770)

Conflict between American colonials and British forces during the American Revolution. On 5 March 1770 an event occurred that fuelled anti-British feeling in American colonies. In Boston crowds were voicing their resentment at the presence of British soldiers when the commanding officer ordered his troops to fire into the crowd. Five were killed in the 'Boston Massacre'.

❖ see AMERICAN REVOLUTION p150

BELOW: *The Boston Massacre of 1770 fuelled anti-British feelings among the American colonialists. This picture is entitled* Bostonians Force-Feeding the Excise Man.

Maratha Wars (1775–82, 1802)

Two wars between the British and the Maratha princes of southern India. Maharashtra is a state in western-central India, dominated by the Maratha people, of Indo-European origin. The Marathas were organized into a loose confederacy under the leadership of various Hindu princes. The Marathas warred victoriously with the Mogul Empire – a situation which brought them up against the British in 1775. The Second Maratha War saw the Marathas defeated by Arthur Wellesley (later Duke of Wellington) and the collapse of Maratha power.

❖ see DUKE OF WELLINGTON p148

American Revolution (1775–83)

Also known as the American War of Independence, the conflict began when British North American colonists revolted against the policies of the British government.

In 1773 an event known as the Boston Tea Party occurred in Boston Harbour. It was a demonstration of the antagonism felt by colonists towards the British parliament for having attempted to introduce a tax on tea. The purpose of the tax was to raise funds to pay for a standing army in North America to fend off threats to the British colonies. The policy backfired, though, serving only to fuel anti-British feelings in the colonies, which were beginning to nurture ideas of independence.

Hostilities between the British and the colonists began on 19 April 1775 when the Massachusetts militia, led by rebel leaders John Hancock and Samuel Adams, attacked British troops in Boston as they attempted to seize military stores. The Battle of Bunker Hill on 17 June, the first proper battle, was a victory for the British, but George Washington was soon to become commander-in-chief to the colonies.

A series of battles over the next three years saw the front line move back and forth, but Washington proved to be a tenacious foe to the British. Following the winter of 1777–78, when Washington reached a low ebb having been deserted by many homesick troops, the French entered the war on his side. The British then had a run of success but the introduction of conscription alienated potential support from loyalist factions. The British general Charles Cornwallis surrendered his army in 1781, leading to peace negotiations. Eventually, at the Treaty of Paris (3 September 1783) American independence from Britain was recognized.

❖ see DECLARATION OF INDEPENDENCE p126

French Revolution (1789–99)

In the latter half of the eighteenth century the common people of France were growing increasingly resentful of the way they were being treated. They lived under a regime of absolute monarchy and were subjected to feudal laws which kept them in poverty whilst those in high

society lived in the lap of luxury.

The French Revolution began on 5 May 1789, when Louis XVI attempted to increase taxation. His 'states general' (political and religious leaders) formed a National Assembly and tried to establish constitutional control at a meeting in Versailles, sensing the unrest of the population. Further repressive measures taken by Louis finally provoked a mob in Paris to storm the Bastille Prison on 14 July. The mob freed seven prisoners and killed the governor and most of the garrison before razing the building to the ground.

In 1791 the National Assembly drew up a constitution ending feudalism, which Louis XVI accepted under duress as a prisoner. 1792 saw France at war with Austria, but the revolution remained on course. The National Convention then declared France a republic and abolished the monarchy.

A mob stormed the Tuileries palace and Louis, along with his wife Marie Antoinette and family, were guillotined for treason in 1793. A Reign of Terror, led by Maximilien Robespierre, lasted until he was overthrown in 1794. A Directory then held power until Napoleon became dictator in 1799.

❖ see STORMING OF THE BASTILLE p127, LOUIS XVI OF FRANCE p81, MARIE ANTOINETTE OF FRANCE p81

BELOW: *European crowned heads began to roll during the French Revolution. This picture depicts the execution of Louis XVI at the guillotine.*

Napoleonic Wars (1803–14)

Series of campaigns fought between Europe and France. Napoleon Bonaparte had been a general in the French Revolution from 1796 and overthrew the ruling Directory in 1799. He made himself dictator and, in 1803, launched a campaign with the aim of conquering the whole of Europe.

Until 1805 the warfare had remained at sea, giving Napoleon the chance to reform France and prepare it for the campaign ahead. In 1804 he crowned himself Emperor Napoleon I and assumed absolute power over his nation. The naval Battle of Trafalgar (1805) was a victory for the British under Admiral Horatio Nelson, ensuring that Napoleon's ambition to conquer Britain was thwarted.

The first land battles came in 1805 when Russia and Austria declared war on France. Napoleon devastated their forces at the battles of Ulm and Austerlitz. By 1806 Napoleon had western Germany and Italy under his control and Prussia was pushed into action.

Before Russian assistance could arrive, Napoleon took on the Prussian army at the battles of Jena and Auerstadt, both on 14 October 1806, defeating it easily. When the Russian army finally arrived, Napoleon and Tsar Alexander I reached stalemate at the battles of Friedland and Eylau. Russia and France became unwilling and distrustful allies, blockading trade with Britain. In 1808 Napoleon invaded Spain, but failed to take Portugal, due to assistance from the Duke of Wellington. He again defeated the Austrians at Wagram (1809), and by 1812 was ready for an invasion attempt on Russia. Napoleon managed to defeat the Russians at Borodino, but casualties were high, leaving him with a diminished army. Then came the Battle of Leipzig, October 1813, where a coalition force of Prussians, Austrians and Russians won a decisive victory.

Napoleon's army found itself attacked from the east and south by an international war machine. Despite a skilful defence of France, Napoleon was forced to abdicate in April 1814, bringing the Napoleonic Wars to an end.

❖ see BATTLE OF AUSTERLITZ p152, NAPOLEON BONAPARTE p81, ADMIRAL HORATIO NELSON p148, BATTLE OF TRAFALGAR p152, BATTLE OF WATERLOO p152, DUKE OF WELLINGTON p148

Battle of Trafalgar (1805)

Battle during the Napoleonic Wars. The entrance to the Straits of Gibraltar, off the coast of Spain, was the scene for the Battle of Trafalgar, 21 October 1805. It was fought by the British fleet against a combined fleet of French and Spanish ships. Clever tactics by Admiral Horatio Nelson divided the enemy fleet and enabled him to get the upper hand, despite having fewer ships. Nelson died in the battle.

❖ see NAPOLEONIC WARS p152, HORATIO NELSON p148

Battle of Waterloo (1815)

Final battle of the Napoleonic Wars. Napoleon was attempting to stage his comeback, having returned from exile and seized power once again in France. In the opening stages of the battle on 18 June 1815 Napoleon had the advantage: he had caught Wellington's British army isolated from Allied forces and launched a direct offensive. Wellington held Napoleon off long enough, however, for German, Dutch and Belgian reinforcements to join in the fray. The victory saw the final defeat of Napoleon.

❖ see NAPOLEON BONAPARTE p81, DUKE OF WELLINGTON p148

Opium Wars (1839–42, 1856–60)

Two wars between Britain and China over the import of opium. At the start of the nineteenth century opium became big business as a trade commodity in the Far East. Britain used opium produced in British India as currency for imports from China, such as tea, silk and porcelain. However, China closed its ports to British ships, prompting the First Opium War in 1839. Britain won the war three years later and enforced the opening of five Chinese treaty ports and took over Hong Kong as a British Crown colony. The Second Opium War saw Britain and France allied against China. China was forced to expand trade with Europe thenceforth.

ABOVE: *The Battle of Waterloo marked Napoleon's biggest defeat, just 100 days after his return from exile.*

ABOVE: *During the Second Afghan War, British troops once again began pushing into Afghanistan and eventually recaptured the capital city of Kabul.*

ABOVE: *The Maori Wars were fought in New Zealand between European settlers and native Maoris who were perceived to be uncultured savages.*

Afghan Wars (1839–42, 1878–80, 1919)

Three wars between Afghanistan and Great Britain caused by the threat of increasing Russian influence in British India. In the early nineteenth century Britain had a garrison of soldiers at Afghanistan's capital, Kabul. At that time Russia was nurturing ambitions of expansion and its influence was being felt in Afghanistan. India was an important part of the British Empire and the British began to perceive the Russians as a threat so they instigated a war with the Russians. This First Afghan War lasted 1839–42. Britain fared badly, however, losing the entire garrison at Kabul.

For 36 years tension remained between Britain and Russia until Britain decided to enter Afghanistan once more. Under General Roberts (1832–1914), British troops began their push in 1878. The Second Afghan War lasted until 1880 and saw Britain recapture Kabul and install Abdur Rahman Khan on the throne.

Another 39 years of tension passed before Russia and Britain once again did battle over Afghanistan in 1919. Before the year was out, though, Britain had won the Third Afghan War, partly assisted by the appearance of the first aeroplane ever seen in the skies over Kabul. Afghanistan regained its full independence as a result.

❖ see BRITISH EMPIRE p124

Maori Wars (1845–48, 1860–70)

Two wars fought between Maoris and British settlers. The first settlers arrived in New Zealand in 1815, and in 1841 the country became a colony of Great Britain. By 1845 the Maoris began to revolt against the loss of their tribal lands. The First Maori War became known as the Flagstaff War because the first act of defiance from the Maoris came with the chopping down of the Union flag on a pole at a settlement on North Island. Uprisings began again in 1860. The most famous encounter of the Second Maori War was at Gate Pah in 1864 when the British attacked a Maori stockade. Although the stockade fell, the British had lost three times as many men as the Maoris. Permanent peace was finally established in 1870.

❖ see MAORIS p104

Lord Horatio Herbert Kitchener (1850–1916)

British military commander during the Boer War and World War I. The Boer War was brought to a successful conclusion for the British by their commander-in-chief, Lord Horatio Herbert Kitchener, who assumed his role in the war from 1900. Victory was won, in part, by the invention of concentration camps which resulted in the deaths of 26,000 Boer women and children. Kitchener spearheaded the campaign for volunteers at the outbreak of World War I and was British war minister. He died in 1916 on board a ship which was hit by a mine and sank.

❖❖ see BOER WAR p161, WORLD WAR I p164

Crimean War (1853–56)

War between Russia and England, France and Turkey. In 1853 Russia invaded the Balkans, with a view to accessing the Mediterranean sea. Considerable mistrust in Russian ambitions by Britain and France led to their intervention. An Anglo-French expedition force was sent to the Crimea, in the Ukraine, to attack Sevastopol on the Black Sea.

Britain and France declared war on Russia in 1854 and laid siege to Sevastopol in September. There followed a series of battles which saw heavy losses on both sides. They included the battles of Balaclava, Inkerman and Alma. The Crimean War was characterized by negligent mismanagement at the War Office, leading to a long, drawn-out campaign and the loss of far more British and French lives than necessary. The war was ended by the Treaty of Paris in 1856.

❖❖ see BATTLE OF BALACLAVA p155, CHARGE OF THE LIGHT BRIGADE p156, FLORENCE NIGHTINGALE p128

Battle of Balaclava (1854)

During the Crimean War there was a Russian advance on British positions at Balaclava, 10 km south-east of Sevastopol in the Ukraine. The Battle of Balaclava took place on 25 October 1854. A British cavalry unit – the Light Brigade – made a foolish charge at Russian artillery, suffering heavy losses.

❖❖ see CHARGE OF THE LIGHT BRIGADE p156

ABOVE: *The Thin Red Line of the 93rd Highlanders repel the Russian cavalry during the Battle of Balaclava in the Crimean War.*

Charge of the Light Brigade (1854)

Infamous event during the Crimean War. Technology was forcing officers to rethink their strategies for effective warfare in the field of battle by the middle of the nineteenth century. Soldiers still wore brightly coloured uniforms, for example, making them easy targets for long-range rifles. The Battle of Balaclava (25 October 1854) involved a foolish charge by a British cavalry unit, the Light Brigade. Their leader, Lord Lucan, gave the order for them to ride their horses along the North Valley right into the firing lines of entrenched Russian artillery. There were 673 soldiers involved in the charge and 272 ended up as casualties. The Light Brigade would probably have been completely decimated had the French cavalry not come to its aid.

❖ see BATTLE OF BALACLAVA p155, CRIMEAN WAR p155

Indian Mutiny (1857)

Native uprising against the British in India. The uprising is named the Indian Mutiny, the Sepoy Rebellion or the Mutiny Revolt, since the British saw it as a mutinous betrayal. The catalyst was the introduction of a new – paper – rifle cartridge. Muslims believed it to be sealed with pig fat, and Hindus with the fat of cows, thereby causing offence to their respective beliefs. The uprising was quelled, but it led to the end of the East India Company.

❖ see BRITISH EAST INDIA COMPANY p89

General Sir Douglas Haig (1061–1928)

Commander-in-chief of Allied forces during World War I. General Sir Douglas Haig's command has been severely criticized, due to the heavy losses resulting from some of his policies. Haig oversaw the Somme offensive of 1916. It was a success for the Allies, but 600,000 lives were lost. The fruitless Passchendale offensive of 1917 saw a further 400,000 die. Haig's command was taken over in 1918 by Frenchman Ferdinand Foch (1851–1929), who launched the final Allied offensive, winning the war.

❖ see BATTLE OF THE SOMME p167

American Civil War (1861–65)

War between the northern (Union) and southern (Confederate) States in America. The reasons for the Civil War were primarily ideological. The populations of the northern States had a more progressive approach to their politics. They proclaimed the emancipation of slaves in 1863, but this issue became overshadowed by a determination to maintain the Federal Union of the States; the people of the southern States were claiming the right to secede from the Union in order that they be able to satisfy their instincts for political conservatism. This included the continuation of slavery, which was a far more significant

element of society in the south – and the foundation of wealth for many white families. In reality, many northern and southern families were divided on the political issues. This meant that relatives ended up fighting on opposite sides, making the war a bitter struggle.

The war began on 14 April 1861 when President Abraham Lincoln proclaimed a blockade of southern ports in reaction to Confederate rebels taking the Federal-run Fort Sumter in South Carolina. In July the Battle of Bull Run was fought. This first major engagement was won by the Confederate side.

In April 1862, at the Battle of Shiloh, General Grant won a victory for the Union and the Confederates began conscripting men. The next three years saw counter-attack followed by counter-attack, including the decisive Union victory over General Lee at the Battle of Gettysburg in July 1863. Eventually, though, the end of the war was hastened by a further Union victory at the Battle of Petersburg in March 1865. Hostilities stopped in May.

❖ see SLAVERY p104

BELOW: *American Civil War caps. The war was fought between the southern confederate States (the red cap), led by commander Robert E. Lee, and the northern union States (the blue cap), led by US President Abraham Lincoln.*

Franco-Prussian War (1870–71)

Otto von Bismarck (1815–98) became chancellor of the Northern German Federation – Prussia – in 1867. He had ambitions to annex parts of northern France in creating a German Empire. In 1870 Bismarck put forward a German candidate for the Spanish throne which had become vacant at that time. It was a strategic move designed to provoke the French emperor Napoleon III (1808–73) into declaring war.

The Franco-Prussian War began in the same year and lasted until 1871. The Battle of Sedan in the Ardennes, France, saw Napoleon III surrender to Bismarck's army, which then laid siege to Paris. Eventually, the Treaty of Frankfurt was signed in May 1871. The result was that France surrendered Alsace and Lorraine to Prussia, as well as paying a large indemnity. Bismarck became Imperial Chancellor of Prussia. In the same year, William I became emperor of all Germany.

Battle of Little Bighorn (1876)

Battle between white settlers and Native American Indians. The battle has become legendary in US folklore for being such a decisive victory for the Indians. Under the leadership of General George Armstrong Custer, a group of outnumbered US troops faced the wrath of the Sioux tribe at the Little Bighorn river in Montana on 25 June 1876. The Sioux were led by chiefs Crazy Horse and Sitting Bull. Custer and all his men were killed.

❖ see SITTING BULL p84, BATTLE OF WOUNDED KNEE p161

Satsuma Rebellion (1877–78)

Medieval Japanese society was hierarchically arranged. Approximately 92 per cent of the population were commoners and eight per cent Samurai. The Samurai were the elite class, allowed to carry the famous Samurai sword. In around 1700, the Samurai suffered a financial depression, which marked the beginning of their demise. They were eventually stripped of their role as defenders of the Empire. The Satsuma Rebellion was the last effort of the Samurai to restore their power.

❖ see SAMURAI p117, WARLORDS p167

Russo-Turkish War (1877–78)

The Greek War of Independence (1821–29) was fought between the Greeks and the Turks. Allied with Greece during the war were Russia, Britain and France. Conversely, the Crimean War saw Britain and France defend the Ottoman Empire (Turkey) from further pressure by the Russians. The Russo-Turkish War lasted between 1877 and 1878. The Russians compelled Turkey to sign the Treaty of San Stefano in 1878. However, it meant an imbalance of power in Eastern Europe and the other great powers eventually pressured Russia to reach a power compromise at the Treaty of Berlin in the same year.

Zulu Wars (1879)

War between Zululand and Britain. The Zulu kingdom expanded in Natal, South Africa, during the nineteenth century. Cetshwayo, the Zulu king in the 1870s, built a highly trained army of approximately 50,000 men and refused Natal's demands to back down. The British army invaded but complacency enabled the Zulus – despite heavy losses – to wipe out a British column at Isandhlwana on 22 January 1879, seizing their rifles and ammunition. The following day, a further Zulu army was held back in the celebrated engagement at Rorke's Drift. On 28–29 March 1879, the Zulus were defeated at Kambula. By July the British had captured the Zulu capital at Ulundi. In 1887 Zululand was incorporated into Natal.

Vidkun Quisling (1887–1945)

Norwegian fascist. Abraham Lauritz Jonsson Quisling aided the Nazi invasion of Norway and was made Norwegian premier by Adolf Hitler. He was arrested and shot as a traitor in 1945. 'Quisling' has been adopted by the Norwegians as a word meaning 'traitor'.

❖ see ADOLF HITLER p159, WORLD WAR II p172

ABOVE: *Adolf Hitler, surrounded by his henchmen, delivers the nefarious Nazi Party salute to the crowds.*

Adolf Hitler (1889–1945)

Nazi leader. Hitler was born in Austria, spending his early years in poverty in Vienna and Munich. In his mid-twenties he served in World War I as a volunteer and began developing fascist ideas to satisfy his anger at the treatment of Germany after the war. By 1921 he was leader of the National Socialist German Workers Party, which he abbreviated to 'Nazi Party'. Hitler used the Nazi Party as his vehicle for nurturing hatred towards races and creeds that he blamed for the humiliating plight of the German people. By 1933 he had become chancellor of a Nazi-Nationalist coalition. 1934 saw the suppression of the Nationalist contingent and Hitler became Führer. Hitler led the Anschluss with Austria in 1938 and whipped Germany into a frenzy of nationalism in the preparation for World War II. Throughout the war he remained the driving force behind the German campaign, but committed suicide when he realized that the Central Powers were facing defeat.

❖ see CONCENTRATION CAMPS p171, NAZI PARTY p22, WORLD WAR II p172

ABOVE: *Field Marshal Erwin Rommel defined the logistics for the Blitzkrieg.*

Battle of Wounded Knee (1890)

Battle between Native Americans and settlers in North America. Chief Sitting Bull commanded the Sioux at Little Bighorn in 1876 when Custer and his entire regiment were killed. The war was not yet won, however. Fourteen years later Sitting Bull led his people against the US army on the reservation at Wounded Knee, where the tribe had been confined. Sitting Bull was killed in the fray, along with 146 other members of the tribe.

❖ see SITTING BULL p84

Erwin Rommel (1891–1944)

German military commander during World War II. Field Marshal Erwin Rommel was largely responsible for putting tank warfare into practice. He organized spearhead attacks with close-knit packs of Panzers. Having successfully invaded Central Europe and France, Rommel commanded the North Africa campaign, which he eventually lost due to overstretched supply routes. He ultimately committed suicide.

❖ see BATTLES OF EL ALAMEIN p174

Herman Wilhelm Goering (1893–1946)

Prime minister of Germany from 1933 and Nazi leader. Goering had been a flying ace in World War I, and built up the Luftwaffe as commissioner for aviation before World War II. He also directed the construction of the concentration camps. The failure of the Luftwaffe over Britain led to his expulsion from the Nazi Party. He poisoned himself, having been sentenced to death for war crimes at Nuremberg.

❖ see CONCENTRATION CAMPS p171, NAZI PARTY p22, WORLD WAR I p164, WORLD WAR II p172

Spanish-American War (1898)

The colonial presence of Spain in the Americas, which had begun at the start of the sixteenth century, ended in 1898 with the Spanish-American War. At the time, Spain ruled Cuba and the Philippines as well as Guam and Puerto Rico. The brief war saw the USA defeat Spain outright and become a colonial power. The Philippines, Guam and Puerto Rico were ceded to the USA in the Treaty of Paris, and Cuba became independent. As compensation, the USA paid Spain $20 million. The war, which lasted less than four months, saw action in both the Caribbean and the Pacific ocean.

Siege of Mafeking (1899–1900)

Siege during the Boer War. The city of Mafeking was besieged by the Boers on 12 October 1899. The city was being held by British troops under the command of Lord Baden-Powell. He managed to hold the Boers off until a relief column arrived to defend the besieged town. Ultimately the Boer republics were annexed by the British.

❖ see BOER WAR p161

Boer War (1899–1902)

Campaign for control of South African territories between Great Britain and the Boers (South Africans of Dutch descent). Horatio Herbert Kitchener was chief-of-staff to the British forces in South Africa between 1900–02, under Lord Roberts. There had already been a South African War between the British and the Boers in 1881, principally over gold and diamond mines in the area known as the Transvaal.

The Boers were descended from Dutch colonials and had occupied the region since the establishment of the Dutch East India Company in 1652, but had become marginalized by the decline in power of the Netherlands, leading to the sale of Cape Town and its environs to Britain in 1814. Things came to a head once more in 1899 following an attempt by the British Cape Colonials to inspire a revolt against the Transvaal president, Kruger, by the non-Boer immigrants of the area, uitlanders, who were treated as second-class citizens by the Boers. As a consequence, the Boers retaliated by invading British territory.

The Boer War lasted for three years. Ultimately the British defeated the Boers, largely because they outnumbered them. However, Kitchener resorted to the tactic of interring Boer women and children in concentration camps to counter Boer guerilla activity. Some 26,000 women and children died.

❖ see DUTCH EAST INDIA COMPANY p89, LORD HORATIO HERBERT KITCHENER p155

Boxer Rebellion (1900)

Uprising against foreign influence in China. At the end of the nineteenth century European and American cultures were beginning to pervade that of China. Chinese nationalists formed a society known as the I ho ch'uan ('Righteous Harmonious Fists'), nicknamed the 'Boxers' by Europeans.

In 1900 the Empress Tz'u-hsi (c. 1834–1908) instigated the Boxer Rebellion. The European and US embassies were besieged in Beijing. On 14 August an international punitive force captured Beijing, liberating the legations. However, thousands of missionaries and Chinese Christian converts had been murdered by the Boxers and China agreed to pay an indemnity.

Russo-Japanese War (1904–05)

The north-eastern corner of China, Manchuria and Korea (then one country), was of territorial significance to both the Russians and the Japanese at the beginning of the twentieth century. For Russia, possession of the territory meant an improved land link to the Pacific Ocean; for Japan it would mean a foothold on the mainland of the Eurasian continent.

The Russo-Japanese War lasted from 1904–05. Japan besieged Port Arthur (Lushun), occupied by Russia, from May 1904 until January 1905. Japan also won the Battle of Mukden, February–March 1905. Russia surrendered and peace came on 23 August.

Schlieffen Plan (1905)

German offensive strategy for World War I. The Schlieffen Plan was named after its creator, the German chief of general staff, General Count Alfred von Schlieffen (1833–1913). It was a two-pronged European attack: the idea was to stage simultaneous offensives on France and Russia and to deploy all available resources against the latter when France had been conquered. General von Moltke (1848–1916) altered the Plan before it was put into effect in 1914, resulting in its failure. Adolf Hitler's plans for the conquest of Europe in World War II were inspired by the Schlieffen Plan.

❖ see WORLD WAR I p164, WORLD WAR II p172

Battle of Mons (1914)

Early battle of World War I. An Allied force of British and French troops launched an offensive against the invading German army at Mons. However, French reinforcements failed to arrive as planned. In panic the French troops at the front line abandoned their positions, leaving the British vulnerable to encirclement by the Germans.

❖ see WORLD WAR I p164

Battles of the Marne (1914 and 1918)

Campaign during World War I. The First Battle of Marne (6–9 September 1914) saw the Germans make an offensive move, only to be defeated by French and British troops under French general Joseph Joffre (1852–1931). The Second Battle of Marne (15 July–4 August 1918) told a similar story, only with the addition of US troops on the Allied side.

❖ see WORLD WAR I p164

Battles of Ypres (1914–17)

Campaign during World War I. Ypres, a small Belgian town in Western Flanders, has become synonymous with the great losses suffered during World War I. There were three battles fought around Ypres between 1914 and 1917, none of which proved progressive for either the Germans or the Allies despite heavy losses.

The Third Battle of Ypres, October–November 1917, was fought on the Passchendale ridge near Ypres. Passchendale became the object of an Allied offensive because the Germans had an elevated command of the Allied trenches. The Allies managed to capture the ridge but at the cost of 400,000 British lives.

❖ see WORLD WAR II p172

BELOW LEFT: *Beleaguered Russian troops in retreat from Manchuria after Japanese victory at the Battle of Mukden in 1905.*

BELOW: *Poison gas was first unleashed by the Germans on the enemy during the Battles of Ypres.*

WAR

World War I (1914–18)

Global conflict. Although action was seen over the Atlantic and Pacific oceans and over much of western Eurasia between 1914 and 1918, the conflict was not particularly ubiquitous and it was formerly known as the Great War. Following the war of 1939–45, confusion over names led to World Wars I and II being used.

World War I was a worldwide campaign in the respect that the Allies enlisted the help of troops from many colonies and dominions globally in fighting the Central Powers: Germany and Austria-Hungary. In fact, the Central Powers had fewer allies of their own to turn to because they had not invested so greatly in the colonization of new lands historically.

The war began over tensions between Germany and Serbia. Archduke Franz Ferdinand, heir to the Austrian throne, was assassinated in Sarajevo on 28 June 1914. It was the excuse Austria needed to declare war on Serbia exactly one month later. Russia jumped to the defence of Serbia. Germany then declared war on Russia and France and conquered Belgium. On 4 August Britain entered the war and the scene was set for a war on a scale never seen before.

For the first month of action, fighting was quite fluid. On the Western Front the Germans advanced to a point just short of Paris before being pushed back by British and French forces. On the Eastern Front the Germans, under Paul Hindenburg, managed to encircle and defeat the Russian army at the Battle of Tannenburg. Soon, though, trench warfare would become synonymous with the war as commanders on both sides struggled to understand the dynamics of fighting a war with weapons of mass destruction.

While the First Battle of Ypres raged between the Germans and Allied forces in Belgium, Britain declared war on Turkey (November 1914) who had invaded the Caucuses and the Middle East. This led to the disastrous Gallipoli campaign, which saw the Anzacs beleaguered until their evacuation in January 1916. Italy declared war on Austria in May 1915, and Bulgaria joined the Central Powers against Serbia in the same year.

The Western Front moved little throughout 1915. Both sides became entrenched and tens of thousands of lives were wasted in futile attempts to gain or defend territory.

The Second Battle of Ypres witnessed the first use of

poison 'mustard' gas by the Germans. The gas, known chemically as dichloroethyl sulphide, caused agonizing blistering to the skin and damage to the mucous membrane in the lungs, resulting in an excruciating death.

In February 1916, the Germans launched their fierce offensive on Verdun at the Western Front. It was to last until June, and would almost exhaust France of its life's blood of available troops. Somehow the French held on, though, and Verdun became a morale-boosting symbol of French resistance against 'the Hun'. Now it was the turn of the Allies. They launched their own offensive at the Somme in July.

The Battle of the Somme, which ended in November 1916, pushed the German front line eastward by a mere 12 km (7 miles). The human cost to the Allies was 600,000 troops. Coupled with further French success at Verdun and Russian progress in Galicia, the Allies were, at least, gaining the upper hand. The Somme also introduced the tank to warfare. Although notoriously unreliable in this first incarnation it proved useful for crossing difficult terrain under heavy fire.

Another new feature of warfare was the submarine, or U-boat, as the Germans called them. In February 1917, the Germans renewed their campaign of submarine warfare, halted in April 1916. This prompted the USA to join the war in April 1917. On land the Germans withdrew to the Hindenburg line on the Western Front. Meanwhile, in Russia the war was about to lead to the overthrow of the monarchy and the start of the Bolshevik Revolution in November 1917.

In other places the war in 1917 went one way, then the other, seeing victories for both sides, but no decisive progress. When the war spilled into 1918, though, both sides desperately began to seek an end to the bitter conflict. On the Western Front the Germans launched what was designed to be their final offensive. They forced the Allies back to Marne between March and June. The Allies appointed supreme commander General Ferdinand Foch (1851–1929) to co-ordinate their counter-attack and, at last, the Allies received reinforcements from the USA.

By August the Allied counter-offensive had pushed the Germans back east to the Siegfried line, and in September 1918 Hindenburg requested an armistice, which was offered in October. In November both Germany and Austria-Hungary agreed to the terms of the 'Fourteen Point' armistice and fighting stopped on the Western Front. Fighting had already stopped on the Eastern Front in March with the signing of the Treaty of Brest-Litovsk. In 1919 at a peace conference at Versailles, the formalities were sorted out, including demands on Germany that would cause deep resentment and ultimately lead to World War II.

❖ see ARCHDUKE FRANZ FERDINAND p84, GENERAL SIR DOUGLAS HAIG p156, BATTLE OF MONS p163, RUSSIAN REVOLUTION p168, BATTLE OF THE SOMME p167, BATTLE OF VERDUN p167, BATTLES OF YPRES p163

LEFT: *Soldiers lived, fought and died in the trenches during World War I.*

RIGHT: *Recruitment posters were introduced during World War I due to a severe shortage of volunteers – there was no obligatory conscription in Britain.*

Dardanelles Campaign (1915–16)

Unsuccessful Allied campaign during World War I. Britain declared war on Turkey at the close of 1914. The strait known as the Dardanelles, where the Sea of Marmara spills into the Aegean, became a hot spot of bitter fighting. In April 1915, under the command of Sir Ian Hamilton, a joint British, Australian, New Zealand and French force landed on the Gallipoli peninsula. The Turks proved a formidable foe and the Allied forces became entrenched. The beleaguered survivors were eventually withdrawn in January 1916. Some 36,000 Commonwealth troops were lost at Gallipoli. The majority were ANZAC (Australian and New Zealand Army Corps) troops.

❖ see WORLD WAR I p164

Brusilov Offensive (1916)

Russia entered World War I in August 1914. As the Russians mobilized their forces to defend their ally Serbia, the Germans declared war on them. By 1916 the Russians were in the thick of it and launched their Brusilov Offensive against the Ukraine in June. The Ukraine had been united with Russia since 1785 but had become occupied by Austro-Hungarian forces. Under commander Alexei Brusilov the Russian army attacked the Eastern Front (4 June–10 August), pushing back the enemy front line to a point called the Pripet Marshes. Eventually, though, the Russian attack was blunted by the arrival of German reinforcements.

❖ see WORLD WAR I p164

ABOVE: *The Battle of the Somme.*
LEFT: *The Dardanelles strait was the scene of many naval battles between British and Turkish fleets.*

Battle of the Somme (1916)

Allied offensive during World War I. Halfway through World War I, the Allied forces made an offensive move on the Germans at the River Somme in northern France. The Battle of the Somme began on 1 July 1916 and lasted until November. Both sides suffered severe losses, and the Allies advanced a mere 13 km (8 miles). The battle is noted for being the first to involve tanks – originally a code name – which were invented by the British soldier Ernest Swinton. The first day of the Somme is also remembered as one of the most tragic in history in terms of sheer numbers of dead and wounded.

❖ see WORLD WAR I p164

Battle of Verdun (1916)

Campaign during World War I. Verdun, a fortress town in north-east France, was subjected to a fierce onslaught by the Germans in 1916 and it became the symbol of French resistance because it was won by the French without direct assistance from Allied forces. The Battle of Verdun lasted between 21 February and 18 December 1916. There were 400,000 French and German casualties.

❖ see WORLD WAR I p164

Warlords (1916–49)

Independent military commanders in China. Following the death of Yuan Shih-K'ia (1916), many warlords, former officers in the Peiyang army, took power in various provinces. Many served foreign powers, including Japan, Britain and the Soviet Union. None of them was strong enough to destroy the rest, and it was not until 1928 when Chiang Kai-shek reunified China that the warlords were incorporated into his army. Local warlords still existed until the Communist takeover in 1949.

Battle of Arras (1917)

British attack on German forces during World War I. The Siegfried line was a defensive line marked out by the Germans in 1917; it was a sub-division of the Hindenburg Line at the Western Front. In support of a French offensive, British troops launched an attack on the German front line during April and May 1917. The Siegfried line was partially breached during the operation, but casualties were extremely high. About 84,000 Britons and 75,000 Germans were killed or wounded.

❖ see WORLD WAR I p164

Russian Revolution (1917)

Two revolutions resulting in the overthrow of the Russian monarchy. When Russia entered World War I in 1914, the country was on the verge of revolution. Riots broke out in Petrograd (St Petersburg) in February 1917, marking the beginning of the Russian Revolution.

Tsar Nicholas abdicated and a provisional government was established under Prince Lvov. There began a struggle for power between the provisional government and the Petrograd soviet. Vladimir Lenin, who had been exiled in Switzerland since 1914, returned to Petrograd demanding a handover of power to the Petrograd soviet. In July 1917, the Bolsheviks, under Lenin and Leon Trotsky attempted to seize power in Petrograd. But Alexander Kerensky of the provisional government held on to power until November of the same year.

In November 1917, the Bolsheviks began their own revolution. Their military revolutionary committee and Red Guards arrested the provisional government. Lenin, Trotsky and Joseph Stalin emerged as prominent figures in the new government. The Treaty of Brest-Litovsk (March 1918) marked the end of Russia's involvement in World War I. By July the royal family had been murdered and civil war had broken out.

❖ see BOLSHEVIKS p18, VLADIMIR ILYICH LENIN p11, NICHOLAS II OF RUSSIA p84, LEON TROTSKY p13

ABOVE: *Bolsheviks up in arms against the government and the Russian aristocracy during the Russian Revolution of 1917.*

Holocaust (1933–45)

Name given to the persecution and extermination of the Jews during World War II. The 'final solution of the Jewish problem' inspired by Adolf Hitler and the Nazi regime in Germany, killed six million Jews. The Ashkenazi, or North European Jews, suffered particularly in the genocide, with the Jewish population of Poland being virtually exterminated. During that period Jews were taken into slave labour, used for medical experiments and identified and humiliated in public through the wearing of a yellow star. Herded on to trains and taken to concentration camps such as Auschwitz and Treblinka, the systematic killing of Jews, as well as homosexuals and gypsies, continued until the very end of World War II. The profound shock of the event was an important element in the foundation of the state of Israel in May 1948. The Holocaust Memorial (Yad Vashem) in Jerusalem is a potent symbol of that period.

❖ see CONCENTRATION CAMPS p171, ADOLF HITLER p159, NAZI PARTY p22, WORLD WAR II p172

Spanish Civil War (1936)

Between 1873 and 1874, Spain became a republic for the first time, but ended up with the restoration of the Bourbon dynasty. The second republic was proclaimed in 1931, but led to a state of tension, which resulted in the Spanish Civil War.

The republican party, the left-wing Popular Front, won a 1936 election, prompting General Francisco Franco to launch a military rebellion against the government which escalated into civil war. The nationalists under Franco won significant support from the German Nazi Party and Italian fascists, enabling them to defeat the republicans who had limited support from the Soviets. The outcome was that Franco became dictator of a nationalist-fascist regime in Spain. The Spanish Civil War was a particularly barbaric struggle, characterized by 'total war' which saw no distinction between combatants and civilians. Picasso's *Guernica*, 1937, is a poignant comment on the bombing of civilians during the war.

❖ see FRANCISCO FRANCO p16

ABOVE: **The Spanish Civil War began as an anarchic uprising in the streets of Madrid, between the nationalists (fascists) and the republicans.**

ABOVE: *Saddam Hussein, seen in this poster, first came to the world's attention with his ruthless invasion of Iran in 1988.*

Manchuria

European name for the north-eastern region of China. From 1937 the Japanese invaded China as part of their empire expansion, having already set up a puppet state in Manchuria in 1932. The Chinese military commander, Chiang Kai-shek (1887–1975), received assistance from Britain and the USA from 1941. At the end of the war in 1945 Soviets occupied Manchuria. The Manchuria region was eventually returned to Chinese control after Japanese settlers were expelled.

❖ see WORLD WAR II p172

Saddam Hussein (1937–2006)

Former Iraqi dictator. Saddam Hussein came to prominence and power as a politician in 1968. Like all dictatorial figures he had a ruthless nature and suppressed opposition to his ambitions. By 1979 he had worked his way to the presidency. He presided over the Iran–Iraq War of 1980–88. During the conflict Hussein persecuted the Kurdish rebels of northern Iraq. In 1990 Hussein annexed Kuwait, resulting in an offensive by a coalition force, led by the USA (1991). He lost the first Gulf War, but he and his regime were overthrown after another offensive led by the USA in 2003.

❖ see GULF WAR p181

Battle of the Atlantic (1939–45)

Naval campaign during World War II. Essential to the success of any campaign in wartime is the regular supply of fuel, equipment and goods to a fighting force. For this reason battles raged in the Atlantic Ocean throughout World War II. Cargo ships needed to sail between Britain and the USA to keep Allied forces in supplies, so they became prime targets for German warships and submarines. The battle began on the very first night of the war in September 1939 when a German U-boat torpedoed the British ocean liner Athenia.

❖ see WORLD WAR II p172

BELOW: *During the Battle of the Atlantic, cargo ships transporting vital wartime goods to British armies became prime targets for maritime attacks by German bomber planes and submarines.*

Concentration Camps (1939–45)

Concentration camps were nothing new by the time of World War II, but the Nazis, under Adolf Hitler, took them to a new extreme in terms of the brutality meted out to those incarcerated.

Hitler intended to rid his Third Reich of all those people that he viewed as either a threat or as sub-human by race or nature. Those sent to concentration camps included homosexuals, gypsies, vagrants and Jews. Another Austrian Nazi, Adolf Eichmann (1906–62), became the architect of Hitler's extermination system, building death camps. The most infamous of these concentration camps were Auschwitz, Bergen-Belsen, Dachau, Maidanek, Sobibor and Treblinka.

In the concentration camps prisoners were subjected to appalling conditions and treatment. Many were worked to death as slaves. Some were experimented on before execution. Over six million died in these camps. The majority – around four million – were exterminated in gas chambers disguised as showers and by other means.

❖ see ADOLF HITLER p159, NAZI PARTY 22, WORLD WAR II p172

BELOW: *A haunting photograph of undernourished concentration camp victims looking through the barbed wire fence of their prison.*

World War II (1939–45)

Global conflict. Following World War I, Germany was plunged into a deep recession when inflation was so exaggerated that millions of Germans became paupers. As a result, deep resentment was harboured towards the nations that had formed the Allied forces. Adolf Hitler had served as a volunteer in World War I and felt indignation at the post-war treatment of his peoples: Germans and Austrians.

In 1921 Hitler became leader of the National Socialist German Workers (Nazi) Party. Seeing an opportunity to seduce a disillusioned population, he began rallying support by enlisting impressionable youths into his Hitler Youth Movement. The recruits were fed dogma that encouraged thoughts of Aryan supremacy and prejudice towards those of other races and creeds, particularly Jews, who had been seen to flourish during the recession, giving the Germanic people an inferiority complex.

By 1934 the Nazis were in full power, with Hitler as Führer. He called his domain the Third Reich (Third Empire) and began plans for its expansion to become the leading power in Europe. Over the following five years, Hitler prepared for war and consolidated the epicentre of his German empire by annexing neighbouring territory, including Austria, Sudetenland and then the rest of Czechoslovakia. Hitler had also formed alliances with Italy, Hungary, Albania and East Prussia, and signed a non-aggression pact with Russia. Now he was poised and ready for World War II.

In September 1939 Germany invaded its eastern neighbour Poland. This prompted Britain and France to declare war on Germany. The USSR invaded Poland from the east and entered Finland. The Germans launched their Blitzkrieg in early 1940, conquering Denmark, Norway, the Netherlands, Belgium and Luxembourg in only a few weeks, and pushing hard into France. They soon broke the French Maginot line and pushed rapidly westward. From 26 May Britain and France began evacuating troops from the beaches at Dunkirk in northern France, while the Germans' front line moved ever nearer. They took Paris on 14 June 1940.

July–October 1940 saw the Battle of Britain, intended to weaken British air defence before Hitler's planned Seelöwe invasion. When Hitler realized defeat he turned his attentions to Russia instead, influenced by the Schlieffen Plan for World War I. In the later months of 1940 Japan invaded French Indonesia and the Italians made an abortive attempt to invade Greece.

Having gone as far as he could westward and northward – Spain and Sweden being neutral – Hitler used 1941 to make headway in the east and south. By April he had taken Greece and Yugoslavia, and June saw him turn traitor on the Soviets,

ABOVE: *An estimated 40 to 60 million lives were lost during World War II. These German troops advance into a burning forest during the Blitzkrieg.*

launching a major offensive in the direction of Moscow, taking Romania, Bulgaria, Lithuania, Latvia and Estonia along the way.

By December 1941, the Germans had come within 40 kilometres (25 miles) of Moscow, but they had not been prepared for the bitter Russian climate and it had them frozen to the spot. Moscow unleashed its Mongolian troops on the Germans at the eleventh hour, smashing their hopes of victory. Meanwhile, the great Siege of Leningrad (now St Petersburg) had begun. In the Pacific, Japan attacked Pearl Harbor and declared war on the USA and Britain. Germany and Italy declared war on the USA for good measure and a worldwide war was underway.

The year 1942 saw the Axis powers reach their full extent of power and then the tide turned in favour of the Allies. The Japanese conquered the Philippines in January, but lost the Battle of Midway in June, putting them on the defensive for the remainder of the war in the Pacific. Similarly, the Germans lost the Battle of El Alamein in Egypt, from October to November, and were sent on the run westward along the Barbary coast of North Africa.

It was even worse for the Axis powers during 1943. The Russians drove the Germans westward to the Donetz and they were cleared out of North Africa. The campaign against the Japanese in Burma (now Myanmar) was launched and the Italians surrendered to the Allies. Then, in 1944, came the Allied landings. In January the Allies attacked the beaches of Nazi-occupied Italy. Eventually, they won the Battle of Anzio against fierce German resistance. With a foothold in the south, the Allies then launched the D-Day landings on the beaches of northern France. The Germans fought for their lives, but the Allied force was too powerful for them to match, and the counter-invasion of Europe had begun.

By the end of 1944 the Allies and Russians had the Germans surrounded. The Japanese were losing territory as well and the end of the war was in sight. In February 1945 the Russians crossed the German border and headed for Berlin. Hitler took his own life in April and the Germans soon surrendered to the Allies. VE (Victory in Europe) was celebrated on both 8 and 9 May. By July, Japan was surrounded but stubbornly holding on. It took two atom bombs to force a surrender. VJ (Victory over Japan) was celebrated on 2 September.

❖ see BATTLE OF BRITAIN p174, CONCENTRATION CAMPS p171, D-DAY p159, BATTLE OF EL ALAMEIN p174, ADOLF HITLER p159, PEARL HARBOR p174

LEFT: *Benito Mussolini and Adolf Hitler met several times during the course of World War II claiming they favoured 'frequent personal contact' with each other.*

WAR

Battle of Britain (1940)

Aerial battle between the British RAF and the German Luftwaffe during World War II. Having successfully invaded France, Belgium and Holland during the Blitzkrieg, Adolf Hitler set his sights across the Channel. British forces had evacuated mainland Europe and he knew that they presented a considerable threat to his plans for the Third Reich while they had time to muster support and strength.

Hitler had an invasion plan for Britain called Seelöwe ('Sea Lion') but he chose to launch an air attack first to weaken and intimidate British defences. Despite considerable advantage, including 50 per cent more aircraft, the Luftwaffe ultimately lost the Battle of Britain (July–October 1940) due to inferior intelligence.

❖ see WORLD WAR II p172

Pearl Harbor (1941)

Japanese attack on the USA during World War II. While Japanese envoys were holding 'peace talks' in Washington their naval airforce struck a US Pacific naval base called Pearl Harbor, Oahu, Hawaii, on 7 December 1941. Public opinion about entering World War II – which had been against it – was turned on its head in the USA. Some 2,000 US personnel died and the Pacific fleet was severely depleted, sending the Americans into a frenzy of anti-Japanese sentiment. President Roosevelt may have allowed the attack to happen for that very reason.

❖ see FRANKLIN D. ROOSEVELT p14

Siege of Leningrad (1941–44)

Campaign during World War II. On 1 September 1941 the Germans laid siege to the city of Leningrad (St Petersburg) in Russia. Hitler had stated that he wanted to 'wipe Leningrad from the face of the Earth' – but he had not reckoned on the tenacity of the city's inhabitants. An estimated one million people lost their lives in the siege but, despite this, the city was not taken and remained in Russian hands when the siege ended on 27 January 1944.

Battles of El Alamein (1942)

During World War II North Africa presented a new theatre of battle for both Allied and Axis powers. Desert fighting was something not previously experienced in the campaign. The front line moved westward and eastward along the Barbary Coast as each side waxed and waned, but El Alamein, in northern Egypt, proved to be the strategically decisive spot. Both Battles of El Alamein (July and October–November 1942) were won by the Allies, largely thanks to shorter supply lines than Erwin Rommel's.

❖ see ERWIN ROMMEL p161, WORLD WAR II p172

Battle of Midway (1942)

Sea battle between the USA and Japan during World War II. The battle took place in June 1942 in the Pacific Ocean. The war in the Pacific had been turning in favour of the Japanese until the USA decisively defeated them off Midway Island. Japanese naval air superiority was destroyed in a single day, marking the turning point of the conflict.

❖ see WORLD WAR II p172

Siege of Stalingrad (1942–43)

While the Siege of Leningrad cost the lives of a million Russians, the Siege of Stalingrad (Volgograd), in August 1942–43, was not quite so devastating. Although 750,000 Soviets died, the Germans lost 4,000 troops in the campaign, and it marked a significant turning point in World War II. The German army besieging the city was forced to surrender on 2 February 1943 having been surrounded by Soviet forces under General Georgy Zhukov.

❖ see SIEGE OF LENINGRAD p174

Battle of Arnhem (1944)

Allied aerial attack during World War II. The Allied landings of World War II began on 6 June 1944. By September, Allied forces had reached the River Rhine. On 17 September the Allies launched an airborne operation designed to secure a number of bridgeheads over the Rhine, intending to capture the key area of the Ruhr – the industrial heartland of the

German military. The Battle of Arnhem, part of the campaign known as Operation Market Garden, lasted for nine days and resulted in 7,600 Allied casualties. It was judged only partially successful.

❖ see WORLD WAR II p172

D-Day (1944)

Allied offensive during World War II. On 6 June 1944, between 6.30 and 7.30 a.m., the Allied invasion of Normandy was launched against the Germans. A vast American and British invasion force arrived at various beaches between the Orne and St Marcouf.

The Germans put up fierce resistance on D-Day to defend Hitler's 'Fortress Europe' but eventually the Allied forces breached their lines and the way was opened for victory. The term 'D-Day' referred to the first day of the invasion, with subsequent days listed as D+1, D+2 and so on – 'D' being an abbreviation for 'Day'.

To ensure the success of the D-Day landings, artificial harbours called 'Mulberry harbours' were constructed on the English coast and towed across the Channel. They enabled the Allied forces to unload vital military equipment for the campaign. Soldiers were delivered to the beaches in landing craft that ferried them from ships anchored out at sea.

❖ see WORLD WAR II p172

BELOW: *A war veteran pays tribute to those who fell on D-Day, 6 June 1944.*

Atomic Bomb (1945)

Weapon with a huge explosive force released through splitting the nuclear atom. Further destruction is caused by radioactive fallout. The first secret test took place in the desert in New Mexico on 16 July 1945. Two atomic bombs, thousands of times more powerful than any previous weapons, were then dropped on the Japanese cities of Hiroshima and Nagasaki by American aircraft in the final stages of World War II. Bombs were later developed by a number of countries, including the USSR, France and China, which led to a build-up of nuclear weapons. Others, including Iraq and Pakistan, are also thought to be able to manufacture them.

❖ see HIROSHIMA p176, WORLD WAR II p172

Hiroshima (1945)

Japanese city destroyed by the first atomic bomb. On 6 August 1945, US president Harry S. Truman ordered the bombing of Hiroshima when the Japanese army refused to surrender unconditionally. The bomb destroyed most of the city, killed tens of thousands of people instantly and caused many more casualties over time from radiation sickness. Three days later, a second bomb was dropped on the port city of Nagasaki and the Japanese surrendered. Estimates of the number of dead for both cities range between 200–250,000. Hiroshima has been rebuilt, though an area was left in its bombed state to create the 'Peace City' memorial.

❖ see NAGASAKI p176

Nagasaki (1945)

Japanese city destroyed by an atomic bomb. Nagasaki was a major shipbuilding city, chosen as the target for a second atomic bomb dropped on Japan in World War II. The city was bombed three days after Hiroshima, while the Japanese were still debating their response to the first bomb. Nagasaki's size and geography led to a smaller loss of life and destruction, even though the bomb dropped on the city was significantly more powerful.

❖ see HIROSHIMA p176

Korean War (1950–53)

War between North and South Korea. At the close of World War II, Korea was occupied by Japanese forces. Russian and US troops entered Korea and accepted the surrender of the Japanese. They then divided the country in two, at the '38th parallel' due to their divided political interests. North Korea and South Korea were strictly isolated from one another in post-war years.

North Korea effectively became a republic of the USSR, as it had a Soviet-backed provisional government installed which was dominated by Korean Communists trained in Moscow. South Korea, meanwhile, was being set up with a pro-US government and then named itself the Republic of Korea in 1948. North Korea responded by naming itself the Democratic People's Republic of Korea, and Soviet troops departed.

With the lines firmly drawn between the two new countries, tensions began to rise. In 1950 North Korea invaded South Korea with a view to reuniting the two areas of territory under one Communist banner. The North Koreans were backed by their Communist neighbour, China. South Korea quickly found defence support from the United Nations and all-out war began. Still holding on to a small area of territory in the south-east of the Korean peninsula, known as the Pusan perimeter, the South Koreans, with the support of US reinforcements, managed to begin pushing their way northward. By October 1950 the Chinese had become directly involved in the warfare and things reached a stalemate position. Negotiations for a truce began in 1951 but an armistice was not reached until 1953.

Arab-Israeli War (1956–57)

In 1948, following the horrors of the Holocaust during World War II, world leaders made a goodwill gesture to the Jewish survivors by establishing a homeland for them in Israel. Many Palestinian Arabs were forced to become refugees in the Gaza Strip and West Bank areas as a result, causing much resentment and unrest. The Israelis soon nurtured ambitions to take more land. They did so in 1956 by invading Gaza and Sinai. The war that ensued was ended by Israeli withdrawal in

1957 due to Egyptian resistance. In 1967 the Six-Day War saw Israel defeat Egypt and Syria. Much of the land seized has subsequently been returned.

❖ see SIX-DAY WAR p179, WORLD WAR II p172

Bay of Pigs Invasion (1961)

Fidel Castro became prime minister of Cuba in 1959. His government was Communist and the regime he established was seen as a threat to world peace by the USA. From 17 to 20 April 1961, some 1,500 US-sponsored Cuban exiles attempted to invade Cuba and seize power from Castro. The invasion was badly planned, however, and Castro's ill-equipped militia were able to defend the Bay of Pigs, where the landings took place. Adding insult to injury, in 1962 Castro demanded a ransom of $53 million worth of food and medicine from the US government in return for most of the prisoners.

❖ see JOHN F. KENNEDY p20

BELOW: *The Arab-Israeli conflict remains unresolved to this day with deep tensions colouring relations between Israelis, who were given a part of Palestine as their homeland, and Palestinian Arabs, who had that land taken away from them.*

WAR

177

Vietnam War (1963–75)

War between North Vietnam and the South, backed by the United States. Vietnam became a divided country in 1954 in the aftermath of the Viet Minh War (1946–54), in which the Vietnamese, under Ho Chi Minh, resisted French attempts to re-assert colonial control. The country was divided into North Vietnam and South Vietnam, at the 17th parallel. North Vietnam was Communist-controlled and South Vietnam was US-backed, similar to Korea.

In 1963 a military coup took place in South Vietnam, led by Lieutenant General Nguyen Van Thieu, resulting in the overthrow of the leader Ngo Dinh Diem. By 1964 US combat troops were being mobilized to assist South Vietnam. It was a war fought in the jungle – a factor which proved a serious impediment to the US forces.

By 1975, when the war ended, 56,555 US troops had been killed in action. An appalling fifth of them had been killed by their own side, such was the difficulty with directing gunfire in thick vegetation and bombing 'blind' through the canopy of trees. Furthermore, about

200,000 South Vietnamese were killed along with an estimated one million North Vietnamese, who were dubbed the 'Vietcong' (a contraction of 'Vietnamese Communists'). A further 500,000 civilians were slaughtered during the campaign.

The US forces were not defeated, but political pressures, especially domestic, resulted in the USA beginning to pull out troops from Vietnam in 1973 following a peace treaty negotiated by Henry Kissinger, for which he won the Nobel Peace Prize, jointly, with Le Duc Tho. Saigon had been captured by North Vietnam by 1975 and in 1976 the Socialist Republic of Vietnam was proclaimed.

Indo-Pakistan War (1965)

Border war between India and Pakistan. On 14 August 1965 a Pakistani force crossed into Indian territory in an attempt to annex Kashmir as a province of Pakistan. India immediately dispatched an army to block the Haji Pir pass. A second Indian force launched a counteroffensive by crossing the border into Lahore. The tank battles that ensued were extremely fierce. Both sides suffered heavy losses of personnel and military equipment. A treaty – the Tashkent Agreement – was signed in 1966.

Six-Day War (1967)

Third Arab-Israeli war. Ever since the UN voted to partition Palestine and allow the formation of the Independent State of Israel following World War II, there has existed a state of tension between Jewish and Muslim populations in the Middle East. The third Arab-Israeli war, or Six-Day War, (5–10 June 1967), saw a major offensive by the Israelis. In less than a week they had annexed the Golan Heights in Syria, the West Bank and Gaza Strip in Palestine, and the Sinai as far as the Suez Canal.

❖ see ARAB-ISRAELI WAR p176

Yom Kippur War (1973)

Name given to the Fourth Arab-Israeli War. The holiest day in the Jewish year is called Yom Kippur. It is the Jewish day of Atonement. Egypt and Syria chose that date to launch a surprise attack on Israel in October 1973 because it marked a national holiday and was likely to catch the Israelis off guard. It was designed to recapture some of the territory taken by the Israelis during the Six-Day War of June 1967.

❖ see ARAB-ISRAELI WAR p176, SIX-DAY WAR p179

LEFT: *The remains of an American helicopter used during the Vietnam conflict. The war was fought between North (Communist) Vietnam and South Vietnam (aided by the USA and its allies).*

ABOVE: *A British paratrooper opens fire on enemy lines during the Falklands War.*

Falklands War (1982)

Campaign between Britain and Argentina over ownership of the Falkland Islands. The first British settlers arrived at the Falkland Islands, in the South Atlantic, in 1765. The islands had been named after Lord Falkland, treasurer to the British navy, at the end of the seventeenth century. In 1766 France sold West Falkland to the Spanish, who ejected the British in 1770–71, and named the islands Islas Malvinas. British sovereignty was not ceded, however, and the islands became a solely British settlement from 1833 when the last of the Argentines – Spanish descendants – were expelled.

On 2 April 1982 Argentina invaded the Falkland Islands. The United Nations Security Council called for a withdrawal but it was ignored. Britain immediately dispatched a task force of army, navy and airforce personnel to launch an offensive against the Argentinians. The task force took some days to reach the islands, giving the Argentinians time to bring reinforcements in preparation for the battle ahead.

The Falklands War proved to be a fierce conflict. Argentine troops outnumbered British, but the British had the advantage of superior technology. Eventually, between 14–15 June 1982, the Falklands were returned to British rule. A thousand Argentinian and British troops died in the campaign, before the Argentine force, of 12,000, finally surrendered.

Argentina still holds with its claim on sovereignty over the Falklands. In 1990 it created a new state, Tierra del Fuego, and claimed the Falkland Islands and other British-held South Atlantic Islands to be part of it. An agreement on oil rights in surrounding waters was signed in 1995.

Gulf War (1991)

War ostensibly fought over territory, although the real agenda was ownership and control of oil reserves. On 2 August 1990, Iraq, under the leadership of Saddam Hussein, invaded and annexed Kuwait. The move was provoked by a dispute over a shared oilfield.

Iraq found itself isolated, facing a coalition of 28 nations prepared to take action on behalf of Kuwait, and spearheaded by the USA. All had vested interests in maintaining supplies of crude oil to their respective countries. Over the next five months troops piled into Saudi Arabia in preparation for an offensive. By January 1991 there were 500,000 US, 42,000 UK, 15,000 French and 20,000 Egyptian troops, plus smaller forces from other nations in the area.

The United Nations Security Council authorized the use of military force on Iraq if it did not withdraw from Kuwait by 15 January. It did not, and action began the following day. The Gulf War lasted for six weeks and was an easy victory for the Allies. The Iraqi army and strategic targets were subjected to overwhelming bombardment from 'smart' weaponry that totally outclassed anything the Iraqis had to offer. Kuwait was liberated and the war was over by 28 February.

❖ see SADDAM HUSSEIN p170, UNITED NATIONS p25

War in Iraq (2003)

The Gulf War of 1991 left unsolved the problems with regard to Saddam Hussein and his brutal regime in Iraq. The most pressing was his suspected stockpiling of weapons of mass destruction. US President George W. Bush began to push for action to put a stop to Saddam's activities in 2002. Despite worldwide anti-war protests, on 19 March 2003 a coalition of US, British and Polish forces attacked Iraq. By April that year the US had secured Baghdad and Iraqi resistance was hampered by mass desertions. Despite initial success, the war in Iraq has rumbled on, with a growing toll of US and British casualties. Saddam Hussein was captured in December 2003 and, after a lengthy trial, he was finally executed on 30 December 2006.

ABOVE: *The 1991 Gulf War in Kuwait was given the most intensive media coverage of any event in world history.*

GLOSSARY

Absolute Monarchy
Rule by a king or queen whereby they are not subject to the laws of government or parliament.

Afrikaaner
Native of South Africa descended from predominantly Dutch heritage. These people were also referred to as Boers or Voortrekkers.

Allies
Term commonly used to describe the countries opposing the Central Powers during World War I: Great Britain, France and Russia. It was also used in World War II.

Anarchy
Political theory that advocates a society run without the coercive authority from government, religion or education, which imposes limits on the freedom of the individual.

Anthropocentrism
Theory which regards human beings as the most important element of existence.

Anti-Semitism
Prejudice against followers of the Jewish faith. Although persecution of Jews is a feature throughout history, anti-Semitism reached its climax just prior to and during World War II, with Hitler's Final Solution: the planned extermination of the race.

ANZAC
Australia and New Zealand Army Corp. Used to denote members of the armed forces of the Commonwealth.

Atomic Bomb
Bomb in which atoms of either uranium or plutonium are bombarded with neutrons, causing an explosive release of energy as atoms split apart. The current type of bomb is the much more powerful hydrogen bomb. An atom bomb is used to make hydrogen atoms merge in a fusion reaction.

Bronze Age
Period of history characterized by the use of early metals, such as copper and its alloys. The Bronze Age is commonly dated at around 3000–2000 BC, although it began at different times around the world.

Central Powers
Term used to describe the nations of central Europe that formed various alliances between 1882 and 1945. Originally they comprised Germany, Austria-Hungary and Italy. During World War I, Italy was absent, but rejoined for World War II. Austria became a member, independent of Hungary, in 1918.

Civil War
War between the peoples of the same nation, usually proving socially and economically devastating for the country concerned.

Colonialism
Political policy by which one country subjugates another to its own rule, with the aim of creating an empire. This can be by economic, religious or military means.

Conservation
Preservation, protection and efficient management of all natural resources, including that of living organisms. The sustainable use by a country of its natural resources has long been recognized as being essential for economic growth.

Constitutional Monarchy
Rule by a king or queen in which their powers are limited by means of a democratic political system.

Democracy
System of government for the people, by the people, normally through election. The word derives from the Greek words *demos* ('community') and *kratos* ('power').

Desegregation
The reintegration of peoples of different ethnic origins in countries where segregation has been a political force. The best-known examples in modern times are in the United States, where blacks and whites were desegregated in the 1960s after the success of the Civil Rights Movement, and in South Africa with the abolition of the apartheid regime.

Disciples
Anyone who strictly follows the teachings of another person. Usually used to describe the 12 followers of Jesus Christ during his life; these include St Peter, considered to be the founder of the Christian faith, and Judas, who betrayed Jesus.

Divine Right of Kings
Christian political belief that the monarch is God's representative on Earth and is subject to no man's will or laws. Rebellion against the monarch was therefore rebellion against God and thus considered blasphemous.

Ecology
Study of the relationships between all living things and their environment. Ecology is a broad discipline that encompasses many areas of science, such as biology, chemistry, geology and statistics.

Economics
The science and study of wealth: its production, distribution and consumption. The first generally recognized work on economics was carried out by Scottish philosopher Adam Smith, who published *The Wealth of Nations* in 1776.

Ecumenicism
Religious theory that argues for the mass unity of all denominations of Christianity around the world.

Gaul
Area covering largely what is present-day France during the period of the Roman Empire. It stretched into what is now northern Italy and the Netherlands.

Genetics
The study of inheritance, genes and their effects. Inherited characteristics are controlled by genes, which are sections of the DNA molecule which make up particular proteins. Genes can have two or more variants, called alleles, which give rise to alternative characteristics, for example eye colour.

Genocide
Deliberate programme of mass murder designed to exterminate a group defined by race, religion or ethnicity. Genocide is most frequently applied to the Final Solution instigated against the Jewish communities, and other groups considered undesirable, such as gypsies, during Germany's Third Reich.

Geocentric
Scientific theory in which the Sun and other planets all revolve around Earth. The theory was later replaced by Copernicus's heliocentric (Sun-centred) model.

Hebrews
Hebrews – meaning 'wanderers' – refers to the Semites who lived in Palestine and are the descendants of Abraham. Hebrew is the Jewish liturgical language and the national language of Israel. Hebrew kings and prophets emerged c. 1000 BC and so did the concept linking religion with morality.

Heliocentric
Theory of the Universe first propounded by Nicolaus Copernicus, in which the Sun is the centre with the planets (as they were then known) revolving around it. Although the Sun is now known not to be the centre of the Universe, the theory of orbiting planets was correct.

Humanitarianism
Theory that places importance on the interests of humanity as opposed to personal or national interests. Most recently humanitarianism has manifested itself in environmental policies and aid for the Third World.

Ice Age
Periods of time, lasting millions of years, when Earth, its oceans and atmosphere experienced a significant drop in temperature causing the formation of large ice masses. The most recent Ice Age began about two million years ago.

Imperialism
Practice of any one state to influence or conquer another in order to expand its wealth, power and dominions.

Iron Age
Period of history characterized by the use of iron, a development of the bronze previously used. The Iron Age is usually dated at around 1000–500 BC.

Liberalism
Theory that places importance on an individual's civil or political rights, particularly their freedom of speech and expression.

Martial Law
Policy by which law and order are maintained through military means. Some countries live under martial law, others deploy it as a means of control in times of crisis or rebellion.

Mesolithic
Name given to the Middle period of the Stone Age, normally taken to begin when the Ice Age finally receded and Earth's climate took on its present-day status. The esolithic era is normally dated from around 10,000 years ago.

Nationalism
Pride in, and a sense of belonging to, a nation. In extreme forms, nationalism can lead to hatred of other nations and peoples, such as occurred in Nazi Germany.

Neolithic
Name given to the final part of the Stone Age, after the Mesolithic period, normally dated from around 8000–3000 BC. The Neolithic era is characterized by the development of agriculture.

Pacifism
Belief in the immorality of war; that it cannot be in any way justified. During World Wars I and II, pacifism became increasingly widespread, with those refusing to fight on grounds of pacifism called conscientious objectors.

Paganism
Name given to anyone who followed a religion other than Christianity. First used in the fourteenth century, pagans suffered years of persecution after Christianity was established.

Periodic Table
Table listing the chemical elements first devised by Dmitri Mendeleyev. The elements are organized in rows by atomic number, with elements having similar atomic structures and chemical properties appearing in vertical columns.

Prehistory
Period of history that covers the time from when life first formed on Earth (about 3.5 billion years ago) up until human beings began to keep records.

Racism
Belief in the superiority of one race over another; often manifesting itself in social discrimination and giving rise to outbursts of violence.

Reservations
Areas of territory set aside by the United States government on which Native American Indians were forced to live after the expansion of settlers into the West. In theory it was believed that the Natives would continue to live as they had done previously, but in reality they were subject to government laws and continual oppression once inside the reservations.

Reunification
The reintegration of two or more countries that once shared a common government but have, for political reasons, been separated. After World War II Germany was divided – physically and politically – into East and West. With the end of the Cold War and the fall of the Berlin Wall in 1989, the two countries were finally reunified.

Socialism
Political ideal opposing the theory of class and private ownership. Such ideas can be traced back to Ancient Greece and beyond, but became popular only with the Industrial Revolution and large urban populations.

Stone Age
The earliest period of human history. As its name suggests, the Stone Age was characterized by the use of stone tools and implements. The Stone Age encompasses those periods of history known as Paleolithic, Mesolithic and Neolithic.

Suffrage
Term used to identify which citizens are eligible to vote in elections. The UK has universal adult suffrage (over 18 years of age) with a few exceptions. Universal suffrage is a key tenet of modern democracy.

BIBLIOGRAPHY

Adams, R. E. W., *Ancient Civilizations of the New World*, Boulder, 1992

Addington, L. H., *The Patterns of War Since the Eighteenth Century*, Indianapolis, 1984

Bakewell, P., *A History of Latin American Empires and Sequels, 1450–1930*, Oxford University Press, Oxford, 1997

Ball, S. J., *The Cold War: An International History, 1947–1991*, London, 1998

Banks, A., *A Military Atlas of the First World War*, London, 1975

Bechert, H. & Gombrich, R. (eds.), *The World of Buddhism*, London, 1984

Black, C. F., Greengrass, M., Howarth, D. et al, *Cultural Atlas of the Renaissance*, Oxford, 1993

Black, Jeremy (ed.), *The Encyclopedia of World History*, Dempsey Parr, Bath, 1999

Blackburn, Simon, *Oxford Concise Dictionary of Philosophy*, Oxford University Press, Oxford, 1996

Blanning, T. C. W. (ed.), *The Oxford Illustrated History of Modern Europe*, Oxford University Press, Oxford, 1996

Bohlander, R. E., *World Explorers and Discoverers*, New York, 1992

Boorstin, D. J., *The Discoverers*, London, 1991

Bowker, John (ed.), *The Oxford Dictionary of World Religions*, Oxford University Press, Oxford, 1997

Brogan, Hugh, *The Pelican History of the United States of America*, London, 1986

Brogan, Patrick, *World Conflicts*, London, 1985

Bruce, George, *Dictionary of Wars*, HarperCollins, London, 1995

Burkholder, M. A. & Johnson, L. L., *Colonial Latin America* (3rd ed.), New York, 1990

Calvocoressi, Peter, *World Politics Since 1945*, New York, 1991

Cameron, R., *A Concise Economic History of the World: From Paleolithic Times to the Present*, New York, 1997

Carruth, Gorton, *The Encyclopedia of World Facts and Dates*, New York, 1993

Cartledge, P. (ed.), *The Cambridge Illustrated History of Ancient Greece*, Cambridge, 1998

Cavendish, R. et al, *Journeys of the Great Explorers*, Basingstoke, 1992

Chacoliades, Militiades, *International Economics*, New York and London, 1990

Chant, C., & Goodman, D., *Pre-Industrial Cities and Technology*, London, 1999

Clutterbuck, Richard, *International Crisis and Conflict*, London and Basingstoke, 1993

Collier, S., Skidmore, T. E. & Blakemore, H., (eds.), *The Cambridge Encyclopedia of Latin America and the Caribbean*, Cambridge, 1985

Cooper, David E., *World Philosophies: An Historical Introduction*, Oxford, 1996

Cornell, Tim and Matthews, John, *Atlas of the Roman World*, Phaidon Press, London, 1982

Cotterell, Arthur (ed.), *Encyclopedia of Ancient Civilizations*, Rainbird Publishing, 1980

Cotterell, Arthur, *The Encyclopedia of World Mythology*, Dempsey Parr, Bath, 1999

Cross, F. L., *The Oxford Dictionary of the Christian Church*, Oxford University Press, Oxford, 1978

Cunliffe, Barry (Foreword), *The Cassell Atlas of World History*, London, 1997

Davidson, Gienapp, Heyrman et al., *Nation Of Nations: A Concise Narrative of the American Republic*, New York, 1996

Dawson, Lorne L. (ed.), *Cults in Context: Readings in the Study of New Religious Movements*, Toronto, 1996

Day, A. E., *Search for the Northwest Passage*, New York and London, 1986

Douglas, J. D. (ed.), *The New International Dictionary of the Christian Church*, Paternoster Press, 1978

Eliade, Mircea, *A History of Religious Ideas*, Chicago, 1984

Evans, Eric (ed.), *The Illustrated Guide to British History*, Dempsey Parr, Bath, 1999

Fagan, B. M., *Peoples of the Earth: An Introduction to World Prehistory*, New York, 1998

Fage, J. D., *A History of Africa*, Century Hutchinson, London, 1988

Featherstone, Donald, *Colonial Small Wars*, David and Charles Publishing, London, 1973

Flatlow, Ira, *They All Laughed: From Lightbulbs to Lasers*, New York, 1992

Fraser, Antonia (ed.), *The Lives of the Kings & Queens of England*, Weidenfeld and Nicholson, London, 1993

Friend, W. H. C., *The Rise of Christianity*, London, 1984

Gardiner, Judith, *The History Today Who's Who in British History*, Collins and Brown, London, 2000

Gilbert, Martin, *First World War*, HarperCollins, London, 1994

Gilbert, Martin, *Second World War*, London, 1989

Goodman, M., *The Roman World, 44 BC – AD 180*, London, 1997

Grove, Noel, *National Geographic Society: Atlas of World History*, Washington, 1997

Guirand, Felix (ed.), *Larousse Encyclopedia of Mythology*, Paul Hamlyn, London, 1964

Hall, Michael, *Leaving Home*, London, 1997

Hanbury-Tenison, R. (ed.), *The Oxford Book of Exploration*, Oxford, 1993

Harding, David (ed.), *Weapons: An International Encyclopedia from 5000 BC to 2000 AD*, London, 1980

Hart, L., *The History of the Second World War*, London, 1970

Haswell, Jock, *The Battle for Empire*, Cassell, London, 1976

Heath, Ian, *Armies of the Dark Ages*, War

Games Research Group, 1980
Herrin, J., *The Formation of Christendom*, Oxford, 1987
Hillier, Bevis, *The Style of the Century*, London, 1983
Hinnells, John (ed.), *Who's Who of Religions*, Penguin Books, London, 1996
Hobsbawn, E. J., *Industry and Empire*, London, 1990
Hobsbawn, E. J., *The Age of Extremes, 1919–1991*, London, 1994
Holmes, George (ed.), *The Oxford Illustrated History of Medieval Europe*, Oxford University Press, Oxford, 1988
Holmes, Richard, *Battle Plans*, Helicon Press, London
Hopper, R. J., *The Glory that was Greece*, Sidgwick and Jackson, 1980
Hughes, Robert, *The Shock of the New*, London, 1991
Kenyon, N. D. and Nightingale, C., *Audiovisual Telecommunications*, London, 1992
Kinder, Hermann & Hilgemann, Werner, *The Penguin Atlas of World History, Vols. 1 & 2*, London, 1995
La Feber, W., *America, Russia and the Cold War, 1945-1996*, New York, 1997
Langmuir, Erika and Lynton, Norbert *The Yale Dictionary of Art and Artists*, Yale University Press, 2000
Laque, Pierre, *Ancient Greece: Utopia and Reality*, Thames and Hudson, London, 1994
Lenman, B. P. (ed.), *Chambers Dictionary of World History*, Chambers, London, 2000
Ling, Trevor, *A History of Religion East and West*, London, 1977
Litvinoff, M., *Atlas of Earthcare*, London, 1996
Loudon, Irvine, *Western Medicine*, Oxford, 1997
Lundestad, G. *East, West, North, South: Major Developments in International Politics, 1945–1996*, Oslo, 1997
Macfarlane, L. J., *The Theory and Practice of Human Rights*, London, 1985
Maisels, C. K., *The Near East: Archaeology in the Cradle of Civilization*, London, 1993
Mallory, J. P., *In Search of the Indo-European: Language, Archaeology & Myth*, London, 1989
Manners, John (ed.), *The Oxford Illustrated History of Christianity*, Oxford University Press, Oxford, 1990
McEvedy, C., *The Penguin Atlas of the Pacific*, London, 1998
McHenry, Robert (ed.), *Webster's New Biographical Dictionary*, Miriam Webster, Inc., 1988
Messadie, Gerald, *Great Modern Inventions*, Edinburgh, 1991
Messenger, Charles, *The Century of Warfare: Worldwide Conflict from 1900 to the Present Day*, London, 1995
Moore, R. I. (ed.), *The Hamlyn Historical Atlas*, London, 1981
Morison, Samuel Eliot, Commager, H. S. Leuchtenburg, W. E., *A Concise History of the American Republic* (2nd edition), Oxford, 1983
Myers, Bernard, *Art and Civilization*, Paul Hamlyn, London, 1967
Myers, N. (ed.), *The Gaia Atlas of Planet Management*, London, 1985
Nigosian, S. A., *World Faiths* (2nd edition), New York, 1994
Norwich, John Julius (ed.), *The Oxford Illustrated Encyclopedia of the Arts*, Oxford University Press, Oxford, 1984
Ousby, Ian (ed.), *The Cambridge Guide to Literature in English*, Cambridge University Press, London, 1989
Pakenham, T., *The Scramble for Africa, 1876–1912*, London, 1991
Parker, G. (ed.), *The Times Atlas of World History* (4th edition), London, 1996
Porter, A. N., *Atlas of British Overseas Expansion*, London, 1991
Quirke, S. & Spencer, J., *The British Museum Book of Ancient Egypt*, London, 1992
Roberts, J. M., *The Penguin History of Europe*, Penguin Books, London, 1996
Roberts, J. M., *The Penguin History of the World*, Penguin, London, 1997
Sabrine, George H. and Thorson, Thomas L., *A History of Political Theory*, Orlando, 1973
Sasson, J. M. (ed.) *Civilizations of the Ancient Near East (Vol. II)*, New York, 1995
Smallwood, A. D., *The Atlas of African-American History and Politics: From the Slave Trade to Modern Times*, New York, 1998
Solomon, Robert C. and Higgins, Kathleen M., *A Short History of Philosophy*, Oxford, 1996
Spiegel, S. L. & Wehling, F. L., *World Politics in a New Era*, Fort Worth, 1999
Starr, Chester G., *A History of the Ancient World*, Oxford, 1983
Stobart, J. C., *The Grandeur that was Rome*, Sidgwick and Jackson, 1980
Taylor, A. J. P., *From the Boer War to the Cold War*, London, 1995
The DK Science Encyclopedia, London, 1998
The New Grolier Multimedia Encyclopedia, USA, 1991
Thomas, H., *The Slave Trade; The History of the Atlantic Slave Trade, 1440-1870*, New York, 1997
Tomlinson, Jim, *Public Policy and the Economy Since 1900*, New York, 1990
Tucker, S. C., *The Great War*, London, 1998
Weller, P. (ed.), *Religions in the UK: A Multi-Faith Directory*, University of Derby, 1997
Williamson, E., *The Penguin History of Latin America*, London, 1992
Wilson, A., *Transport*, London, 1995
Woolf, Stewart (ed.), *Nationalism in Europe*, London, 1996

AUTHORS

Patrick O'Brien
General Editor

Patrick O'Brien holds the positions of Governor of the Programme in Global History at the Institute of Historical Research, London University, and Centennial Professor of Economic History at the London School of Economics. He has edited and contributed to a wide range of historical journals and encyclopedias.

Guy de la Bédoyère
Royalty

Guy de la Bédoyère is an archaeologist and historian with numerous books to his credit on the Roman world, seventeenth-century literature and World War II aviation amongst others. He has also written numerous travel articles on a variety of historical sites for *The Independent* and has made a number of appearances on television and radio history programmes.

Alan Brown
Religion

Alan Brown is director of the National Society's Kensington R. E. Centre and R. E. (Schools) Officer of the General Synod Board of Education. He has written a great many books about world religions, as well as numerous articles, reviews and booklets. He is also tutor and examiner for The Open University course, 'The Religious Quest'.

Gerard Cheshire
Science & Technology and War

Gerard Cheshire is a specialist science writer. He has written and contributed to many books on the subject, including *Chemical Elements*, as well as magazine articles and part-works. His other areas of research and interest include the history and technology of warfare.

Ingrid Cranfield
Exploration & Empire and Industry

Ingrid Cranfield is a full-time writer and editor. Her works include *The Challengers*, a survey of modern British exploration and adventure. She contributes to books, magazines and periodicals on a regular basis.

Judith Hodge
Politics

Judith Hodge has worked as a freelance writer and editor for 15 years, both in the UK and New Zealand. She writes on a range of subjects for websites and magazines, including history, education, health and business. Judith is the author of a number of non-fiction titles for children.

Michael Kerrigan
Art & Culture

A contributor to the *Time–Life History of the World* series, Michael Kerrigan has written extensively on aspects of life and culture from the earliest times to the present day. His books cover everything from world literature to the history of torture; he writes regularly for *The Scotsman* and *The Times Literary Supplement*. He lives in Edinburgh.

Jon Sutherland
Society

Jon Sutherland is an experienced writer and lecturer in business studies. He has written and contributed to over 100 books and encyclopedias on a wide range of subjects, including social and military history.

CREDITS

Picture Sources

The Art Archive: AA: 5; AA/Museo Tosio Martinengo Brescia/Dagli Orti: 6; AA/Cava dei Tirreni Abbey Salerno/Dagli Orti: 39; AA/Bibliotheque Universitaire Geneva/Dagli Orti: 46; AA/Egyptian Museum Cairo/Dagli Orti: 52 (l); The Art Archive: 56; AA/Museo Capitolino Rome/Dagli Orti: 57 (t); AA/ Victoria and Albert Museum: 59; AA/Bibliotheque Nationale Paris: 60; AA/Galleria Degli Uffizi Florence/ Dagli Orti: 66; AA/Musée du Chateau de Versailles/Dagli Orti: 68; AA/Museo del Prado Madrid Album/Joseph Martin: 73 (r); AA/Galleria degli Uffizi Florence/Dagli Orti: 79 (l); AA/Miramare Palace Trieste/Dagli Orti: 83 (r); AA/Museo Tosio Martinengo Brescia/Dagli Orti: 90 (r); AA/Dagli Orti: 107; AA/Mireille Vautier: 108; AA/British Library: 114-115 (t); AA: 123; AA/RAMC Historical Museum/Harper Collins Publishers: 128; AA/London Museum: 130 (t); AA/British Library: 143; AA/British Library: 144; AA/Harper Collins Publishers: 146; AA/Museo del Prado Madrid/Josse: 147

Christie's Images Ltd: 3, 70, 80 (r), 88 (b), 88 (l), 102-103, 118, 138-139, 145, 153

Graham Stride: 7, 53, 112-113 (b)

Impact Photos: Simon Shepheard/Impact: 24; Caroline Penn/Impact: 28-29; Mark Cator/Impact: 29; Piers Cavendish/Impact: 31; Geraint Lewis/Impact: 34 (r); Mark Henley/ Impact: 48-49; Simon Shepheard/Impact: 52 (r); Alain le Garsmeur/ Impact: 109; Fabrizio Bensch/Impact: 127; John Arthur/Impact: 132 (b); John Cole/Impact: 137; Colin Jones/Impact: 155; Caroline Penn/ Impact: 170; Alexis Wallerstein/Impact: 175; Colin Jones/Impact: 178-179; Julian Calder/Impact: 180; Ben Edwards/Impact: 181

Mary Evans: 4, 8-9, 11, 12 (l), 13, 14 (r), 18, 20, 21, 23, 32-33, 34 (l), 35, 38, 40, 42, 44-45, 50-51, 54 (t), 57 (b), 58, 62, 64, 67, Mary Evans/Edwin Wallace 69, 71, 73 (l), 74 (t), 75, 77, Mary Evans/Edwin Wallace 79 (r), 80 (l), 82 (l), 84 (l), 84 (b), 85 (b), 89, 90-91 (b), 92 (tr), 93 (t), 93 (b), 95,

96 (l), 97 (t), 97 (b), 98 (b), Mary Evans/Explorer Archives 98 (t), 99, 117 (b), 125 (t), 125 (b), 126 (b), Mary Evans/Sigmund Freud Copyrights 129, 130 (b), 131, 133, 141, 142, 149, 150-151, 154 (t), 154 (b), 159, 162, 163, 171, 172, 173, 188

Topham Picturepoint: 12 (r), 14 (l), 15 (l), 15 (r), 16, 17 (l), 17 (r), 19, 22, 25, 26, 27, 30, 36, 37, 41, 54 (b), 55, 61, 72, 74 (b), 78, 81 (b), 81 (t), 82-83, 85 (t), 86-87, 91 (t), 92 (b), 92 (tl), 96 (r) 100, 101, 104, 105, 106, 110, 111 (b), 111 (t), 112 (t), 113 (r), 115 (b), 116, 117 (t), 119, 120, 121, 126 (r), 132, 134, 136, 156-157, 160, 164, 165, 167, 169, 170 (b), 177

INDEX

Aboriginals 105
Abraham 34
Acropolis 110, 113
Actium, battle of 54, 55, 56, 140
Adolphus, Gustavus, King of Sweden 76
Afghan wars 154
Agincourt, battle of 66, 144, 145
Agrarian Revolution 91
AIDS 137
Akhbar, Emperor 71, 75, 142
Akhenaten 52, 106
Alcuin of York 60
Aldrin, Edwin 'Buzz' 100
Alexander the Great 54, 106, 107
Alfred the Great 61, 114
American Civil War 105, 156–57
American native population 104
American Revolution 80, 126, 149, 150
Ancient Egypt 52, 106
Ancient Greece 88, 110, 113, 130, 140
Ancient Rome 56–57, 111, 112, 140 see also Romans
Anglo-Dutch wars 147
Anglo-Saxons 58–59, 61, 114–15
Antony, Mark 54, 140
apartheid 132, 135
Aquinas, St Thomas 114–15
Arab-Israeli Wars 176–77, 179
Arab League 23
Archimedes 88
Argentina 21, 180–81
Aristotle 88, 110
Armstrong, Neil 100
Arnhem, battle of 174–75

Árpád 114
Arras, battle of 167
Arthur, king of the Britons 58–59
Asoka of India 54
Assyrians 106, 108, 109
Atlantic, battle of 170
atomic bomb 176
Attila the Hun 142
Augustine, St, Bishop of Hippo 37
Augustus Caesar 54, 55, 56, 111, 112
Aurangzeb, Emperor 78
Austerlitz, battle of 152
Austrian Succession, War of 79, 148
Aztecs 68, 115, 119

Babar, Emperor 71, 75, 142
Babbage, Charles 93
Babylonians 53, 108, 109
Baha'i 47–48
Baird, John Logie 98
Balaclava, battle of 155, 156
Barbarossa 145
Bastille, storming of the 81, 127, 150–51
Batista, Fulgencio 16, 17, 22
battles 138–81 see also under named battles
Bay of Pigs Invasion 20, 29, 177
Becket, St Thomas 41
Becquerel, Antoine Henri 96
Bell, Alexander Graham 94
Benedict XVI, pope 48–49
Benedictine Order 38
Berlin Wall 19, 24, 27, 28, 127
Bible, the 34, 36, 45, 47 see also Christianity; Jesus Christ
Bill of Rights 126
Billy 'the Kid' Garrat 130

Bismarck, Otto von 158
Blériot, Louis 97
'Bloody Sunday' 30
Boer War 12, 155, 161
Boers 161
Bolsheviks 11, 18, 19, 78, 84, 168
Bonaparte, Napoleon 81, 127, 152
Boston Massacre 149
Boudicca 113
Bourbon Dynasty 76, 169
Boxer Rebellion 162
Brandenburg Gate 126–27
Brandt, Willy 19
Britain
politics 10, 11, 12, 18, 19, 21, 23, 25, 28
religion 34–35, 39, 40, 44, 47
royalty 58–59, 61, 63, 64–65, 66, 68, 70–71, 72, 73, 74, 75, 76–77, 78, 80, 82–83, 85
science and industry 89, 90–91, 92, 93, 94, 98, 99, 101
society and culture 114, 122, 124, 125, 130
war and conflict 142, 143, 147, 148, 155, 156, 158, 181 see also World War I; World War II
Britain, Battle of 172–73, 174
British East India Company 89, 147, 148, 156
British Empire 26, 83, 124, 154
Brusilov Offensive 166
Buddhism 37, 49, 54, 58, 59, 61
Bush, George Snr. 26
Byzantium 66–67

Caesar, Augustus 54, 55, 56, 111, 112
Caesar, Julius 55
Calcutta, Black Hole of 81, 148

Caligula 56
Calvin, Jean 44, 45, 47, 147–48
Cambodia 31
Canute, King 61, 114
Capone, Al 132
Carnarvon, Lord 52
Carolingian Empire 59, 60
Casas, Bartolomé de la 121
Castro, Fidel 16, 22, 29, 177
Catherine the Great 78, 80
Ceausescu, Nicolae 20
Chamberlain, Neville 10
Channel Tunnel 101
Charge of the Light Brigade 155, 156
Charlemagne, Emperor 59, 60
Charles I of England 65, 76–77
Charles II, Holy Roman Emperor 60
Charles II of England 77, 78, 122
Charles V, Holy Roman Emperor 44, 67
Charles V of France 65
Charles VI, Holy Roman Emperor 79, 147
Charles IX of France 46, 66, 76
Chernobyl 101
Chiang Kai-shek 19, 167, 170
Ch'ing Dynasty 53, 56, 85, 109
China 10, 19, 31, 53, 56, 61, 66, 85, 109, 119, 137, 152, 162, 167, 170
Chou Dynasty 53, 56
Christ see Jesus Christ
Christianity 34, 35, 36, 37, 38, 39 see also Counter-Reformation; Reformation; Roman Catholicism
Churchill, Sir Winston 12, 24, 25

189

civil rights movement 132, 134–35, 136–37
civilizations and cultures 102–37
Classical period 110, 113
Clement VII, pope 42, 44, 66
Cleopatra 55, 106, 140
Clinton, Bill 26
Clive, Robert 81, 148
Cold War 14, 15, 19, 24, 26, 27, 28, 29, 100, 127
Columbus, Christopher 67
Commonwealth Games 130
Communism 10, 13, 16, 20, 24, 26, 31, 130
Communist Revolution 129
concentration camps 22, 159, 161, 169, 171
Concorde 101
confederacy 10, 156–57
Confucianism 61, 137
Conquistadors 117
Constantine, Emperor 36–37, 67
Constitution, United States 126
Copernicus, Nicolaus 88
Cortés, Hernán 68, 119
Cossacks 121–22
Counter-Reformation 47, 73
Crécy, battle of 64, 144
Crimean War 128, 155, 156
Cromwell, Oliver 77
Crusades 35, 39, 41, 63, 142
Cuba 16, 22, 177
Cuban Missile Crisis 20, 29, 100
Cultural Revolution 16, 137
culture and society 102–37
Curie, Marie and Pierre 96
Custer, George Armstrong 84, 104, 158
Cyrus the Great 53, 108
Czechoslovakia 23, 27, 137

D-Day 15, 173, 175
Da Gama, Vasco 121
Da Vinci, Leonardo 118–19
Dalai Lama 49

Danegeld 114
Dardanelles Campaign 12, 166
Dark Ages 113, 114–15
Darwin, Charles 93
Davy, Humphrey 92
De la Casas, Bartolomé 121
Declaration of Independence 126
Descartes, René 122, 123, 125
Diaz, Bartholomew 121
Diet of Worms 44, 68
Dome of the Rock 35
Domesday Book 63, 116
Dual Entente 16, 18
Dutch East India Company 89, 147, 161

Easter Rising 20
Edict of Nantes 46
Eddington, Arthur 98
Edison, Thomas Alva 94–95
Edward I of England 63
Edward II of England 64
Edward III of England 143, 144
Egypt 23, 28, 124, 173, 174, 176–77
  Ancient 52, 106
Einstein, Albert 90, 96, 98
Eisenhower, Dwight 15
El Alamein, battles of 161, 173, 174
Elizabeth I of England 70, 71, 72, 73, 74, 75, 89, 147
Elizabeth II of England 85
English Civil War 77, 78
Enigma machine 99
Enlightenment 124–25
Entente Cordiale 18
Ethelred II, the Unready 61
ethnic cleansing 36
Etruscans 110–11
European Union (EU) 31

Falklands War 180–81
Faraday, Michael 93
Fascism 158, 159
Ferdinand, Archduke Franz 64, 84, 164–65

Ferdinand II and Isabella of Spain 67, 68
feudalism 113, 116
Five Year Plans 14, 17
Fleming, Alexander 98
Ford, Henry 96
'Fourteen Point' armistice 10, 165
Fox, George 47
France 15, 16, 18, 19, 23, 28, 46, 60, 62–63, 65, 76, 78, 81, 94, 96, 97, 101, 127, 143–44, 145, 151, 152
Francis of Assisi, St 42
Franco, Francisco 16, 169
Franco-Prussian war 82, 158
Franklin, Benjamin 91, 126
Frederick the Great 75
French East India Company 89
French Revolution 81, 127, 150–51
Freud, Sigmund 129, 130

Gagarin, Yuri 100
Galileo Galilei 88, 89
Gama, Vasco da 121
Gaulle, Charles de 15
Gandhi, Indira 15, 20
Gandhi, Mahatma 15
Garibaldi, Giuseppe 83
genetic engineering 101
Geneva Convention 135
George III of England 80, 82
German Democratic Republic 27
Germany 19, 22, 23, 24, 25, 27, 28, 62–63, 68, 96, 98, 126–27, 132, 146–47 see also World War I; World War II
Gettysburg, battle of 156–57
Ghandi, Mahatma 10–11, 26
Goering, Herman Wilhelm 161
Gorbachev, Mikhail 100
Great Depression 14, 99, 132, 134
Great Exhibition 83
Great Fire of London 122
Great Pyramid of Giza 106

Great Schism 42, 44
Great Wall of China 56, 109
Greece, Ancient 88, 110, 113, 130, 140
Gregory IX, pope 42
Guevara, Ernesto 'Che' 22
Gulf War 23, 170, 181
Gupta Empire 58
Guru Nanak 42

Habsburg Empire 63, 64
Hadrian, Emperor 56–57, 111
Haig, General Sir Douglas 156, 164–65
Haile Selassie, Emperor 48
Halley's Comet 90
Hanging Gardens of Babylon 106–7, 108
Hannibal 140
Harold II of England 142
Hastings, battle of 63, 142
Heisenberg, Werner 98
Henry V of England 66, 144, 145
Henry VIII of England 42, 44, 47, 71, 72, 73
Herod the Great 34, 35, 55
Hinduism 58
Hirohito, Emperor 85
Hiroshima 85, 176
Hitler, Adolf 22, 158, 159, 169, 171, 172–73
Hittites 52, 107, 108, 109
Ho Chi Minh 130, 178
Holocaust 169
Holy Roman Empire 44, 59, 60, 62–63, 64, 68, 142, 148
Home Rule 11
Hudson's Bay Company 90, 124
Huguenots 46, 76
human rights 121, 130, 132, 134–35, 136–37
Hume, David 125
Hundred Years' War 64, 65, 66, 143–44, 145
Hussein, Saddam 170, 181
Huygens, Christian 89

Incas 117
Indian Independence 10, 15, 26, 124
Indian Mutiny 89, 124, 156
Indians, Native American 104, 158, 161
Indo-Pakistan War 179
Indus Valley civilizations 108
Industrial Revolution 90–91
industry and science 86–101
Innocent III, pope 41, 42
Inquisition 42, 67, 73
Iran 17
Iraq 23, 109, 170, 181
Ireland 11, 20, 30
Iron Curtain 24, 28, 100
Islam 17, 34, 35, 38, 47–48, 104
Israel 23, 34, 176–77, 179
Italy 14, 41, 42, 44, 83, 97, 173
Ivan III of Moscow 66–67
Ivan IV, 'the Terrible' of Moscow 74

Jacobites 124
Japan 85, 122, 173, 176
Jenner, Edward 92
Jerusalem 34–35
Jesus Christ 35, 36, 45
Joan of Arc, 144
John Paul II, pope 48
Judaism 34, 35
Julius Caesar 55
Jung, Carl 129, 130
Justinian, Emperor 59

Kant, Immanuel 125
Kennedy, John F. 20, 29
Khair-ed-Din (Barbarossa) 145
Khan, Genghis 63, 75, 117–18, 142
Khomeini, Ayatollah Ruh Allah 17
Khrushchev, Nikita 16
King, Martin Luther 132, 134–35, 137
Kitchener, Lord Horatio Herbert 155, 161
Khmer Rouge 31

Knights Templar, Order of 41
Korean War 15, 100, 176
Ku Klux Klan 10
Kuomintang 19

League of Nations 10, 21 see also United Nations
Leipzig, battle of 152
Lenin, Vladimir Ilych 11, 13, 18, 168
Leningrad, seige of 173, 174
Leonardo Da Vinci 118–19
Lincoln, Abraham 105, 156–57
Lister, Joseph 94
Little Bighorn, battle of 84, 104, 158, 161
Louis XIV of France 46, 76, 78–79, 147
Louis XVI of France 76, 81, 127, 150–51
Louisiana Purchase 128
Luther, Martin 44, 45, 47, 147–48

Maastricht Treaty 31
Mafeking, seige of 161
Magyars 113, 114
Maharajas 54
Malcolm X 132
Manchuria 170
Mandela, Nelson 132, 135
Mao Zedong (Tse-tung) 16, 19, 137
Maoris 104
Maori wars 104, 154
Maratha wars 150
Marconi, Guglielmo 97
Marie Antoinette of France 81, 150–51
Mark Antony 54, 140
Marne, battles of 163
Marshall Plan 100
Marx, Karl 10, 11, 129
Marxism 10
Mary I of England 72, 73
Mary, Queen of Scots 74, 75
Maximillian I 68

Maxwell, James Clerk 94
Mayan civilization 108–9
Medici family 66, 76
Mendeleyev, Dimitri 94
Michelangelo 42, 118–19
Middle Ages 114–15
Midway, battle of 174
Ming Dynasty 66
Missouri Compromise 128
Mogul Empire 71, 75, 78, 142
Mohammad, Prophet 38, 104
Mongol Empire 109
Mongols 63, 66, 117–18
Mons, battle of 163
Montezuma II 68–69, 119
Moors 116
More, St Thomas 44
Morse, Samuel 93
Mother Teresa of Calcutta 48
Muhammad, Prophet 38, 104
Munich Pact 10, 23
Mussolini, Benito 14

Nagasaki 85, 176
Napoleon III 82
Napoleonic wars 81, 148, 152
Nasser, Abdel 21, 28
Native American Indians 104, 158, 161
NATO 15, 26, 27, 100
Nawab of Bengal 81, 148
Nazi Party 22, 23, 132, 159, 161, 169, 171, 172–73
Nazi-Soviet Pact 23
Nefertiti 52
Nehru, Jawaharlal 15, 20
Nelson, Admiral Horatio 81, 148, 152
neo-Nazi movement 10, 22
Nero 56
New Deal 14, 135
Newcomen, Thomas 92
Newton, Isaac 88, 90, 98, 125
Nicaea, Council of 36
Nicholas II of Russia 12, 18, 78, 84, 168
Nietzsche, Friedrich 128–29
Nightingale, Florence 128, 155

Nixon, Richard 19, 29, 30
Nobunaga, Oda 122
North Atlantic Treaty Organization (NATO) 15, 26, 27, 100
Nostradamus 120, 121
Nuremberg Trials 135
Olmec civilization 109
Olympic Games 130–31
Opium wars 152
Organizations of American States (OAS) 26
Ottoman Empire 72

Pakistan 26, 179
Panama Canal 10, 130
Pankhurst, Emmeline 130
Paracelsus 88
Paris, Treaty of 124, 148
Passchendale 156
Pasteur, Louis 94
Paul III, pope 42
Pearl Harbor 14, 173, 174
Perón, Eva 21
Persia 53, 108, 140
Persian Wars 54, 72, 140
Peter I of Russia 79
Phillip II of Spain 73, 74, 147
Phoenicians 107, 140
Pilate, Pontius 35, 36
Pizarro, Francisco 117
plague 122
Planck, Max 96
Plassey, battle of 81, 148
Plato 88, 110
Poitiers, battle of 64
Pol Pot 31
politics 8–31 see also war
Pompeii 112
Potsdam Conference 24
printing 119–20
Prohibition 132, 134
Protestantism 45, 47
Pu Yi 85
Punic wars 111, 112, 140

Quakers 47
quantum theory 98

INDEX 191

Quisling, Vidkun 158
Qur'an 38
rail travel 92, 94
Rameses II 52, 106
Rasputin 12, 84
Rastafarian faith 48
Reformation 44, 45, 47, 62–63
Regency period 80, 82
religion 32–49
Renaissance 44, 110, 118–19
Restoration 65, 78, 122
Richard I of England 39, 63
Richard III of England 68
Roman Catholicism 42, 47, 48, 73
Romania 20, 27
Romanov Dynasty 78
Romans 36, 54, 55, 56, 59, 111, 140 *see also* Ancient Rome
Rommel, Erwin 161, 174
Roosevelt, Franklin D 14, 25, 135, 174
Roosevelt, Theodore 10
royalty 50–85
Russia 10, 11, 12, 13, 16, 19, 22, 23, 27, 78, 79, 84, 121–22, 155, 168, 174 *see also* Soviet Union; USSR
Russian Revolution 16, 18, 19, 84, 121–22, 168
Russo-Japanese War 10, 78, 162
Russo-Turkish War 13, 158

Sack of Rome 44
Safavid Dynasty 72
Saladin 35, 63, 142
Samurai 117, 158
San Stefano, Treaty of 13
Sargon the Great 52
Satsuma rebellion 117, 158
Schindler, Oskar 132
Schlieffen Plan 162, 172
science and industry 86–101
Seven Years' War 75, 80, 124, 148
Severus, Septimus 57
Shah Jahan, Emperor 76, 78

Shakespeare, William 119
Siddhartha Gautama (the Buddha) 37
Sikhism 20, 42
Sitting Bull 84, 104, 158, 161
Six-Day War 21, 176–77, 179
slavery 104–5, 121, 128, 156–57
Sluys, battle of 144
Smuts, Jan Christian 12
society and culture 102–37
Somme, battle of 156, 164–65, 167
Song Dynasty 61
Soviet Union 10, 11, 22, 23, 24, 27, 29 *see also* Russia
space race 100
Spain 67, 73, 74, 76, 79, 146, 147, 152, 169
Spanish-American War 161
Spanish Armada 73, 74, 146, 147
Spanish Civil War 16, 169
Spanish Inquisition 42, 67, 73
Spanish Succession, War of 79, 147
Stalin, Joseph 13, 14, 24, 25, 100, 168
Stalingrad, seige of 174
Storming of the Bastille 81, 127, 150–51
Strategic Arms Limitations Talks (SALT) 29
Stuart Dynasty 65, 124
Suez Canal 96, 124
Suez Crisis 21, 28
Suleiman the Magnificent 72
Sumerians 106, 107, 108, 109

Taiping Rebellion 10
Taj Mahal 76
Tamerlane 142
T'ang Dynasty 59
Tatars 66–67
technology and trade 86–101
Tenochtitlán 68, 119
Teresa of Calcutta, Mother 48
Thatcher, Margaret 181

Thermopylae, battle of 140
Thirty Years' War 63, 76, 146, 147–48
Tiananmen Square Massacre 31
Tibet 49
Titanic 99
Tito, Marshal 16
Toltecs 115
trade and technology 86–101
Trafalgar, battle of 148, 152
'Trail of Tears' 104
Trevithick, Richard 92
Triple Entente 16, 18, 19
Triumvirate 54, 55, 56
Trojan war 110, 140
Trotsky, Leon 13, 168
Truman, Harry S 15, 24, 100, 135, 176
Tse-tung, Mao 16, 19, 137
Tudor Dynasty 71
Turing, Alan 99
Tutankhamen 52, 106

United Nations 12, 21, 25, 181
United States Constitution 126
Urban VI, pope 42
US 28, 84, 93, 94, 96, 97, 99, 100, 104–5, 128, 132, 134–35, 136–37, 149, 150, 158, 161, 176, 177, 178–79, 181
politics 21, 25, 26, 29, 30, 126
presidents 10, 14, 15, 19, 20, 26, 150, 156–57, 176
World War I 165
World War II 172–73, 174, 176
USSR 14, 16, 17, 23, 24, 27, 176 *see also* Russia

Valois Dynasty 65
Vasco da Gama 121
Verdun, battle of 164–65, 167
Versailles 78

Victor Emmanuel II 83
Victoria, Queen of England 82–83
Vietnam War 100, 130, 135, 178–79
Vikings 60, 61, 113, 114

Wall Street Crash 99, 132
war 138–81 *see also* politics; under named wars
warlords 122, 158, 167
Warsaw Pact 27
Washington, George 150
Watergate 19, 30
Waterloo, battle of 81, 148, 152–53
Watt, James 92
Wellington, Duke of 81, 148, 150, 152
Westphalia, Treaty of 47
William I, 'The Conqueror' of England 63, 114, 116–17, 142, 143
Wilson, Woodrow 10
Wonders of the Ancient World 107
World War I 10, 12, 16, 18, 19, 21, 78, 84, 121–22, 155, 156, 161, 162, 163, 164–65, 166, 167
World War II 12, 14, 15, 16, 22, 23, 24, 25, 26, 27, 85, 96, 121–22, 132, 135, 158, 159, 161, 162, 163, 169, 170, 171, 172–73, 174, 174–75, 175, 176
Wounded Knee, battle of 158, 161
Wright brothers 97

Yalta Conference 14, 25
Yeltsin, Boris 22
Yom Kippur War 179
Ypres, battles of 163, 164–65
Yugoslavia 16, 36

Zedong, Mao 16, 19, 137
Zulu wars 158